Sex, Death and Resurrection
in *Altered Carbon*

Sex, Death and Resurrection in *Altered Carbon*

Essays on the Netflix Series

Edited by ALDONA KOBUS *and* ŁUKASZ MUNIOWSKI

McFarland & Company, Inc., Publishers
Jefferson, North Carolina

LIBRARY OF CONGRESS CATALOGUING-IN-PUBLICATION DATA

Names: Kobus, Aldona, 1988– editor. | Muniowski, Łukasz, editor.
Title: Sex, death and resurrection in Altered carbon : essays on the Netflix series / edited by Aldona Kobus and Łukasz Muniowski.
Description: Jefferson, North Carolina : McFarland & Company, Inc., Publishers, 2020. | Includes bibliographical references and index.
Identifiers: LCCN 2019055145 | ISBN 9781476679624 (paperback : acid free paper) ∞
ISBN 9781476638461 (ebook)
Subjects: LCSH: Altered carbon (Television program)
Classification: LCC PN1992.77.A A52525 2020 | DDC 791.45/72—dc23
LC record available at https://lccn.loc.gov/2019055145

BRITISH LIBRARY CATALOGUING DATA ARE AVAILABLE

ISBN (print) 978-1-4766-7962-4
ISBN (ebook) 978-1-4766-3846-1

© 2020 Aldona Kobus and Łukasz Muniowski. All rights reserved

No part of this book may be reproduced or transmitted in any form or by any means, electronic or mechanical, including photocopying or recording, or by any information storage and retrieval system, without permission in writing from the publisher.

Front cover image © 2020 Shutterstock

Printed in the United States of America

McFarland & Company, Inc., Publishers
  Box 611, Jefferson, North Carolina 28640
    www.mcfarlandpub.com

Table of Contents

Introduction
    ALDONA KOBUS *and* ŁUKASZ MUNIOWSKI   1

Sex

"Technology advances, but humans don't": Neo-Noir Women, Psychoanalysis and Transhuman Love
    ALEXANDER N. HOWE   15

The Flinching Edge: Sex, Consensual Death(lessness) and the Limit-Experience in *Altered Carbon*
    KWASU DAVID TEMBO   27

Functions of Sex Scenes in *Altered Carbon*
    MICHAŁ KLATA   39

Sleeves

The Materiality of Reality: The Floating Consciousness in *Altered Carbon*
    ESRA KÖKSAL *and* BURCU BAYKAN   51

Embodiment in *Altered Carbon*
    LARS SCHMEINK   67

Wearing Wellness on Your Sleeve: On Meths, Self-Control and Capitalism
    ŁUKASZ MUNIOWSKI   81

New (Cloned) Bodies for the Old: Biopolitics in *Altered Carbon*
    ALINE FERREIRA   90

"Meths" versus "Quellists": *Altered Carbon* as the Battleground
of Two Ideologies
    Damla Pehlivan   105

Look Who's Talking: Haunted Bodies and Uncanny Voices
in *Altered Carbon*
    Dariusz Brzostek   118

Cyberpunk

Cyberpunk Resleeved: How Netflix's *Altered Carbon* Reformats
Its Cyberpunk Ancestry
    Adam Edwards   129

Another Kind of War: The Manufacturing of History
in *Altered Carbon*
    Kenneth Matthews   144

The Present of the Dead: Spectral Ideology in *Altered Carbon*
    Aldona Kobus   155

Nevermore! Poesque Thanatophobia as Counter-Narrative
    Fernando Gabriel Pagnoni Berns
    and Emiliano Aguilar   177

About the Contributors   191
Index   195

Introduction

ALDONA KOBUS *and* ŁUKASZ MUNIOWSKI

Altered Carbon, the Netflix series based on the 2002 science-fiction novel written by Richard Morgan, was met with mixed reviews. Benjamin Lee of the *Guardian* called it "stylish yet often silly," Julie Muncy of *Wired* characterized it as "a generally interesting, if sometimes plodding, popcorn show with a few great ideas," whereas Jen Chaney of *Vulture*, while critical of the show as a whole, appreciated it for its visual candy and philosophical subtext. We find this philosophical subtext so engaging that we are willing to look past the series' flaws and use *Altered Carbon* as the basis for an exploration of diverse ideas. The show's flaws are all too obvious, so it will be best to get them out of the way early on.

Apart from the idea of stacks and sleeves, the future presented in the show does not seem that original or distinct from other, lackluster cyberpunk series, novels or films. The main problem of the series is the lack of coherence between the message and the plot. The story of bodily control and enhancement revolves around unwanted pregnancy, an idea seemingly taken directly from a 19th-century novel. Some of the more interesting observations also seem to be at odds with the plot. They stay unexplored, sacrificed for a rather generic story where the motivations of most of the characters are often just absurd. The dialogue is sometimes clunky and ridiculous. The visuals are too reliant on sex and violence, which rarely serve any purpose for the plot. The characters are bland and stereotypical. And yet, underneath all these imperfections, are issues that beg for in-depth analysis.

The world of *Altered Carbon* presents a reality where immortality is only achievable through technology. An invention called cortical stacks allows for the digital storage of human consciousness and the ability to download it into new bodies, called sleeves. Most people can afford just a few resleevings but are financially unable to upgrade their bodies through genetic and cybernetic manipulations. These enhancements are the domain of wealthy Meths, a social class named after the biblical Methuselah. The rich are able to remotely store the back-ups to their minds in satellites, ensuring that even if their stacks are damaged, they can still enjoy the luxury of resleeving. Due to their longer lifespans (or sleeve-spans), Meths are able to acquire more wealth and power than an average person, which also allows them to sustain extravagant habits. As a result, they live above the law.

One of the richest and oldest Meths, Laurens Bancroft, uses his influence to resleeve a presumed war criminal, Takeshi Kovacs, and hires him to solve the mystery of the unsuccessful attempt to murder Bancroft. We get to know the fascinating futuristic world of the series alongside Kovacs, as well as unwrap the classic murder mystery with its many suspects and motives, because *Altered Carbon* fuses the core of cyberpunk ethos—a dystopian vision of the techno-revolution—with the plot of a proper crime novel.

Altered Carbon can be seen as a show advocating for transhumanism as well as a satire aimed at its basic assumptions, especially stark anthropocentrism and the discontention between the body and the mind/soul. It is a fascinating subject of scholarly reflection, furnishing ideas that can be analyzed through the lenses of cognitive science, posthumanism, postgenderism, psychoanalysis, or the theories of social control. The series also problematizes the cyberpunk genre, most notably the above mentioned extreme presentations of violence and sexualization, two grand marks of the hypermasculine face of mainstream cyberpunk, which have been previously recognized by Karen Cadora (1995, pp. 357–358).

It is also important to notice the intertextual dimension of *Altered Carbon*, presented in the form of visual and literary quotes. The series is strongly rooted in the history of the genre, beginning with Edgar Allan Poe's proto-crime novels, such as *The Murders in the Rue Morgue*, *The Mystery of Marie Rogêt* and *The Purloined Letter*, going through classic noir movies from the '40s—the title of every episode of the series is also the title of a famous noir movie—and ending with TV series and movies crucial for cyberpunk works from the '80s and the '90s. This ideological and cinematic mixture, which *Altered Carbon* undoubtedly is, is also the result of an attempt at overcoming the impasse of the genre, the clash of the techno-revolution of tomorrow with not-so revolutionary ideology (Cadora, 1995, p. 357).

We consider this Netflix-produced series substantially relevant, since it takes on a plethora of current issues, from the critique of neoliberalism, through the ethical aspects of biotechnology, up to issues regarding thanatology. It provokes questions about what it means to be human in a world in which death basically does not exist. The same goes for the limits of defining the construction of identity, be it gender, sexual and/or ethnic. Primarily, it is a show about the relationship between the mind, the body and the machine. *Altered Carbon* stays true to cyberpunk's ethos, as it metaphorically presents a reality dominated by consumerism, where one's life expectancy is dependent on one's economic status.

The series can also be seen, similarly to *Snowpiercer* (2013), *Ghost in the Shell* (2017) or *Blade Runner 2049* (2017), as a vital element of the cyberpunk renaissance, which begs the question: is this mainstream revival a sign of cyberpunk's transgressive aspects, reminiscent of the novels, graphic novels and movies of the '70s and '80s, or is it the opposite, and the genre's failure to successfully criticize modernity is precisely the reason it has been embraced by today's movie studios, directors and audiences?

In order to analyze these issues we have divided the essays in this collection into three sections devoted to sex (obviously); sleeve technology (the most promising idea of the series); and cyberpunk (which is quite obvious as well). Through this organization, the contributors and ourselves were able to explore the genre, philosophy and visuals of *Altered Carbon* all in one collection.

The issue of sex in *Altered Carbon* seems to be the most urgent, considering the harsh responses from critics on that aspect of the series. The show was accused of indulging itself with violence, nudity and sex scenes. The contributors examined the validity of such accusations and questioned whether there is more to it than simple cyberpunk clichés. This section starts with Alexander N. Howe's "'Technology advances, but humans don't': Neo-Noir Women, Psychoanalysis and Transhuman Love," where we first encounter the recurrent thought of this collection, the intersection between the futuristic imagery of *Altered Carbon* and its very contemporary issues of construction of human consciousness, morality and mechanisms of psyche. Howe focuses on the character of Kristin Ortega, who he calls "a rather rare construction of female detective in the context of hard-boiled fiction." Howe's two-way analysis addresses the roots of the cyberpunk genre as well as the posthuman conception of the psyche. Howe proves that *Altered Carbon* stays true to its cultural heritage with the character of Ortega. He develops a sophisticated gender methodology to study the question of the place of the female character in neo-noir fiction. He also notices that "the question of embodiment is more significant for the female detective as she must negotiate not only her defense against the hostile world, but also a merger with her loved ones." Complications of embodiment result in the reinterpretation of cyberpunk. Considering that with the character of Ortega the technocybernetic revolution faces the traditional conditions of the human psyche brings us back to posthumanism as the core of the cyberpunk genre. The technology of stacks and sleeves might suggest that bodies are redacted to interchangeable sleeves but the relationship between Ortega and Ryker (or Kovacs in Ryker's sleeve) could be read as the Lacanian return of the Real, the core of romantic involvement. Howe's use of Lacanian psychoanalysis offers interesting insight into the world of *Altered Carbon* but, more importantly, it illustrates one of the fundamental mechanisms of the human psyche: the relationship with the Other.

Kwasu David Tembo offers an engaging analysis of immortal sexuality (or Meth sexuality) in "The Flinching Edge: Sex, Consensual Death(lessness) and the Limit-Experience in *Altered Carbon*." Tembo goes back to Michel Foucualt's conceptions of biopower and biopolitics to consider their mechanisms in a world where bodies' possibilities are potentially limitless. Foucault's and Bataille's conception of the limit-experience, which confronts the subject with the limits of her subjectivity, is used to understand the condition of self in *Altered Carbon*. One must agree that stack and sleeve technologies violate the limits of known subjectivity when reduced to the experience of a single body. Tembo theorizes three interconnections between Meths: as comprehensive examples of the posthuman condition; the stack and sleeve technology; and sexuality in relation to the limit-experience, which also best sums up the Meth condition in a nutshell—the possibility to live through the death of the body and the mind. Tembo recognizes the transmission of consciousness and the liberation from the limits of singularity as the most radical statement in the world of *Altered Carbon*, which brings him to the concept of Meth sexuality as a consequence of disintegration of subjectivity.

Finally, Michał Klata proposes a very formal type of cinematic analysis, rooted in classic theory of montage developed by Sergei Eisenstein, as well as Laura Mulvey's concept of the male gaze, which he applies to the "infamous" sex scenes. "Functions of Sex Scenes in *Altered Carbon*" could be read as a direct response to the aforementioned reviewers' critiques of the show. To these Klata replies with his own accusations of the superficial reception of the series by the reviewers. He also clarifies reasons for such harsh critique and presents the importance of sex scenes in serving to advance the plot. His insight offers a new perspective regarding the evaluation of the cinematic merit of the series, presenting the clever ways is which *Altered Carbon* uses cinematic language. Despite being rooted in a very classic methodology, Klata offers one of the most radical reinterpretations of the series. This essay is also the first to raise the issue of another recurring theme, the relationship between Eros and Thanatos, and how it is presented in the world of *Altered Carbon*.

The second section—"Sleeves"—theorizes the focal point of the Netflix production, which is the stack and sleeve technology. Already described by Tembo as the most far-reaching element of *Altered Carbon*, it returns yet again with a full focus on the consequences of disconnection between the mind and the body. At first glance the stack and sleeve technology presents disembodiment as a way of living, a posthuman utopia of free mind, limitless in a digital environment. As Paweł Frelik puts it, "traditional cyberpunk is privileging the mind and reviling the body" (2010, p. 185). Cyberpunk is a fantasy about escaping embodiment but the issue of the body is the flipside of the stack and sleeve technology, and the following essays are determined to prove that. The first two essays in this section present the issue of subjectivity in the conditions of disembodiment of the subject, detailing the potential changes undergone by the human condition in a world in which the self is separated from a singular body. These analyses discredit the radical dissonance between the body and the mind, which became the basis for the formation of the Cartesian subject and, in effect, influenced the transhuman perception of the self. The other four essays analyze the consequences of the stack and sleeve technology in various contexts: market, ideological, psychoanalytical, as well as in the light of the broadly understood phantasm of death avoidance. The most promising aspect of these essays is not their exploration of the future as it is presented in *Altered Carbon*, but their usage of the series as a lens highlighting the political, economical and philosophical issues of today.

Esra Köksal and Burcu Baykan focus on subjectivity in the context of the stack and sleeve technology. In "The Materiality of Reality: The Floating Consciousness in *Altered Carbon*," they oppose the typical cyberpunk understanding of bodiless and freed consciousness with Donna Haraway's concept of cyborg subjectivity, and N. Katherine Hayles' interpretation of posthumanism. This significantly complicates the context of the series and allows us to see *Altered Carbon* as a unique voice in cyberpunk discourse. Intertextuality of the series again becomes clearly visible, since the Netflix production opposes traditional elevation of the mind at the expense of the body. Embodiment and consciousness are two distinct dimensions of human subjectivity but since René Descartes we tend to understand the unified subject as bodiless. Haraway's cyborg rejects this essentialism and dualism, as well as ontological boundaries, which allows Hayles to theorize posthuman consciousness as a collective, de-centered and heterogeneous entity. Reconfiguration of the human condition through the installation of stacks only seemingly frees the subject from the boundaries of the body. In reality, stacks and sleeves are connected and complement each other, neither is self-reliant. Through their in-depth analysis Köksal and Baykan prove that the stacks and sleeves technology "provide[s] the foundation for the growth of the cyborg subjectivity" and by that they unveil corporality upon subjectivity.

Lars Schmeink continues the analysis of the posthuman treatment of the mind/body relationship in the series in "Embodiment in *Altered Carbon*." For Schmeink, the Netflix series presents a posthuman nightmare, a hypercapitalist fantasy of commodification of bodies where an obviously flawed posthuman vision of bodiless existence intersects with "the complete embrace of capitalist, neoliberal notions of human ownership and mastery of the body."

Schmeink takes various aspects of the series under consideration, devoting special attention to those pursuing the posthuman narration of interchangeable bodies (mostly Meths) and those focusing on the importance of corporeality in creating a person's consciousness. The coexistence of both points of view in the series is not a matter of inconsequence but a response to the social inequalities and the treatment of the upgraded sleeve as a premium commodity. The posthuman vision of consciousness freely drifting between bodies, etheric and bodiless at its core, turns out to be a capitalist fantasy which can become a reality when one possesses sufficient assets. Only the rich can afford to control the body on a level in which they actually trick themselves into believing that they have mastered the biological tool, to the point of it becoming a material expression of their existence. Schmeink notices that Meths are actually prone to bodily impulses, even though they think they are the ones in control. The commodification of the body is based on the modern discourse of the triumph of the mind over the body, which leads us straight to the trap of posthumanism.

Łukasz Muniowski also focuses on the material dimension of the slack and sleeve technology. "Wearing Wellness on Your Sleeve: On Meths, Self-Control and Capitalism" puts resleeving in the context of market forces of late capitalism. Muniowski remarks that sleeves are just commodities, while the best, luxury products are available only to the chosen few. The quality of a sleeve is what marks the difference between the rich and the poor. It corresponds with the neoliberal concept of wellness as self-control and self-responsibility, but in the world of *Altered Carbon* a perfect body is not the consequence of strong will and hard work, just wealth. The slogan "You Deserve This Sleeve!" is the embodiment of internalized capitalism, a system that ultimately commodifies everything. Muniowski's analysis evokes Foucault's idea of biopolitics, the concept of the "productive body" as market value. This essay also points to the gender double standard in the Netflix production. The sleeve commercial is aimed at (heterosexual) men. It flatters their vanity, reassures them that they deserve only the best sleeves on the market. But at the same time female sleeves are advertised with the slogan "Put Your Wife in Me," which compromises every trace of female agency, even in the wealthy class of Meths. Presenting the body/sleeve as a product also underlines the economic gap between classes, and the fact that wellness and immortality are available only to a select few in the world of *Altered Carbon*.

Aline Ferreira offers a unique perspective on posthumanism in terms of thanatology. "New (Cloned) Bodies for Old: Biopolitics in *Altered Carbon*" focuses on the phantasmatic aspects of the series, seeing in it the realization of the eternal fantasy of escaping death. The Netflix series stands out in regard to other realizations of that motive due to the superficial egalitarianism of the technology allowing eternal existence. This leads to the creation of a society which is not afraid of death. Ferreira ponders the social and psychological consequences of such a state of affairs in regard to Freud's diagnosis of the human condition as fueled by the death drive. In the Western philosophical tradition mortality is the basis and ultimate point of human existence, that which gives life meaning. The lack of the inevitable vastly influences the society of *Altered Carbon*. Those who are the closest to reaching immortality in every sense of that word—the wealthy Meths—are completely devoid of morality, at least as we understand it, which gives way to an eternal indulgence in hedonistic pleasures. Unequal distribution of wealth and the gradual degeneration of the "mortals" turn *Altered Carbon* into a cautionary tale about the dangers of posthuman fantasies coming true.

"'Meths' versus 'Quellists': *Altered Carbon* as the Battleground of Two Ideologies," by Damla Pehlivan, offers a unique reading of the Netflix series through the lens of Gnosticism—religious ideas and systems based on a duality between the material universe and spiritual transcendence. Pehlivan analyzes the series' take on the materiality of human existence, which corresponds well with previous essays. The essay is also a compelling approach to the sleeve and stack technology as the answer to a millennia-old inquiry of whether human transcendence can be reached through knowledge (*gnosis*) or technology. Pehlivan begins with similarities between the information society and Gnostic apotheosis of knowledge. The world of *Altered Carbon* turns out to be "a Gnostic-ornamented realm" where "a technologic transcendence is combined with Gnostic symbolism." Moreover, it is possible to ascribe Gnostic values to two main ideologies in the world of *Altered Carbon*, Meths and Quellists, groups that represent different understandings of humanness. For Meths the stack and sleeve technology is another step toward the improvement of the human race; for Quellists it is a part of the process of self-dehumanization. Both groups also strive to reach transcendence from the constraints of the human condition which results in two very distinctive uses of Gnosticism. In this essay it becomes clear that the Netflix series wisely utilizes the elements of the past—genre conventions, ideologies and the construction of time itself—to tell the story about the future of mankind. To decipher Gnostic elements in *Altered Carbon* as another layer of meaning is fascinating by itself but it also contributes to a broader reading of the series.

Dariusz Brzostek's "Look Who's Talking: Haunted Bodies and Uncanny Voices in *Altered Carbon*" also focuses on a "millennia-old question" of identity, as well as a fundamentally anthropological question of who is actually speaking. Brzostek uses psychoanalysis to answer the inquiry about the notion of identity inscribed in the body and the voice. This essay moves beyond the stack and sleeve technology, and sees the transfer of consciousnesses not only as a technological process, but also, simultaneously, as a part of non-scientific, religious or metaphysical discourse which explains why Neo-Catholics refuse to be resleeved. In the context of psychoanalysis and horror, resleeving is akin to the mediumship phenomenon of using the voice of the spirit or the Other. The general idea of Richard Morgan's novel and the Netflix series is the relationship between the self and the body, while the main uncanny motif in the story is someone else's voice haunting the body. This essay explores the soundscape of the *Altered Carbon* universe in the context of the psychoanalysis of human voice and Derrida's idea of hauntology, rethought by Colin Davis in his *Haunted Subjects*.

The third section—"Cyberpunk"—focuses on the metatextual dimension of *Altered Carbon*. The series was criticized for the display of quasi and direct quotes from paramount cyberpunk texts, without contributing any new perspectives to cyberpunk's exploration of the socio-cultural concerns surrounding technology. The spirits of *Blade Runner* and *Ghost in the Shell* are present within the cityscape of Bay City as well as within the main motifs and themes of the series. The genre references are not empty dingbats, however. They run far deeper than critics of the series have noticed, which is proven by the essays in this section. It may even be said that *Altered Carbon* is haunted by its cyberpunk past. Articulations of this haunting result in a reformulation of the genre. *Altered Carbon* is a textbook example of what cyberpunk is but is also an attempt to remold the genre within the new expectations from the not-so-distant future. The series actively seeks to reimagine the structure and narration of cyberpunk in the light of postmodern fears and hopes associated with the posthuman condition.

Adam Edwards' "Cyberpunk Resleeved: How Netflix's *Altered Carbon* Reformats at Its Cyberpunk Ancestry" argues that the Netflix series builds upon the audience's previous engagement with iconic cyberpunk texts to "refresh dialogues about dystopian technology and press such discussions into a distinctly contemporary context." Edwards looks upon not only well known mainstream titles such as *Blade Runner*, but also the cult-classic British series *Max Headroom: 20 Minutes into the Future*. Edwards' use of Fredric Jameson's distinction between *parody* and *pastiche* and Linda Hutcheon's theory of parody, to analyze *Altered Carbon* precisely as a parody recognizes at least two layers of the parodic mechanism: parody of the transhumanist ideology regarding technology that allows escaping embodiment and, more importantly, a "self-aware and *useful* parody of the genre itself." Hutcheon understands parody as a "repetition with critical distance," which actually comes close to irony. In this essay *Altered Carbon* becomes an ironic series, strategically parodist and thus reformulating cyberpunk's traditional tropes. Subtle changes in the narration, as well as the structure of the plot and the characters are the subject of Edward's analysis, through which he demonstrates the shift from "the violent detective's world, to the more recognizable family space," from exploitations of the techno-revolution to a very personal impact of it on our everyday lives; from androcentric cyberpunk rooted in hard-boiled fiction to challenging and engaging speculative fiction.

Kenneth Matthews argues that the concepts of time and history are central to *Altered Carbon*, and analyzes the work of ironic distance in the series. "Another Kind of War: The Manufacturing of History in *Altered Carbon*" transcribes the mechanism of parody as repetition with changes to the subplot of the series regarding the reconstruction of history, be it the personal history of Takeshi Kovacs, lost memories of Laurence Bancroft or the change in understanding of the Uprising by future generations. Matthews reads the series through a lens of New Historicism, which reveals a complex manufacturing of history that is dependent upon the complexity of power in the present. Even with the stacks and sleeves technology, past is mostly constructed, not remembered. And as such, history escapes the linear way of thinking. The series puts a lot of effort into presenting this peculiar attribute of history by reassembling fragments of its timeline and charging the audience with the responsibility of putting them in the correct order. In Matthews' words, "the world of *Altered Carbon* shows how history is manufactured through the manipulation (both intentional and unintentional) of the past during the present," which is related to "contemporary concerns of misinformation in the post-truth political environment." This can serve as an illustration of Edwards' idea concerning reformulating cyberpunk within *Altered Carbon*, in accordance with contemporary sensitivity. This essay also stands on its own as the beginning of an analysis of how carefully crafted the relation between past, present and future in the Netflix series actually is.

Aldona Kobus continues this thread of reasoning in the essay "The Present of the Dead: Spectral Ideology in *Altered Carbon*." The Derridean metaphor of haunting stands here for the past that becomes visible in the present in order to hold us accountable. The transmission of consciousness between sleeves through stacks has all the characteristics of haunting. This essay analyzes various forms of haunting, ghost-like characters and the purpose of the perpetual returns of the past in the world of *Altered Carbon*: the specter of Poe, the ghostly existence of Lizzie Elliot, and the haunting of Takeshi Kovacs. Specters in the series appear as *revenants* as well as *arrivants*, reminders of the past and heralds of the future that is supposed to come. In that world, time is defragmented, and chronological, linear order is not the reality. Hauntology makes it possible for us to reinterpret the past and use it as a tool for change. Repetition with change—*difference*, a very Derridean notion indeed—seems to be a recurring theme in this section and the core of the reformulation of the cyberpunk genre. The core of Derridean hauntology is the relationship between responsibility and inheritance, which rightly sums up the condition of the series. Kobus writes that *Altered Carbon* is haunted by the ghosts of cyberpunk and its roots, including the proto-crime stories of Edgar Allan Poe and classic noir films. The series takes on its heritage and uses it to activate the untapped potential of the genre. This is achieved through the emotional dimension of the Gothic, which translates to the motivations of characters and a different construction of the main character, who rejects the toxic masculinity inherent to traditional noir detectives. The haunting of Kovacs is similar to the female characters' relationships with specters, at least in the form presented by modern television. Derridean hauntology reveals another layer of the feminist dimension of *Altered Carbon*. It is also quite surprising how accurately Derridean theses are presented in the series.

The ghost of Edgar Allan Poe comes back in the final essay of the book, by Fernando Gabriel Pagnoni Berns and Emiliano Aguilar, "Nevermore! Poesque Thanatophobia as Counter-Narrative." The authors analyze in depth the Gothic heritage presented in the Netflix series, its aesthetics and ethos, which are deeply rooted in late Gothic novels. Poe, an AI character, serves as a reminder of what is seemingly missing in the world of *Altered Carbon*: death. Pagnoni Berns and Aguilar read Poe's presence as a counter-narrative that parallels and challenges the neoliberal discourse framing the show. The neoliberal thinking that imposes itself through Meth ideology rejects the ethics of death, burial and mourning, transforming life into something that can be extended to the infinite. In other words, the show reveals deep thanatophobia—excessive fear of death—inscribed in our current culture. As death is mastered through the show and presented as nothing more than exciting exoticism, Poe's counter-hegemonic narrative disrupts this neoliberal logic. This essay analyzes the different spectral traces of Poe in the show: fear of death, metempsychosis, the importance of the letter "L" in the names of the female characters such as Lizzie, among others. It also concludes the concatenation of Eros and Thanatos, a motif mentioned in several earlier essays. The Gothic take on the relationship between erotica and death makes for an acute and interesting analysis of those two dimensions of human existence. Pagnoni Berns and Aguilar see the relationship between the two as necessary for the reveal of the fundamental feature of thanathopobia—fear of death is unequivocal with the fear of life. This is the most vital lesson of this futuristic vision of a society without death, responsibility and consequences, as presented in *Altered Carbon*.

The essays in this collection vary when it comes to methodology, approach and context but they serve as a deep and comprehensive analysis of fascinating issues, motifs and problems presented in the Netflix production. Their relevance goes well beyond the series itself—the tools used and conclusions reached here may as well be applied to other mainstream titles. The fact that we have not exhausted the underlying topics of *Altered Carbon*, combined with the announcement of a second season and an animated series, leaves the door open for further analysis and publications devoted to the topic. At a closer look, *Altered Carbon* has more to offer than initially noticed. We are hoping future seasons will offer just as many hard questions and complicated solutions.

REFERENCES

Cadora K. (1995). Feminist cyberpunk. *Science Fiction Studies*, 22(3), 357–372.
Chaney, J. (February 2, 2018). Altered Carbon is an over-stacked cyberpunk mess. *Vulture*. Retrieved from https://www.vulture.com/.
Frelik, P. (2010). Woken carbon: The return of the human in Richard K. Morgan's Takeshi Kovacs trilogy. In G. Murphy & S. Vint (Eds.), *Beyond cyberpunk: New critical perspectives* (pp. 173–190). New York: Routledge.
Lee, B. (February 1, 2018). Altered Carbon review—Ambitious Netflix sci-fi is flashy, flawed and fun. *The Guardian*. Retrieved from https://www.theguardian.com/.
Muncy, J. (February 2, 2018). Altered Carbon may not be the cyberpunk show you're looking for. *Wired*. Retrieved from https://www.wired.com/.

Sex

"Technology advances, but humans don't"

Neo-Noir Women, Psychoanalysis and Transhuman Love

Alexander N. Howe

Since the release of Ridley Scott's groundbreaking and visually stunning *Blade Runner* (1982), neo-noir science fiction films have necessarily engaged the hard-boiled thematics of time, mortality, and empathy, all of which were very much a part of the original early and mid-century hard-boiled and noir texts that inspired Scott's film. While the world-weary neo-noir male hero is a "stacks" character type, the neo-noir female detective is a far rarer construction, despite the fact that as the hard-boiled and noir genres develop throughout the twentieth and twenty-first centuries, such characters appear with increasing frequency. One of the great accomplishments of *Altered Carbon* (Lenic & Kalogridis, 2018–) is the creation of a deeply complex female hard-boiled detective, Kristin Ortega (Martha Higareda), that draws significantly from this tradition, particularly the genre's focus on relationships and private and domestic life. In this essay, I will argue that while Ortega at first glance reads as a sort of redemptive touchstone of the series, her reflections on her past love relationship with Elias Ryker (Joel Kinnaman) increasingly reveal the Lacanian *Real of the drive* as a machinic and alien experience that is at the core of all love relationships. This opens an interesting reassessment of neo-noir posthumanism, while Ortega productively engages with the technological amplification of embodiment at the heart of the series by reminding us of more traditional (and low tech) uncanny impasses of the psyche.

Altered Carbon: *"I'm asking you to be human"*

Stack technology offers a novel take on the issue of embodiment, and serves as a useful mirror in a time of omnipresent screens, when our physicality is significantly devalued and disavowed. The reduction of the body to interchangeable sleeves in Netflix's *Altered Carbon* figures this devaluation quite well. Indeed, characters with the appropriate financial means might play dress-up with bodies just as easily as children play with old clothes, and should their current sleeve become damaged beyond repair, they can simply be transferred into a new one. However, while bodies might be arbitrary within the series, they are nevertheless necessary, first and foremost because humans choose embodiment when technology makes it possible to upload human consciousness into the infinity of virtual, bodiless space. Disembodiment within a virtual space, or being placed "on ice," is actually a form of imprisonment and often torture in the series. For the Meth characters, veritable immortality assures that human decadence finally knows no bounds, and sexualized violence and murder become a diversion of the mega-rich, allowing customers to rage against embodiment, which remains an impediment of one kind or another. The possibility of "real death" or destruction of an individual's stack, in these murderous sessions heightens the drama of this pursuit. The body, and our most basic condition of embodiment, is not so easily left behind, despite the fact that stack technology ostensibly promises exactly this possibility.

Promising Monsters: The Body in Trans- and Posthumanism

Celebratory trans- or posthumanism might be typified by Hans Moravec's 1990 declaration that it will one day be possible to download a human consciousness onto a computer (1990, p. 123), a possibility that had long been common for sci-fi and cyberpunk speculative fiction. Posthuman extropian philosophy, based on the work of futurist Max More, offers a similarly optimistic promise that humans might live indefinitely through the rational use of technology. As More declares in his manifesto:

> Extropy means designing and managing technologies not as ends in themselves but as effective means for improving life. Applying science and technology creatively and courageously to transcend "natural" but harmful, confining qualities derived from our biological heritage, culture, and environment [More 2003].

Technology and rationality promise life beyond all limits, and More's own engagement with cryonics demonstrates the extremes of this faith. Such claims about technology are unmistakably fantasy constructions that promise to return a missing wholeness to individuals. This prospect plays upon an age-old transferential relation to science as messianic, and one that inevitably places the body at the forefront, be it as the object of mesmerism or the vitamin industry. Posthumanism of this type reduces the body to a problem that must be solved and escaped through the rational application of technology—only then can we at last be our best selves—and as several critics have identified, it amounts to simply another brand of humanist progression through reason.

However, Suzanne Dow and Colin Wright suggest that there is a "critical posthumanism" that "interrogates the imbrication of the embodied human with other entities—potentially animate, inanimate, informatics—and the extent to which this imbrication militates in favor of a perhaps more radical de-centering of the human than poststructuralist itself envisioned" (Dow & Wright, 2010, p. 302). Such work does not promise to return a missing wholeness to the subject; rather, it examines the ways in which our inherently limited subjectivity is all the more bound to technological and informatic interfaces. In so doing, we reclaim our flawed embodiment, something that is increasingly disavowed when the bulk of our time is spent screening our virtual identities. As Jacques Lacan reminded early in his seminar, "we are embodied beings, and we always think by means of some imaginary go-between, which halts, stops, clouds up the symbolic mediation. The latter is perpetually ground up, interrupted" (Lacan, 1988, p. 319). Today more than ever, the screen is the site of our fantasies of subjective completeness—technologized go-between's in a process that Lacan acknowledges is essential to the subject. The body is undoubtedly a sharp reminder of the limits of screen life, particularly at a time when symbolic mediation (that is, a realization that our fantasies are just that—fantasies) is perhaps more easily disregarded in the apparently seamless virtual spaces we inhabit. However, critical posthumanism of the sort proposed by Dow and Wright likewise acknowledges that the body itself is transformed, reimagined, and re-deployed as a thinking, desiring, and enjoying entity through contemporary technological interfaces. In other words, the uncanny return of the body will be technologized.

The stack technology of *Altered Carbon* is a perfect mechanism for considering the complexities of embodiment in critical posthumanism. It should ultimately remind us of the ways in which we are newly (or further) embodied—and not disembodied—by our increased reliance upon technology. As *Altered Carbon* emphasizes, our minds do in fact need bodies, and, interestingly, the apparent immortality of jumping from sleeve-to-sleeve, or body-to-body, underscores the imperfections of this arrangement. The condition of "sleeve sickness" occurs for those who make the jump too frequently and are thus disoriented beyond comfort by their new incarnation. This is a shrewd reminder that the human condition is to be not-at-home in body or mind, which is the most basic psychoanalytic insight. Interestingly, we are told that jumping into cloned bodies of oneself (i.e., a copy of one's own body) does not result in this condition; however, the Bancroft family, who have the means to indulge in this way, give ample evidence that this practice is not so comfortable as it may appear. This, then, is the greater posthuman insight of *Altered Carbon*: technology will not free us from our bodies; quite the contrary, it requires us to rethink the parameters of our embodiment.

Feminine Forms: Noir Bodies and Hard-Boiled Kindred

This foregrounding of embodiment through technology in the series is amplified by the neo-noir mode in which it is told. Ridley Scott's *Blade Runner* (1982) brilliantly merged the genres of dystopian science fiction and film noir, and produced a benchmark against which all similar projects must be measured. *Altered Carbon* contains numerous atmospheric allusions to Scott's film—often to the point of distraction—and each of its episodes is named after a famous film noir. Noir films of course originated during the Second World War in America, with strapped Hollywood budgets and a somber national mood resulting in a stark cinema where light and shadow become as meaningful as set pieces and narrative. John Huston's 1941 film version of Dashiell Hammett's *The Maltese Falcon* is an essential early example of the genre. Here, all the key components of noir are present: visually, the play of shadows in the film mimics the protagonist's struggle to remain good in a morally ambiguous world.

Humphrey Bogart's portrayal of Sam Spade is similarly genre-defining. The character's tough, world-weariness is obviously an enduring movie trope—one that interestingly undermines a good deal of Hammett's own characterization of the detective, who is more beleaguered than Bogart, particularly at the conclusion of the novel. What likewise becomes a hallmark of the genre is the anti-climax of the detective story within the film; that is, the recovery of the Maltese Falcon statue itself, which turns out to be counterfeit. Such thwarted detections are common to the genre, which is, in the end, an anti-romance featuring the failure of knowledge. It is precisely because of this failure of knowledge, and ultimately the order of law, that the detective becomes all the more embodied. The threat of violence and death is ubiquitous in this world and is, of course, quite frequently represented in film noir by the *femme fatale* character who endeavors to seduce, use, and ultimately kill (or frame) the detective.

The role of women in film noir is fascinating, both within the films themselves and in the scholarship devoted to the genre. Indeed, feminist film criticism in the 1970s was built largely through an ongoing debate on the status of women in these works. Noir women are inevitably captivating and powerful, at the level of the narrative and the frame, so much so that their allure often overshadows the shortcomings of some of the plots of such films. They nevertheless remain objects of desire and play for the men in the stories. A woman remains an object that is seen and produced in this seeing. Janey Place summarizes the uniqueness of noir women who are "active, not static symbols, are intelligent and powerful, if destructively so, and derive power, not weakness, from their sexuality" (1998, p. 47). And naturally, it is because of this activity that "men need to control women's sexuality in order not to be destroyed by it" (Place, 1998, p. 49). Nonetheless, Christine Gledhill suggests that the femme fatale's characterization is far more nuanced and idiosyncratic to each film. The only commonality with which we might group these women is through their "unstable and fractured characterization" (Gledhill, 1998, p. 31), a conclusion that Ann Kaplan similarly reaches in the introduction to the 1998 edition of her famous anthology, *Women in Film Noir*: "Given generational, racial, class, and sexual-orientation differences among women, I would argue that film noir offers a space for playing out *various* gender fantasies" (Kaplan, 1998, p. 10)—for both women and men. Critics of detective fiction have made a similar argument regarding women in hard-boiled and noir works, and Lee Horsley in particular has demonstrated the more nuanced presentation of the femme fatale in fiction, which avoids the simple villain-virgin option for women and implicates the detective (and culture) in such gendered categories (Horsley, 2005, p. 154). In fact, a good deal of recent work has been devoted to the ambiguity of the male detective's own body and pleasure (e.g., Plain & Forter), providing a more complex reading of gender across the genre.

The hard-boiled mode itself undoubtedly functions as a space for mediating various gender fantasies, as Kaplan suggests of film noir, and a historical shift within the genre is particularly important for understanding *Altered Carbon*. In the late 1970s, women and minority authors begin producing works featuring women and minority detectives—that is, individuals who were formerly reduced to objects and villains within the hard-boiled world suddenly took center stage as investigators. Marcia Muller, Sue Grafton, and Sara Paretsky are pioneers to these ends, and female sleuths continue to grow in popularity the world over. These new detectives share many of their male counterparts' qualities of wit, intelligence, and perseverance; however, often developed over several novels in lengthy series, their characterization is unsurprisingly more complex than in the original works. Of particular importance here is the foregrounding of family and sustained love relationships. Whereas the original hard-boiled protagonists were largely blank professionals without a past, these new detectives enjoy fuller and varied lives open to the accidents (and perils) of fortune. The question of embodiment is, then, all the more significant for the female hard-boiled detective, as she must negotiate not only her defense against a hostile world, but also a merger with her loved ones. This includes scripting her own active sexuality, but likewise maintaining ties with friends and family to build community rather than retreat from it, as was the case with the original hard-boiled dicks.

Female Hard-Boiled Detectives: Officer Kristin Ortega

In *Altered Carbon*, Officer Kristin Ortega of the Bay City Police Department is brilliantly cast as a noir investigator that draws significantly from this tradition of the female hard-boiled detective. Her lines are clever, snide, and powerful, much like the original detectives and femme fatales. Appropriately, she has a lengthy history of problems with authority including her supervisor, Captain Tanaka (Hiro Kanagawa), and the Bancroft family, whose indulgences frequently skirt the law. She lives alone in a sparsely furnished apartment that was once a retail space, littered with still unpacked moving boxes—a smart set piece that merges public and private in keeping with the original hard-boiled ethos. Her partner, Samir Abboud (Waleed Zuaiter), often chides her about her solitary life, and he maintains a relationship with Ortega's mother that seems closer than her own. These hard-boiled tropes are summarized well in Episode 2, "Fallen Angel," when Ortega—who has woken up early to practice kickboxing with Abboud before work—suggests that he needs to stay out of her personal life, to which he replies: "And what personal life would that be?"

While this collapse of the private into the personal is the hallmark of early hard-boiled works, Officer Ortega is far more complex and interesting, infusing the neo-noir aspects of the series with many elements of contemporary hard-boiled detective fiction. She maintains a strong, if quarrelsome, connection with her family—particularly her mother who intrudes frequently with motherly advice and convenient expositions in the form of debate on stack technology. In Episode 3, "In a Lonely Place," Ortega amusingly has her dead grandmother's stack "spun up" and resleeved into the body of a street thug she found at the police station to celebrate *Dia de Los Muertos*—a common practice for those who cannot afford to be resleeved indefinitely. The dinner scene that follows is wonderfully humorous, as the doting grandmother in the body of a brutish, tattooed criminal drinks heavily and is reunited with her great-grandchildren. The Ortega family are, for the most part, devoutly Neo-Catholic and have consequently opted out of stack technology; however, the grandmother renounced this "coding" after her husband died, choosing instead the option of resurrection—a choice that infuriates her extremely conservative daughter Alazne, Kristin's mother, to no end. Kristin and her grandmother have a revealing conversation shortly before the evening ends, and the grandmother speaks of the trauma of losing the great love of her life, Kristin's grandfather. After speaking of their joy and conflicts, she asks to never be brought back again, explaining: "No matter how long you live, you never finish. You have to let the world continue. Accept that death is part of life" (*AC* 3, "In a Lonely Place"). The grandmother is a fantastic figure of play and openness, who offers a less-dogmatic insight into the biological limits of the human. She clearly is a source of strength and wisdom for Kristin, and their conversation suggests the possibility of love and connection for the detective.

Such an unchaining of the professional and private is in effect a neo-hard-boiled character arc and promises a more fulfilled and broadened experience. Indeed we learn that Ortega has already made such a connection with fellow police officer, Elias Ryker; the two were in a long-term committed relationship and had recently made the decision to move in together. Ryker has unfortunately been jailed for a murder that he did not commit, and incarceration in the future amounts to the deep (or big) "sleep" of having one's stack placed in hibernation. Kristin was in love with Ryker and actually went so far as to pay the rent on his sleeve storage to ensure that his stack and body could be reunited should she find evidence to acquit him. Unfortunately, Laurens Bancroft has Kovacs cruelly resleeved in the body of Ryker to punish Ortega for repeatedly harassing his family. This painful joke accounts for Ortega's interest in Kovacs, and she actually goes so far as to put a tracking device on him, presumably so she can keep an eye on her lover's sleeve, in addition to keeping tabs on the Bancrofts, whom she suspects had something to do with framing Ryker.

Unsurprisingly, the sexual tension between the two characters develops rapidly, and in Episode 5—aptly titled, "The Wrong Man"—the two have sex soon after Kovacs learns the origin of his current sleeve. Shortly before this he also eerily sees a clone of his own original sleeve in an underground flesh market, an experience that emphasizes just how far both he and time are out of joint. In the seduction scene at Ortega's apartment, Kovacs at one point asks what she sees when she looks into his eyes. She sharply responds that they are not his eyes; however, it is clear that she has developed a connection to Kovacs, despite the fact that he inhabits Ryker's body. The uncanniness of the disembodiment—or better, mis-embodiment—here is downplayed, somewhat, by the characters for whom resleeving is an everyday occurrence; however, their union suggests an inherently uncanny aspect to all love and attraction.

The nature of this connection between Ortega and Kovacs becomes an ongoing question for the remaining five episodes, and is often contrasted with flashbacks of Kovacs' prior relationship with the revolutionary, Quellchrist Falconer (Renée Elise Goldsberry), the founder of the Envoys, an elite counter-military organization. In these flashbacks, Takeshi Kovacs is played by Will Yun Lee. The dialogue in these sequences is at times melodramatic, a tone typified by Falconer's claim that "a man who doesn't love isn't a man" (*AC* 6, "Man with My Face"), a comment made in response to Kovacs's own assertion that "a man who doesn't love, gives no hostage to fortune." Despite the strained emotion, it is clear that the series wishes to pose love as a question, and the Ortega and Kovacs relationship becomes all the more powerful when Ortega is violently attacked at the police precinct, forcing Kovacs to rush to her aid. In her delirium after emergency surgery, Ortega looks at Kovacs and calls him "Elias" (Ryker), and Kovacs walks out, noticeably dejected. Elsewhere, this connection is comically downplayed, as people repeatedly call Ortega Kovac's "girl," a moniker that both renounce—Kristin goes so far as to exclaim, in one instance, "I don't even like him"—although it is obvious that they both protest too strongly. Ortega's grounded family life and fidelity to her partner, her work, and her boyfriend further suggest that she is a sort of sentimental moral center to the series. However, by way of conclusion, I would like to argue that her love for Kovacs, and the posthumanism of *Altered Carbon* itself, are far more interesting and demands recourse to psychoanalysis.

Psychoanalysis, Love and Posthumanism

In her essay, "Love and Sexual Difference: Doubled Partners in Men and Women," Renata Salecl discusses the barriers to love men and women so frequently create. Fiction and film—romantic or not—are inevitably built around such obstacles to love, and the desire created by these impossibilities all too often drives the larger plot, as well. As Salecl suggests, women in love illustrate well the Lacanian notion that desire is inevitably the desire of the Other, that is, women love, in part, by imagining the way in which they embody the *objet petit a* of their lover's desire—and thereby their lack, in Lacan's reckoning of the subject. Because the woman understands that this object must remain open, she does all within her power to be elusive, and doubled partners, often in a classic Hollywood-esque love triangle, is one such strategy (Salecl, 2000, p. 307; p. 315). From a psychoanalytic perspective, this type of love is more closely aligned with the experience of desire and is prone to any number of misfires that doubled partners are meant to conceal—"loving" the impossible lover in the midst of an oppressive marriage, for example. This romantic or courtly love attempts to take the lover as whole—as "the One" that will complete the subject. In the case of women, they must play the object to the man's One, and in this way access the Other's fantasy of wholeness.

However, Salecl speaks of a second variety of love in psychoanalysis, love as sublimation. In this instance, the lover approaches the partner as an object, "driven by the fact that the object can never be reached because of its impossible, horrifying nature," making love an "impossible mediator" between desire and drive (Salecl, 1998, p. 19; 2000, p. 48). In Lacan's work, desire functions as a structuring absence of the sort found in romantic love. Drive on the contrary is a presence of uncanny and often disturbing enjoyment. Love thus occupies that interstitial distance between the object of love as ordinary and transcendent. Alenka Zupančič summarizes this well when she suggests: "In love, we do not find satisfaction in the other that we aim at, we find it in the space or gap, between, to put it bluntly, what we see and what we get (the sublime and banal object)" (Zupančič, 2002, p. 77). The partner is enjoyed apart from the piecemeal fantasy of prohibition that organizes romantic love, leading Salecl to conclude that in love as sublimation, what we "love" in the other is the drive itself. In a like manner, Jacques-Alain Miller offers a rather lyrical description to the convergence of varieties of love aligning in sublimation (that is, as absent object of desire, demand for love, and present object of drive): "The labyrinths of amorous life are made from the articulation of these three levels, at time united, at times separate, permanent here, temporary there, whether pure, whether mixed. This is how one obtains in amorous lives meetings of infinite variety" (Miller, 2013).

Psychoanalysis suggests a useful disruption of celebratory posthumanism's narcissism, which is always a variety of love, that imagines wholeness for the subject when freed from the limits of the body. Toward similar ends, Jerry Aline Flieger writes of analysis's ability to disrupt the "flatness of the mirror reflection [in celebratory posthumanism] between the human Creator and his (*sic*) machines. Freud showed us, after all, that when we seem to exercise the greatest control over our world, and our own discourse, a 'slip' may remind us of just how wily the unconscious is, and just how human we remain" (Flieger, 2010, p. 364). Love itself is precisely an experience of this slip, as attraction, desire, and enjoyment occur at disruptive times and in unexpected embodiments. With this psychoanalytic insight, posthuman love is, then, a detour through technology that promises mastery and (re)union with all that we have lost and offers instead a reminder of the inherent limits that are the very foundation of our (often uncanny) humanity as subjects of the unconscious.

Conclusion

As with all good science fiction, *Altered Carbon* begins with a transcendence of fundamental human limits through the use of technology—in this case, mortality itself. The Neo-Catholics of the series protest the use of stack technology as inhuman, and even the Envoys were originally a terrorist organization which sabotaged stacks to ensure that everyone lived only one lifetime. A frequent refrain throughout the series is the monstrousness of human nature that is displayed when time is no longer a factor. Indeed, what is no longer possible when we are given unlimited time? For Kristin Ortega, the question of limits and love is similar. Her relationship with Elias Ryker seemingly contains all the usual hesitations and blockages, particularly regarding their moving in together. With his imprisonment, their love becomes literally impossible, reducing her to a pining romantic lover—a brief condition that does not diminish her numerous and innovative neo-hard-boiled and noir traits. Just before her sexual encounter with Kovacs (in Ryker's body), she mentions that it had been a long time since someone looked at her the way he does—that is, since she was the object of desire for another. Kovacs is, then, a doubled partner that allows Ortega to maintain her desire (and love) for Ryker.

That Kovacs inhabits Ryker's body is Lacanian through and through, as the doubling spoken of by Salecl takes place literally within the same body. It is tempting to argue that Kovacs represents the drive of Ryker; however, such a seamless alignment of narrative and theory is unnecessary. At the conclusion of the series, as she and Kovacs finish unpacking the apartment, Kristin is clearly anxious about Ryker's return. It remains to be seen whether or not she will traverse this blockage in favor of a revivified relationship with her boyfriend, but it is clear that she understands the emptiness of the romantic structure that formerly sustained her, even in her solitude. This insight undercuts the broad gesture to romantic love that seems to conclude the first season, as Kovacs speaks of setting off in search of Falconer, whom Reileen resurrected and hid away as a sort of insurance policy. These gestures outward into the sunset or even into the infinity of immortality are, as Ortega's grandmother concludes, ultimately inhuman. Juxtaposed with this is an enjoyment in presence that Kristin's relationship with Kovacs in her boyfriend's sleeve has suggested. Lacan's notion that love means giving what you do not have is exactly what occurs in *Altered Carbon* (Lacan, 2015, p. 34). Kovacs, in effect, "gives" Ryker to Ortega (or the vice versa—it amounts to the same thing), and it is through this that she regains her love.

Posthumanism requires us to reflect upon the bodily effects of our technologized and virtual existences, just as psychoanalysis reminds us that our bodies are marked, and therefore limited, by both drive and language. Quite apart from a humanist notion of the soul and the unwavering improvement of humanity, both psychoanalysis and critical posthumanism show us that the very notion of our unique humanity is a function of an overarching, machine-like structure. To these ends, less utopian renderings of technology are instructive and, truth be told, increasingly familiar to us all as the luster of mid-90s promises of virtual life and cyberpunk fantasies have faded in the blue glow of our collective system crashes. As we know well, our online technology is inevitably flawed and halting, and this experience is as instructive as utopian science fiction narratives. As Dow and Wright suggest, here borrowing from a point made by Slavoj Žižek, the more "we are confronted in our daily lives with the over-functioning futility of gadgetry, not to say the piles of waste that it produces, the closer we get to the kind of subjective destitution at which psychoanalysis itself aims in the clinical setting" (2010, p. 306). Psychoanalysis thus reveals that technology neither corrects nor extends; rather, it embodies—as much through its failures as its success—the horrifying death drive at the core of the subject, an encounter that analysis is itself ultimately to provide. Kovac's voiceover narration that begins Episode 2, "Fallen Angel," asserts that "Technology advances but humans don't," a statement that exemplifies this psychoanalytic assessment of posthumanism well, and serves as a fitting summary of *Altered Carbon*'s final reading of technology.

References

Deeley, M. (Producer), & Scott, R. (Director). (1982). *Blade Runner* [Motion picture]. United States: Warner Brothers.

Dow, S., & Wright, C. (2010). Introduction: Towards a psychoanalytic reading of the posthuman. *Paragraph*, 33(3), pp. 299–317.

Flieger, J.A.(2010).Is there a doctor in the house? Psychoanalysis and the discourse of the posthuman. *Paragraph*, 33(3), pp. 354–375.

Forter, G. (2000). *Murdering masculinities: Fantasies of gender and violence in the American crime novel*. New York: NYU Press.

Gledhill, C. (1998). *Klute* 2:Feminism and *Klute*. In E.A. Kaplan (Ed.), *Women in film noir* (pp. 99–114). London: BFI

Horsley, L. (2005). *Twentieth-century crime fiction*. Oxford: Oxford University Press.

Huston, J. (Director). (1941). *The Maltese Falcon*. [Motion picture] United States: Warner Brothers.

Kaplan, E.A. (1998). Introduction to new edition. In E.A. Kaplan (Ed.), *Women in film noir* (pp. 1–14). London: BFI

Lacan, J. (1988). *The seminar of Jacques Lacan: Book 2: The ego in Freud's theory and in the technique of psychoanalysis, 1954-1955*. J.-A. Miller (Ed.) & S. Tomaselli (Trans.). Cambridge: Cambridge University Press.

_____. (2015). *The seminar of Jacques Lacan: Book 8: Transference*. J.-A. Miller (Ed.) & B. Fink (Trans.). Cambridge: Polity.

Lenic, J.G. (Producer), & Kalogridis, L. (Creator). *Altered Carbon*. (2018–). [Series]. United States: Netflix.

Miller, J.-A. (2013). Love's labyrinths: The symptom 16 (Summer). Lacan.com. Retrieved from http://www.lacan.com/.

Moravec, H. (1990). *Mind children: The future of robot and human intelligence*. Cambridge, MA: Harvard University Press.

More, M. (2003). Principles of extropy: An evolving framework of values and standards for continuously improving the human condition. *The Rational Argumentator*. Retrieved from http://www.rationalargumentator.com/.

Place, J. (1998). Women in film noir. In E.A. Kaplan (Ed.), *Women in film noir* (pp. 47–68). London: BFI.

Plain, G. (2001). *Twentieth-century crime fiction: Gender, sexuality and the body.* Chicago: Fitzroy and Dearborn.
Salecl, R. (1998). *(Per)version of love and hate.* New York: Verso.
―――. (2000). Love and sexual difference: Doubled partners in men and women. In R. Salecl (Ed.), *Sic 3: Sexuation* (pp. 297–316). Durham, NC: Duke University Press.
Zupančič, A. (2002). On love as comedy. *Lacanian Ink,* 20, pp. 62–79.

The Flinching Edge
Sex, Consensual Death(lessness) and the Limit-Experience in Altered Carbon

Kwasu David Tembo

> His generation was addicted to sorcery, and Methuselah apprehended that his grandson might be bewitched if his true name were known, wherefore he kept it a secret.
> —Chapter IV, "Noah—The Birth of Noah," from *The Legends of the Jews* by Louis Ginzberg (1909)

> Poetry leads to the same place as all forms of eroticism—to the blending and fusion of separate objects. It leads us to eternity, it leads us to death, and through death to continuity. Poetry is eternity; the sun matched with the sea.
> —Georges Bataille, *Erotism: Death and Sensuality* (1962)

"The Ruinousness of Our Extravagance": Introduction

Leata Kalogridis' Netflix adaptation of Richard K. Morgan's *Altered Carbon* (2002; 2018–) is set nearly 400 years in a future dystopian rendering of San Francisco or Bay City. In the world of *Altered Carbon*, a human being's consciousness and personality (specifically memories) can be removed, stored, and redistributed using devices known as "stacks." These devices are surgically removed and/or implanted in the back of the neck of a body known as a "sleeve." To remove a stack is to desleeve, while to insert a stack into a different body is to resleeve an individual. Within the series diegesis, the stacks are of extraterrestrial origin, and are reverse engineered for human use in the mass production of sleeves. While sleeves and stacks may be transferred and/or mechanically reproduced, an individual may still be killed should their stack be destroyed. In view of the fact that the lore of *Altered Carbon* permits the mechanical reproduction of the "soul," both the physical and temporal limits acting upon what we could call single-sleeve life are undone by the reproducability and transferability of the stack itself. In short, the combination of stacks and sleeves opens up the possibility of human immortality. However, like all things sociopolitical, economic, and cultural, immortality is a privilege meted out on the grounds of capital. Only the wealthiest individuals, known as "Meths" (a reference to Methuselah of the Torah and Old Testament, renowned for his longevity), possess the capital to achieve immortality through the use of sleeve clones and off-world satellite facilities in which to store backups of their consciousnesses (a process known as Needlecasting). By keeping their selves in remote storage, Meths may be resleeved even in the event of the destruction of their stacks. Meths, who typically reside in gargantuan hypertechnological cloud-piercing complexes (known as the Aerium), are contrasted with "grounders," lower class citizens who reside on the Earth's surface, seen in the show as high density settlements scattered across and covering what once was the Golden Gate Bridge. The series follows Takeshi Kovacs (Joel Kinnaman/Will Yun Lee/Byron Mann), a highly skilled operative known as an Envoy, who is tasked to investigate the apparent murder of a wealthy and powerful 300-year-old Meth named Laurens Bancroft (James Purefoy). Bancroft reveals to Kovacs that while he was resleeved, his stack was destroyed. The 48-hour back-up schedule of his resleeving results in Bancroft having little to no recollection of the two days preceding his death.

In "The 'Experience Book,'" in *Remarks on Marx: Conversations with Duccio Trombadori* (1991), Michel Foucault describes the concept of a limit-experience (*expérience limite*) as "the point of life which lies as close as possible to the impossibility of living, which lies at the limit or the extreme" (Foucault, 1991, pp. 30–31). For Foucault, the limit-experience is primarily concerned with the paradoxical moment in which the subject is confronted with the limits of her or his own subjectivity. In both Michel Foucault's and George Bataille's respective approaches, the limit-experience has eschatological undertones, latently suggesting that in a single act, the self can, paradoxically, experience its own self annihilation and/or overcoming. Among the series' underlying philosophical engagements with questions of consciousness and biotechnology, *Altered Carbon* explores the consequences of the continued existence of the conscious self in multiple embodied selves. The implication here is that the experiences of that self must also violate the limits of subjective experience as sequestered to the life of a single body.

Thematically, the series' investigation of Bancroft's death draws together sexuality, technology and power. From a Foucauldian perspective, it could be argued that in the show's diegesis, sexuality is a technology of biopower, one shown to be insidiously exploited by the Meth elite. Bancroft is shown to indulge in brutally violent sexuality to and beyond the point of death. Being that sleeves that house stacks are disposable, Meths are able to explore and exploit the interstices between sex and death on account of their socioeconomic, cultural, and political ability to purchase and/or manufacture replacement sleeves. Moreover, being that sleeves *are* disposable, the psychosexual and emotional limits of distress, pain, and fear individuals are willing to endure and exploit are influenced—arguably broadened—by the persistence of the self-in-stack following the death of a sleeve.

This essay seeks to theorize the relationship between Meths, stacks, sleeves, sexuality, and violence in relation to the theoretical concept of limit-experience. In doing so, it suggests that, in the world of *Altered Carbon*, a combination of sociopolitical, economic, and cultural power and onto-existential difusion (stack consciousness and sleeve embodiedness) is still not enough to ensure that every ethical, moral, and indeed, legal prohibition may be transgressed in the future. While Meths may theoretically live forever, the main narrative thrust of the series illustrates, in a rather utopian gesture, that Meths cannot outlive the various ethical, moral, and judicial ideological limits they have, ironically, internalized over time. This essay will refer to the works of French theorists Michel Foucault, George Bataille, and Roland Barthes, as well as German philosopher Walter Benjamin to: (1) theorize the onto-existential (that means physical and psychical) consequences of the combination of stack and sleeve in relation to limit-experience, particularly subjective singularity. Here, I will examine how the technological constituents of being in *Altered Carbon* transgress the limits of a single body and a single human lifespan; and (2) theorize the nature of limit-experience in relation to Meth sexuality.

The Worm in the Fruit: Limit-Experience, Embodiedness and the Biopolitics of Future Human Sexuality in Altered Carbon

This essay opens by contending that any question concerning the sociopolitical, cultural, and economic issues and debates, including the future of human sexuality, in the *Altered Carbon* diegesis redound to a single dialectic: embodied/disembodied. In Bay City, a world controlled by an ultra-elite free of death, masters of interstellar influence, possessors of radical and transgressive technologies, both consciousness and its embodiedness are necessarily under the jurisdiction of biopolitical determinations. The combination of stack and sleeve in conjunction with Meths' sociopolitical, economic, and cultural power allows the rarefied elite to exert "contemporary commodification of the human biological body by scientific advancements and the political economy [and in so doing, instigates an] anatamo-politics of the body" (Godamune, 2011, p. 23). In Foucauldian thought, biopower and biopolitics are inextricable from one another. The former term first appears in *The History of Sexuality (Volume 1)*. Foucault describes biopower and biopolitics as praxes employed by modern nation states for the regulation of their subjects through

> an explosion of numerous and diverse techniques for achieving the subjugations of bodies and the control of populations, a number of phenomena that seem to me to be quite significant, namely, the set of mechanisms through which the basic biological features of the human species became the object of a political strategy, of a general strategy of power, or, in other words, how, starting from the 18th century, modern Western societies took on board the fundamental biological fact that human beings are a species [Foucault, 1978, p. 14].

Biopower describes the ways in which human beings exist within the realms of society and the politics that govern its determinations. Included in this definition is an understanding that humans are also complex biological entities whose manipulation and control is seen as politically valuable. According to Foucault, biopower expresses itself in two main ways. First, the process of amalgamating political and biological phenomena with one another occurs at the level of the individual. Foucault calls this form of biopower "anatomo-politics of the human body" (Foucault, p. 139). Here, biopower seeks to discipline, optimize, and exploit the human body, using various ideological and repressive apparatuses to ensure and consolidate efficiency and economic control thereof. Second, the process of amalgamating political and biological phenomena with one another occurs at the level of populations. This form of biopower seeks to manage a population or populations. This is primarily achieved by removing individuals and other social factors that would or could act as impediments to the control of populations of which they are part of. The ideological and repressive apparatuses brought to bear in this type of biopower include sociopolitical, economic, and cultural forces concerning reproductivity, health, mortality and mass well-being.

Applying Foucault's thoughts to *Altered Carbon* offers incisive critical insights into the functioning of power in the series. The combination of stack and sleeve not only divides the notion of self from singularity, but also disentangles the limit of life, as understood heretofore in terms of "typical human lifespan," from death via reproducible "sleeve-spans." As a result, the stack and the sleeve divide the population, creating a sociopolitical, economic, and cultural double-caesura. On the one hand, the combination of the stack and the sleeve separate the contemporary understanding of human onto-existential experience as typically marked by brevity, precariousness, a single body, an approximately 70 year lifespan, and the inescapability of death at its terminus. On the other hand, the combination of stack and sleeve further separates these technologically altered bodies, ones whose "humanity" is placed under erasure and reconstruction, and therefore necessarily diffuse and indeterminate, into supposedly superior (Meth) and inferior (grounder) populations. What ultimately separates these populations is their proximity to death. Being that the average citizen in Bay City may be able to resleeve their stack once or twice, Meths can, with the aid of their sociopolitical, economic, and cultural affluence, theoretically maintain this process indefinitely. As such, manipulating, exploiting, and indeed killing the grounder population becomes more acceptable in relation to Meth immortality because grounders are, literally and figuratively, closer to death. As a result, the biopolitics of Bay City suggest that an antagonistic relationship between Meths and grounders must be necessarily maintained, in order to supply Meths with stacks and sleeves to destroy for their sexual gratification.

Every aspect of life in Bay City, from its violence to its pleasure, falls under the purview of the Meths' sociopolitical, economic, and cultural control, exploitation of consciousnesses, as well as the bodies which house them. Not only is bare life necessarily concerned with the onto-existential, psycho-emotional, and sociopolitical issues and debates related to biopower in the series, but "the discipline, regulation and economic exploitation of biological bodies of both individuals and populations by political powers as such are also the main concerns of the philosophy of biopolitics." (Godamune, 2011, p. 11). At the same time, however, the combination of the stack and the sleeve necessarily allows new forms of subjectivity to emerge that can, as the series shows, be used to resist Meth biopower.

The existential and ontological consequences of the technological reproduction of self are also addressed by Roland Barthes and Walter Benjamin. From a Barthesean perspective, the process whereby a stack is resleeved is not unlike a process of writing and/or printing. As Barthes suggests, "writing is the destruction of every voice, of every point of origin" (Barthes, 2010, p. 1322). The implication here is that the sequestration of a human consciousness to a disk of reverse engineered alien technology first troubles the distinction between the subsequent humanity and Otherness of a stacked consciousness. Second, the resleeving of said stack troubles the understanding of human individuality and subjectivity as limited to a single body that exists for a determinate span of time. The combination of the stack and the sleeve, therefore, acts as a "neutral, composite, oblique space where our subject slips away, the negative where all identity [in a singular sense] is lost, starting with the very identity of the body writing" (Barthes, 2010, p. 1322). While it could be argued that the stack is the "transcendent" element of self that recurs, reemerges, and/or resurrects after sleeve-death or resleeving, the influence of embodied experience on consciousness and individuality must also necessarily affect consciousness. In other words, while the stack appears to be more fundamental, more onto-existentially sovereign than the sleeves it inhabits, sleeve-embodiedness necessarily influences the memories, and therefore the "self," contained within said stack.

From a Benjaminian perspective, the process of the technological reproduction of objects, including selves, necessarily erases the authenticity, sovereignty, and authority of origins. Applied to *Altered Carbon*, the technological violation of the limits of time and space facilitated by the combination of stack and sleeve means that "technological reproduction can place the copy of the original in situations which the original itself cannot attain" (Benjamin, 2010, p. 1054). The implication here is that human subjectivity is liberated from the limits of singularity, both of body and time. Kovacs is a perfect example of this consequence. The interstice of embodiedness between sleevings, that is, the gap in time between his experiences of having a body, is 250 years in the series. Resleeving his stack in a different body in a different time means that Kovacs has access to times and experiences unavailable to an individual whose consciousness was limited to a single body which lived for a set amount of time. The technological dissolution of self as singularly embodied phenomena is perhaps the most radical aspect of the series. While the audience perceives the character as a single individual for the predominance of the series, the audience is simultaneously aware that the "individuality of the individual" has been diffused throughout supplementary selves (Ryker, Kovacs and the clone of his resleeved self he prints and double-sleeves with), whose "identity" or "subjecthood" does not properly belong to a singular entity (Benjamin, 2010, p. 1060). Used creatively, this radical dissolution of self can give a skilled individual, like an Envoy, the tactical advantage of literally being in two places at once. It is a tactic Kovacs brings to bear in his investigation of Bancroft's death and, in fact, is essential to solving the case by employing Meth privileges, such as double-sleeving, against them. The very notion of subjectivity itself is radically disintegrated in *Altered Carbon*'s vision of the future which is ultimately governed by the combination of the stack and the sleeve. Stack and sleeve technology allow individuals to escape subjectivity as a phenomena of spacio-temporal singularity. However, instead of facilitating radically different forms of subjectivity not beholden to the limits of capital, the series shows the exact opposite to be the case: wealth, influence, and longevity act as a new economy to which all life, onto-existentially singular or technologically diffused, is still ultimately subject. If one has enough money, like a Meth, one can purchase a stack and a sleeved individual to dominate, degrade, and ultimately destroy.

For Foucault, the concept of a limit-experience represents a type of somaesthetic "edgework" that goes on to test the limits of an individual's experience of ordered reality (Foucault, 1978, pp. 30–31). Inherent in the concept's latent erasure of ordered reality is limit-experience's reference to classical notions of onto-existential dissolution, including, but not limited to the sublime, madness, abandonment, and fascination. The outcome of each instantiation of limit-experience is "an invitation to call into question the category of the subject, its supremacy, its foundational function" as well as "calling the subject into question meant that one would have to experience something leading to its actual destruction, its decomposition, its explosion, its conversion into something else" (Gutting, 2007, p. 340). In the cyberpunk futurity of *Altered Carbon*, limit-experience is a phenomena mediated by the technological constituents of stack and sleeve, the transgressing self reterritorialized in the onto-existentially disposable domain of the technologically reproductive body. Resleeving a stack is itself a limit-experience, one which "has the function of wrenching the subject from itself, of seeing to it that the subject is no longer itself, or that it is brought to its annihilation or its dissolution" (Foucault, 1978, p. 241). What it means to be a person in a world whereby the presiding technology that reproduces, stores, and redistributes consciousness and bodies constitutes "direct experiences aimed at pulling [oneself] free of [oneself], at preventing [one] from being the same," is rendered radically indeterminate by stack and sleeve in this way (Foucault, 1978, p. 241).

The pursuit of limit-experience, therefore, inherently suggests a type of transcendentalism or what Elisabeth Roudinesco (2005) refers to as a "dark mysticism" (p. 166). The reverential and indeed resentful sentiments Meths illicit in "grounder" or proletariat public opinion, the mystique, influence, and longevity of the Meths portrays them as masters of a type of dark technomysticism and/or as pseudo-benevolent gods of technology. While Foucauldian limit-experience helps us theorize the onto-existential transgressions inherent to the idea of technologized immortality, George Bataille's exploration of limit-experience in specifically erotic terms helps us theorize the nature and influence of limit-experience in Bancroft's death. According to Bataille, eroticism has latently transgressive effects in that much of the phenomena collectively known as human sexuality engender the dissolution of boundaries between subjectivity and humanity, the thinking subject and the (sexually) ecstatic being. While always *temporary* in its effects, the limit-experience of eroticism is exacerbated by "the desire that triumphs over the taboo. It presupposes man in conflict with himself" (Bataille, 1957, p. 256). While I have placed Bataillean limit-experience under the aegis of sexuality, Bataille holds that limit-experience goes beyond simple sexual *activity*, suggesting instead that "eroticism is assenting to life even in death" (1957, p. 11).

When one considers the fact that Meths are practically immortal, one can begin to conjecture what sort of erotic experiences would continue to stimulate them over a three century sleeve-span. For both Miriam (Kristin Lehman) and Laurens Bancroft, Meth-eroticism is as much concerned with power, volume, variety, and death as it is with sexual acts themselves. Throughout the series, Meth-eroticism is presented as excessive, violent, and sadistic. It is shown to always be seeking to transgress not simply the moral-ethical laws they, as Meths, have simply outlived, but the limits between life and death both internally within themselves, and externally over other bodies. In this way, Meth-eroticism is shown to fetishize that which is abjectly unattainable or outside of Meth experience, namely, death which, for Meths, has been rendered obsolete by technology. Despite this, however, Bancroft is shown to have a psychic "break" after being confronted with the reality of his violence and sexuality which confirms his violation of a taboo he has internalized in the face of his immortality. What is revealed in this impasse-in-the-limit is the fact that

> there is always some limit which the individual accepts. He identifies this limit with himself. Horror seizes him at the thought that this limit may cease to be. But we are wrong to take this limit and the individual's acceptance of it seriously. The limit is only there to be overreached. Fear and horror are not the real and final reaction; on the contrary, they are a temptation to overstep the bounds [Bataille, 1957, p. 144].

As such, Meth-eroticism is shown to delight and despair in its very transgressiveness, or, as Bataille would put it, "the truth of eroticism is treason," and "the urge towards [pleasure], pushed to its limit, is an urge toward death" (1957, pp. 42; 171).

Beauty Befouled, Limit Overreached: Sex, Immortality, Meths and Morality in Altered Carbon

Being immortal opens up a multitude of onto-existential opportunities and possibilities of being. These include physical and psychical violence and pain, as well as physical and psychical pleasure. Being that a Meth is not pressed for time, so to speak, she or he is, should she or he choose, able to dedicate whole sleeve-spans to experimentation in this regard. As they have the means, both in terms of pecuniary and temporal capital, the Bancrofts, as Meths, can be thought of as attendees of an eternal party on account of their immense sociopolitical, economic, and cultural influence. The very same power engenders boredom, violence, and a desire to violate *all* moral, ethical, and cultural boundaries, legal and illegal alike. This pseudo-godlike status is expressed by Reileen (Dichen Lachman) who declares "I'm a Meth.

I take what I want" (*AC* 10, "The Killers"). Earlier she reiterates this sentiment and lays out, in simple terms, what could be described as the ethics of being a Meth when she claims to Kovacs, "you'll get it, when you live long enough. There are no rules. We do what we want" (*AC* 9, "Rage in Heaven"). While the series only offers a glimpse into a specific cross-section of Meth life, one filtered through the familial intrigues and personal conspiracies of the Bancrofts and their associates, the real question pertaining to Meths in the series is whether they are all as bored, lascivious, immoral, and violent in their sexuality as Laurens, Miriam, and/or their associates such as Oumou Prescott (Tamara Taylor).

From details revealed in Episodes 3, 8, 9, and 10, Meth being is in certain ways an exacerbation of the typical onto-existential experience, forces, and pressures acting on mortal being: sex, violence, law, family, and power. There are numerous examples of sexual violence in the series, embodied and enacted both in real life and virtual reality, by various characters. Instances of this kind include the psycho-emotional and physical sexual torture of Lizzie Elliot, Miriam Bancroft's drugging of Kovacs for sexual ends (without his consent), and the amoral sadism of the Prick Up VR brothel. The sociopolitical consequences of the elision of sex and violence are widespread, enabled, and enjoyed by Meths and non–Meths alike. The issues and debates surrounding sexual violence in the series are really distilled by Bancroft and his experiences in Head in the Clouds (a highly exclusive Meth brothel) shown in flashbacks in Episode 9. Before this, however, Kalogridis provides the viewer with various clues that offer insight into Meth sexuality and eroticism; that is, precisely what stimulates an individual who has lived multiple conventional lifetimes in and through a variety of bodies.

Bancroft's sexual profile is, for the preponderance of the series, hinted at, particularly through Kovacs' droll albeit deeply critical jibes. For example, Episode 3 features the following exchange between Kovacs and Bancroft:

> KOVACS: I thought you were gonna tell me about your habit of going to bio-cabins and beating women nearly to death? Didn't consider it to be particularly important.
> BANCROFT: Yes, I have spent some time in purchased sexual release, both virtual and real. But then, I've also spent time off-world gambling or indulging my passion for null-gravity knife fighting [...] But I have never taken a single life. Unlike you, I have a line that I am very careful not to cross [*AC* 3, "In a Lonely Place"].

Kovacs offers the following details of his investigation to Bancroft: "From the beginning of this case, the details just didn't add up. All the evidence said suicide. It was neat, tidy, perfect.... But how could you possibly bring down Laurens Bancroft? This is a VR jack-in brothel called Prick Up. It specializes in simulated rape and murder. It's the last place you visited before you died"

(*AC* 8, "Clash by Night"). Later in the episode, Kovacs offers Bancroft further evidence to support the conclusions of his investigation. Handing Bancroft a document, Kovacs states: "It's a bill for damages. Signed by you. Damage from the sleeve being strangled and raped" (*AC* 8, "Clash by Night"). In flashbacks highlighting Bancroft in the midst of a violent sexual encounter in Episode 9, "Rage in Heaven," the fish-eye effect employed, in conjunction with Purefoy's sweaty, grunting excessiveness, registers Meth sexuality as all consuming, animalistic, impersonal, and, like all other Meth vices and privileges, gratuitous.

In essence, the crux of the series, in part, redounds to a number of questions: is the boundary crossing inherent to practical immortality actually free of the prohibitions of guilt? Is morality eternal? Is morality the limit of experience, Meth and non–Meth alike? I contend that the last question is latently a subject/object problem, that is, the eternal consciousness contra the seeming transhistoricism of ideology carried *within* the consciousness, mortal and immortal alike. This is a radical supposition. But what does it have to do with sex and violence? The implication here is that even the most violative expressions of sexuality unmoored from temporal constraints—what in essence amounts to a timeless sexuality—is still bound to moral interpretations thereof. What results here is an essential paradox between proclivity, will, and prohibition. In a very real sense, the entire series is predicated on Bancroft's sexual limit-experience, one which involves sex, violence, and death.

"You have to kill me": The Iridium Package as Limit-Experience in Altered Carbon

In Episode 10, Kovacs infiltrates Head in the Clouds with the help of all three Elliots, his own double-sleeved clone, the AI of the Raven Hotel (Chris Conner), and Mickey (Adam Busch), a Bay City Police tech expert. Going undercover as a five star general, Vernon enters the establishment under the pretence of seeking out the Iridium Package. The Iridium Package is the most expensive sex package offered by the brothel and requires its exclusive clientele to undertake several introductory sessions which are implied to condition said clients in experiencing and enjoying the most morally and ethically extreme sexual acts. This extremity is symbolized by the fact that acts ranging from peadophilic encounters to sexualized murders are offered in the Iridium Package. It is again further reiterated toward the end of the episode where the Pleasure Concierge (Peter Woodward) says to a clearly distracted and uncomfortable Vernon, "perhaps we can find you another young lady? Or a man? Or perhaps a child?" (*AC* 10, "The Killers"). As Vernon plays out the ruse, he, and his team listening/watching via retinal technology, learn that his Iridium Package experience involves a 19-year-old girl and a torture case. This case contains various implements including a bullwhip, plasma cutter, a tactical serrated back knife, and a captive bolt pistol. While all the implements contained in the case are used for construction, discipline, or killing, the last of these symbolically suggests that Head in the Clouds' Sleeved sex workers are considered little more than livestock for slaughter, consumption, and disposal. When Vernon encounters the girl he "purchased" named Belle (Lexi Atkins), she does not reveal the true extent of Meth-eroticism, nor its violence. What she ultimately reveals to him in their brief albeit revelatory encounter is the fact that Meth-eroticism uses the combination of stack-sleeve immortality to fully pursue eroticized death. Vernon opens by asking Belle how old she is. Belle replies, "I'm not some old hag resleeved into this. This is my flesh. All 19 years of me. But if you don't wanna take me first I guess we can get right to it … Iridium Experience. I'm all yours…. Is that what you want? Huh? Then you can. You could cut holes in me anywhere. Fuck me in them. Tear me apart, General. Rip me open with that big dick. Do you want me to scream? … Beg? Please. Please, don't. Please. [CRYING] Please. Please, don't. Please. Please. Please. Please" (*AC* 10, "The Killers"). In response, Ava remarks incredulously "Head in the Clouds runs its girls as snuff whores!?" (*AC* 10, "The Killers"). That Belle is concerned that she ruined the general's fantasy, as well as the fact that she has been instructed that said fantasy is not complete *without* the general killing her, reveals that the Iridium Package is not fundamentally about sexual acts themselves, regardless of how simple or complex they are. The question here is what exactly is the fantasy? Does the fantasy pertain to a sexual partner whose life is in one's hands? If this is the case, even simple erotic asphyxiation can offer similar experiences by eliciting similar effects. I argue, therefore, that the Iridium Package is primarily concerned with *total* stack-sleeve domination and power; that is, to control someone's body and soul, so to speak. It is primarily concerned with death whereby the eroticism thereof occurs after the fact. Moreover, Belle's statements here suggest, ironically, that in the near deathless world of *Altered Carbon*, death itself can only express itself as integrated fully into the praxis and enforcement of elite sex work. As Mickey notes, this conglomeration of phenomena is shown to be extremely effective with Meths: "That's why you have to qualify. They must put the johns through virtual first, because the ones that come sniffing back will pay anything for the real thing. Killing a girl who doesn't know that she'll never come back" (*AC* 10, "The Killers"). The suggestion here is that it is precisely *because* the victim of Meth-eroticism does not know that her death is final that she gives herself over to performing for the john with the illusion of regenerative certainty. This is the core power dynamic, the real titillation of the Iridium Package.

The Meth johns are suggested to relish the simulation of the finality of their financial, sexual, and epistemological domination of the young girl. In this sense, death becomes the ultimate expression of sexuality possible: the Meths have fully integrated power over life and sex under capital.

In conclusion, looking at the services provided by the Head in the Clouds, one is tempted to ask what are the implications of its menu, so to speak? One possibility is, I contend, that the temporal intervention represented by the stack-sleeve combination not only pushes the concept of mortality beyond "natural" boundaries, but also pushes sexuality and the pursuit of pleasure beyond *both* mortality *and* morality. Without the prohibitive fear of death, all possibilities that two bodies have in terms of what they can do to one another to inflict both pain and pleasure, aided by paradoxically external internal apparatuses like VR, the limits of feeling, embodiedness, and, in the last extent, Being, are explored *past* death and morality. The unknown element is whether or not pleasure, violence, eroticism, and indeed power plateau if endless. In view of the fact that Season 2 of the series is set to air in 2020, in a very practical sense, only time will tell.

References

Barthes, R. (2010). The Work of Art in the Age of Its Technological Reproducibility. In *The Norton Anthology of Theory and Criticism: 2nd Edition*. V.B. Leitch (Ed.). United States: W.W. Norton & Company, pp. 1322–1326.

Bataille, G. (1962). *Erotism: Death and Sensuality*. M. Dalwood (Trans.). San Francisco: City Lights Books.

Benjamin, W. (2010). The Work of Art in the Age of Its Technological Reproducibility. In *The Norton Anthology of Theory and Criticism: 2nd Edition*. V.B. Leitch (Ed.). United States: W.W. Norton & Company, Inc, pp. 1051–1071.

Foucault, M. (1978). *The History of Sexuality Volume I: An Introduction*. R. Hurley (Trans.). New York: Random House, Inc.

_____. 1991. The Experience Book. In *Remarks on Marx: Conversations with Duccio Trombadori*. R.J. Goldstein & J. Cascaito (Trans.) New York: Semiotext(e).

Godamune, V. (2011). *Biopolitics in Science Fiction Films: An Exploration of the Representation of the contemporary Politicization of Human Biological Life In Cinema*. (Master's Thesis). London: London Metropolitan University

Gutting, G. (Ed.). (2007). *The Cambridge Companion to Foucault*. Cambridge: Cambridge University Press.

Lenic, J.G. (Producer) & Kalogridis, L. (Creator). *Altered Carbon*. (2018–). [Series]. United States: Netflix.

Roudinesco, E. (2005). *Lacan: In Spite of Everything*. G. Elliot (Trans.). London: Verso.

Functions of Sex Scenes in *Altered Carbon*

Michał Klata

> *[L]uridly veers from gratuitous nudity to gratuitous violence to gratuitous silliness.*
> —Benjamin Lee, *The Guardian*
>
> *Find what others have missed.*
> —Laurens Bancroft

Upon its release, the critical reactions to the *Altered Carbon* series were not favorable. The main accusations concerned too many clichés and sex scenes (Lee, 2018; Hale, 2018). It may be argued, however, that this kind of reading is too superficial, and a closer analysis may show that there is more to it than meets the eyes of the critics. As for the first argument, suffice it to say that most of the elements pointed out in the reviews are actually crucial for the cyberpunk genre. Callbacks to both classic noir films as well as *Blade Runner* or William Gibson's novels are fairly justified, as these are the pillars of the genre (Yuen, 2007, p. 98; Tatsumi, 2006, pp. 43–44). As for the second argument-this is the subject of the analysis presented in this essay. The purpose of the following analysis is to determine the functions of the sex scenes in the series.

The first step of my analysis is a thorough plot segmentation with the purpose of determining the importance of the sex scenes in advancing the narrative. Then the scenes are analyzed within the framework proposed by Roger Crittenden (1991). Additional angles are provided by Laura Mulvey's (1989) theory of the "male gaze" and Sergei Eisenstein's (1997) theory of montage. Scene typology proposed by Robert De Natale (2018) helps to clarify the results and classify the functions of said scenes.

The Shower Scene

The first sex scene appears almost at the very beginning of the first episode. It would have been the first scene of the series, if not preceded by the opening credits and a sequence showing Kovacs' new sleeve in a pool of liquid. At the end of the sequence a cloud of bubbles appears right in front of the camera, some of them too close to be in focus. An editing trick turns the ones closest to the viewer into whitish hexagons. Then it cuts to a shot of water streaming from the shower. The hexagon returns later in the scene as a tile pattern on the walls and on the floor. This is an example of an interesting modification of Eisenstein's tonal montage. The Soviet filmmaker used a common visual or auditory motif to connect two seemingly different shots (Eisenstein, 1997, p. 75). Here we have two visual tones—water and the hexagon pattern. The former will later provide a thread woven into all the episodes of the series.

The sex scene in the shower is the first of the series of flashbacks presenting Kovacs' memories, serving as this character's backstory. Falconer's monologue against the background of ambient music can be heard. Her first words: "The first thing you'll learn is that nothing is what it seems" may be read in multiple ways. This is the first of a series of flashback "lessons" helping Kovacs deal with new situations. It is also a clue for the viewers, telling them through a number of flashbacks and virtual realities that the world of *Altered Carbon* is a mystery to be solved, and nothing can be trusted here. The third possible meaning results from the connection between Falconer's words and the images on the screen. The beginning of the monologue is accompanied by a sound of a woman gasping and a shot of a hand inside the cabin, sliding against the wet, translucent wall—an image invoking the idea of sex. It turns out that Falconer's warning is directed at the naïve spectator, hoping for a sex scene … or is it?

The camera cuts to the inside of the shower, and we can see Kovacs in his original Envoy sleeve with a woman called Sarah (her name does not appear in any of the dialogues but it is credited). It turns out that they do not have sex (for the time being), but the scene is not as "innocent" as it could have been; the two are washing the blood covering their bodies, and camera close-ups show stacks scuttled on the floor, a scar at the back of Sarah's neck where one of the devices was implanted, and a piece of human flesh in her hand. One of the close-ups shows another important element—a tattoo of a snake biting its tail, Ouroboros, folded in the shape of the number "8," a symbol of the recurring past, continuity, eternity and infinity.

The blood and human flesh are in sharp contrast with the gentle lovemaking that follows. It is clear that Kovacs and Sarah have sex, but the act is not presented as overtly as those later on in the show. The activity can be inferred from the movements of the bodies, suggesting pelvic thrusts, and open mouths, indicative of sexual ecstasy, but nothing is shown explicitly. Close-ups focus on faces, arms, and backs, and during a medium-shot there is a stream of water between the camera and the lovers. Even the kiss in a close-up is "censored" by the mouth covered by Sarah's thumb. Nevertheless, the scene is quite "steamy," not just because of the setting, but also thanks to the details in presentation that make it more sensual, in both meanings of the word. The limitations of the sight are compensated by other senses. There is sighing and panting against the sound of the water streaming down. The scene appeals also to the imaginary sense of touch, as the camera closes up on the drops of water or sweat rolling down Kovacs' face.

The scene under the shower cuts to flashbacks of Kovacs having sex with Falconer. The montage here is of an intellectual variety, defined by Eisenstein as a technique connecting two sequences with an idea rather than a simple auditory or visual motif (Eisenstein, 1997, p. 82). Sex is not the only principle connecting the two sequences. They are also connected by other elements. The water from the shower is juxtaposed with the fire we can see behind Falconer's back. The principles of the "180 system," according to which the camera can move only within one side of the axis connecting the two characters, alternating shots between them (Bennett, Hickmann, Wall, 2007, p. 49) are used here to create an interesting illusion. The two couples are "mixed" together, with the camera placed behind Kovacs' back in the shots with Falconer and behind Sarah's back in the shots under the shower.

The shower scene with Kovacs and Sarah, along with his flashbacks to the intercourse with Falconer, serve many functions. Based on two instincts which, if we are to believe Sigmund Freud, are the most important in humankind, Eros and Thanatos (Freud, 1961, p. 38), the scene introduces themes of sex and violence, love and death. Other themes introduced by the scene are water, stacks and the ideas of a recurring past and infinity symbolized by the Ouroboros snake. The scene introduces two characters: Kovacs in his original sleeve and Quellchrist Falconer. Important as the above-mentioned elements are, the role of sex itself in the narrative at this point is limited only to one of the many themes woven into the fabric of the plot, and apart from that it seems to be gratuitous.

At the Raven Hotel

The next sex scene takes place at the end of the second episode. This time the intercourse is between Kovacs and Mrs. Miriam Bancroft, who visits him in his apartment in a hotel called the *Raven*, run by an AI fittingly named

Poe, as it is modeled after the famous writer. This time gratuity is balanced with a healthy dose of narrative functions.

Poe lets Mrs. Bancroft in when Kovacs is absent. When the hero enters the apartment, Miriam stands on the balcony, silent, and does not even look at him. The camera stays on her for a moment, taking Kovacs' perspective. Miriam may be silent, but the seduction is already suggested by the soundtrack, as a soft saxophone music starts to play. According to David Bordwell and Kristin Thompson, the "oleaginous saxophone" is a cliché often used in such scenes (Bordwell, Thompson, 1990, p. 214). When the silence between the two is finally broken, Miriam gives a rather lame excuse regarding her visit, telling Takeshi that she came here to ask about the progress in the investigation, as she is worried about her husband. However, she does not waste her time and quickly proceeds to proper seduction.

After turning the direction of the conversation to sexual matters, Miriam starts undressing Takeshi, taking off his shirt, unmoved by the fact that he wants her to stop ("I think that's enough"—he says; "Enough? It's an interesting word. I'm not familiar with it"—she replies). For the time being, the visuals do not conform to Mulvey's thesis (p. 19)—this is the time for the "female gaze," an opportunity to admire the muscular male body. Miriam explains how her sleeve was developed in such a way that it produces a powerful drug called Empathin, allowing for an enhanced experience during intercourse and making other people more susceptible to her suggestions. This is when the scene becomes significantly more daring than the one from the previous episode. The camera shows Miriam putting her fingers into her mouth, to moisten them with her saliva, after which she smears them on Kovacs' lips. For all his strong will and "Envoy intuition," he gives his consent, licking the fluid.

The impact of the drug is marked with a change in the sound, which becomes more spacious, endowed with a psychedelic echo. Another editing technique applied is slow motion, often used in films for dwelling on moments of spectacle or to achieve dreamlike quality (Bordwell, 1990, p. 317). Here it plays both roles. The slightly blurred image also contributes to the overall mood. The form matches the daring content. When the two kiss, there is no "censorship," like there was in the scene with Sarah and Quell. The audience is spared neither the sound of the word "cunt" uttered by Miriam explaining where else the substance is being produced, nor the sight of the signified.

Given the above, it seems Mulvey's thesis is not entirely invalid in the world of *Altered Carbon* (p. 20). Male and female bodies are presented differently. A good example is the way the genitals are presented—only the female organ is visible here. Apart from the reservation above, both bodies are exposed to a similar degree.

Between the seduction and proper intercourse there is a cut to Ortega at the confessional. Its function is to create suspense, a break during which the audience anticipates the climax of the sex scene. Moreover, Ortega's words during the confession can be read in multiple ways, and one of the possible readings shows that they might be used to describe what happens between Kovacs and Mrs. Bancroft. When Ortega says "Forgive me father, for I have sinned: I've had lustful thoughts," (*AC* 2, "Fallen Angel") and the camera cuts back to the lovers, the ideas of sin and lust are the only connecting principles, justifying the cut to the church. This intellectual montage can be read as suggesting that cheating is a sin. Another possible interpretation is that it was Kovacs who was the object of the "lustful thoughts," which suggests the possibility of him and Ortega being lovers in the future.

Whereas in the scene from the first episode the purpose of the close-ups was to conceal the more daring elements of the intercourse, here the camera shows what is most important from the erotic point of view. The close-ups focus on the faces, mouths open in ecstasy, and the changes in positions are clearly visible in the long-range shots. The main principle of montage, linking shots of different positions on the bed is a single phrase uttered by Miriam. In the shots that start and finish the montage Miriam is shown saying the words, laying under Takeshi in a missionary position, and in the intervening shots the sound of her voice is non-diegetic. This type of montage contributes to the psychedelic quality of the scene's mood. During the intercourse, the soundtrack becomes more ominous, suggesting the potential danger. The grim sounds are combined with occasional cuts to icicle-like decorations hanging down from a lamp nearby. The overall effect clues the audience to think about the possible consequences of the intercourse (Bancroft's revenge, most likely), and make them wonder about the role of the lamp in the whole scene. One of possible interpretations is that there the ice-like decorations correspond with the certain emotional coldness of the act (unlike in the scene in the first episode, here the lovers do not show each other too much affection). Later it would turn out there is more to it than meets the eye.

There are more cuts after the sequence showing the intercourse. The purpose of juxtaposing different situations is to present a variety of possible meanings, explanations of events, and future scenarios. In the confessional, Ortega says she has done "violent things," and there is a cut to a naked female body in the morgue, from which she has taken a stack. The body is clearly visible, along with genitals. The sight of the corpse, with a close-up showing the dirt on the skin and the ugly wound where the stack was cut out contrasts with the intercourse. The themes of sex and death are combined again. There is also a cut to a shot showing the bloodstain at the place where Bancroft died. The shot begins, *nomen omen*, with a sound of a gunshot—the theme of death again. In the next shot, Bancroft looks at the camera. A lot of questions arise at this stage. Is there a connection between the corpse and Bancroft's death? Is the "violent thing" Ortega talks about Bancroft's murder? Was it a suicide? Is the powerful Meth spying on the lovers? At least one of the mysteries is explained right away—the significance of the lamp. The last shots of the scene show a tiny drone, sitting there and spying on the lovers.

The scene may be gratuitous to some degree, but here the sex itself also plays an important role. For the time being, it seems the intercourse may play an important role in the plot. Given the fact that the whole act was recorded, it may lead to a conflict between Kovacs and Bancroft, once he learns that his wife cheated on him. However, it turns out to be a "red herring"—Bancroft tells him later he does not want the two to have sex, but the conflict does not really affect the plot. It is more important for Bancroft that Kovacs solves the murder and makes Ortega suffer because of his sleeve being the one of Ryker, her (ex-)partner. This scene is also inconsequential for Miram's character—her agency in the encounter with Kovacs goes unpunished, contrary to what Mulvey has observed (Mulvey, 1989, p. 21).

One of the consequences of the intercourse is that now Kovacs has an ally and his choices become more complicated. Later Miriam offers to give him a new identity so that he does not have to work for Bancroft anymore. The relationship between them, established with the intercourse, will help Kovacs distract his opponents when the team attacks Head in the Clouds, as Kovacs, double-sleeved, pretends he is with Miriam. Another function is combining the themes of stacks, death, and sex again.

The scene at the Raven Hotel establishes the relationship between Kovacs and Mrs. Bancroft, hints at a possibility of a future relationship between him and Ortega, as well as advances the plot (although in ways surprising for the audience). The montage with a lot of cuts to other situations maintains the mood of a grim world where the motives of sex and death are inevitably connected, contributing to the vision of the decadent future typical of the cyberpunk genre (Yuen, 2007, p. 98). Last but not least, the scene entertains the audience with gratuitous displays of the erotic, in ways which leave more room for female agency than in the case of old Hollywood classics analyzed by Mulvey (p. 19).

In the next episode, Poe tells Kovacs about the drone which "acquired the footage" of the intercourse between him and Mrs. Bancroft (*AC* 3, "In a Lonely Place"). There is a single flashback shot of the lovers. It serves to remind the audience about the event. Upon learning about the footage, Kovacs is frightened. To add to the tension, Bancroft invites the protagonist to a party. For the time being, Kovacs believes the powerful Meth wants to kill him in revenge. Ortega learns there is going to be some "organic damage" at the party. All of this suggests that the events presented in the sex scene from the previous episode are going to have serious consequences for the plot. However, as already mentioned, it turns out later that it is enough for Bancroft to just draw a clear line, and he does not want to exercise any revenge. According to Bordwell and Thompson, "we can expect that any one element in a film will have some justification for being there" (Bordwell & Thompson, 1990, p. 133). Sometimes tapping into those expectations proves to be a trick on the part of the filmmakers.

Bancroft's Party

The next sex scene takes place at the party thrown for the other Meths by Bancroft. Kovacs spots another woman who looks like Miriam. Takeshi follows her and discovers a secret passage, leading to a room. The mysterious woman does not waste time—by the moment the protagonist gets there, she is already having sex with Curtis, one of Bancroft's bodyguards. The music, creating a mood of mystery and tension, which grows louder and louder since Kovacs decided to follow the woman, stops the moment he opens the door. In the silence the sighs of the lovers and the sounds of bodies pounding each other are clearly heard. What the sounds reveal is concealed from the sight. The lovers are in the doggy-style position, facing the door, with their clothes on. The only shot from behind shows only a fragment of Curtis' arm.

When Curtis leaves, the woman reveals her identity and then explains why she is wearing that particular sleeve, touching her breasts to show how beautiful it is. There is no doubt the scene provides an opportunity to admire the beauty of the female body. It is interesting, however, that the gaze in the scene does not work in the way it does in the films analyzed by Mulvey. The author of the "male gaze" theory writes that the gaze of the male protagonist is usually combined with shots from his point of view, presenting the female body from his perspective (1989, p. 18). This is not the case here. When the two stand facing each other, judging from the direction we can guess that Kovacs looks at her breasts. However, it is not accompanied with the shots of the above-mentioned type.

A sleeve which is biologically identical with the one Miriam wears could be used to open the safe where the gun was stored. Thus, Kovacs learns that the woman had the means to commit the murder. During the party, Kovacs learns a lot about possible motives for killing Bancroft, but this is the only lead so far that combines the motive with the possible means (apart, of course, from the suicide hypothesis). As Bordwell and Thompson put it: "filmmakers want us to construe the story, moment by moment, in a certain way, and that way can involve a lot of diversions and blind alleys" (1990, p. 14).

The scene helps in building the mood of the party, where Meths indulge in a range of decadent activities, from sex, through showing off, often at the expense of the grounders, to watching fights. Although the themes of sex and death are connected in that they all belong to the range of entertainment activities mentioned above, they are not directly connected in the scene. The only connection here between Eros and Thanatos is that one of the lovers is the person who might have killed Bancroft. The intercourse may serve as a form of entertainment as well, but seems to be fairly justified by the plot and the social mechanics of the world of *Altered Carbon*. It is worth noting that the intercourse is not very explicit, devoid of any nakedness.

Ortega's Flat

The next sex scene appears in the fifth episode. Here the intercourse is between Kovacs and Ortega. At the end of the previous scene, Ortega sees blood dripping from the protagonist's hand and decides she has to stitch him up. The two scenes are connected by means of two kinds of montage: tonal (the motif of blood returns later in the scene) and intellectual (the dripping blood is connected with the action of stitching up). When the two get to Ortega's flat, Kovacs discovers a photograph of Ortega with Ryker, and seems to be jealous. Old motifs are brought back, as Ortega begins the treatment where the snake tattoo is. The dialogue that follows plays an important role in the scene. The two hesitate, visibly aroused, but unsure what to do with the fact that Kovacs is in Ryker's sleeve. Ortega says that when she looks in "his eyes" (Ryker's, that is), she sees Kovacs "looking back at her as no one has for a very long time" (*AC* 5, "The Wrong Man"). It seems that to her this is proof that there is more to their relationship than just her attraction to the body, and there is more to Kovacs than just a former terrorist and now a blunt instrument in the hands of a Meth. When Kovacs still seems confused by the situation, she says "just shut the fuck up," with a peculiar mixture of anger, tenderness, and sensuality, and starts kissing him.

The montage between the part of the scene described above and the proper intercourse combines the motives of blood and sex. In the medium-range shot, showing the two kissing on the sofa, a carpet is visible. The next shot is a close-up on the carpet, showing the stains of blood, which is combined with the sound of the lovers sighing. A cut follows to the two having sex. The tenderness and warmth of the intercourse contrast sharply with the one with Miriam, where a certain coldness and distance are present even though they were both under the influence of Empathin. The camera does not shy away from nakedness, leaving only the genitals concealed.

The cooperation between Ortega and Kovacs, which up to this moment was still a bit reluctant, is from now on firmly established. Themes of Eros and Thanatos are combined again. The snake returns, bringing back the themes of recurring past and infinity. The scene develops the character of Kovacs, as he proves to be capable of really caring about Ortega. The scene reveals more about the backstory of Ortega and Ryker. One of the functions of sex in the scene is entertainment, but it does not seem gratuitous as the focus here is on emotions, not nakedness—bodies may be visible, but the camera does not linger on them.

There is only one sex scene in the whole second half of the season. In a flashback in the seventh episode, there is an intercourse between Kovacs and Quell at the waterfront. This is the same event that was presented in a flashback during the shower scene from the first episode. There is even more tenderness than in the scene with Ortega. The themes of Eros and Thanatos are combined in a more abstract manner—the scene takes place in the night before Kovacs is to embark on a suicide mission. There is not much nakedness in the scene—only backs, faces, and hands are visible. There seems to be, however, a gratuitous element in the way the camera lingers on Quell's face, mouth open in ecstasy. Unlike in the previous sex scenes, there are no elements on which the camera focuses apart from the lovers. No stacks, bloodstains or lamp decorations. This seems to indicate that this is how "true love" is—a feeling which sweeps away all the external world, so that nothing else matters.

Although placed in the past, the scene does not reveal any new information about the backstory. The way sex is depicted in the series suggests that this was the only "true love" of Kovacs' life, but it is possible to infer it from the many flashbacks and the conversations he has with Quell in his mind. The fact that the intercourse takes place on what is supposed to be the last night of his life maintains the dark mood of the series and keeps the themes of love and death connected. There is not much nakedness, which seems to suggest the "purity" of their feeling, however there is still some gratuity in the way camera looks at Quell's face.

Conclusions

As the analysis reveals, the sex scenes in the *Altered Carbon* Netflix's series serve many different purposes, only one of them being gratuity. It is worth noting that not all sex scenes are explicit, meaning nakedness is not always openly presented. In most of the episodes there are no sex scenes at all, which helps to break the stigma of *Altered Carbon* being simply a series focused just on "sex and violence." The probable reason for the stigma may have been the fact that most of the scenes were concentrated in the first half of the series and were heavily featured in the marketing campaign. The functions played by the sex scenes in the narrative are: presenting the backstory of the characters, creating the mood of the dystopian cyberpunk world, and connecting the recurring themes, most important of them being Eros and Thanatos.

One can wonder why the critics fixated so heavily on the sex themes in the series, and why they attributed them such a negative connotation from the start. As we can see, such a sex-negative attitude is not supported by the facts. For a show that is supposed to be abundant in sexuality, not only are there long stretches where it is completely devoid of it but when it is there, it is usually presented with significance to the plot and maturity on the part of the creators.

REFERENCES

Bennett, P., Hickman, A., & Wall, P. (2007). *Film Studies: The Essential Resource.* New York: Routledge.
Bordwell, D., & Thompson, K. (1990). *Film Art: An Introduction.* New York: McGraw-Hill.
Crittenden, R. (1991). *Manual of Film Editing.* Thames and Hudson.
DeNatale, Bob. (2013). Functions of a Scene. *Bob DeNatale.* Retrieved from http://www.bobdenatale.com/.
Eisenstein, S. (1977). *Film Form: Essays in Film Theory.* J. Leyda (Trans.). New York: Faber & Faber.
Freud, Sigmund. (1961). *Beyond the Pleasure Principle.* J. Strachey (Trans.). Liveright Publishing Corporation.
Hale, M. (2018, February 1). Review: 'Altered Carbon,' Netflix's 'Blade Runner' Replicant. *The New York Times.* Retrieved from https://www.nytimes.com/.
Lee, B. (2018). Altered Carbon Review—Ambitious Netflix Sci-fi Is Flashy, Flawed and Fun. *The Guardian.* Retrieved from https://www.theguardian.com/.
Lenic, J.G. (Producer) & Kalogridis, L. (Creator). *Altered Carbon.* (2018–). [Series]. United States: Netflix.
Mulvey, L (1989). *Visual and Other Pleasures.* Bloomington: Indiana University Press.
Tatsumi, T. (2006). *Full Metal Apache: Transactions Between Cyberpunk Japan and Avant-Pop America.* Durham: Duke University Press,
Yuen, W.K. (2007) 'On the Edge of Spaces: 'Blade Runner,' 'Ghost in the Shell' and Hong Kong's Cityscape, In: Redmond, S. *Liquid Metal: The Science Fiction Film Reader.* London: Wallflower Press.

Sleeves

The Materiality of Reality
The Floating Consciousness in Altered Carbon

ESRA KÖKSAL *and* BURCU BAYKAN

Introduction

This essay takes a closer look at the technologically altered human subjectivity as it is portrayed in the Netflix series *Altered Carbon* (Lenic & Kalogridis, 2018–). Based on the 2002 novel by Richard K. Morgan and recently adapted by Laeta Kalogridis, the series depicts an intriguing, punchy and convoluted story that is simultaneously dark and alluring. At the same time, it contributes to the ongoing cultural debates about humans' changing relationships with science and technology. Set in a speculative future world, *Altered Carbon* presents a highly technologized daily life, replete with cybernetic and biochemical modifications, man-machine interfaces, digitalized environments and even pure artificial intelligence bodies. It envisions a social reality in which cutting-edge digital technologies enable the extraction of the mind from the body, which in turn allows humans to cheat biological death through transferring their consciousness to other bodies. Thus, not surprisingly, the show deals with controversial issues regarding the concepts of human identity, embodiment, selfhood, life and mortality in a futuristic context.

Altered Carbon can be framed within the context of "cyberpunk"—a sub-genre of science fiction that takes place in future urban settings. According to Veronica Hollinger (1990, pp. 30–31), "the central 'generic' feature of cyberpunk" is its focus on "the potential interconnections between the human and the technological," which is manifest in its portrayals of bodily transformation and explorations of the nebulous boundaries between "the natural and the artificial, the human and the machine." Indeed, the cyberpunk genre has been particularly concerned with the manipulation of human bodies through hard science and information technologies, as well as the resulting fragmentation of the fixed human subject. However, the genre has perhaps come to be identified mostly by its explorations of the motif of cyberspace—virtual environments that promote disembodied states of being. Accordingly, cyberpunk focuses on the possible futures of mankind in a way that is not considered by other derivatives of science fiction: by exploring the Cartesian separation of the mind from the body. Hence, the narratives of traditional cyberpunk are accurately characterized by Paweł Frelik (2010, p. 185) as "privileging the mind and reviling the body" and being dominated by "characters seeking to escape embodiment" in favor of an incorporeal existence in cyberspace. Altogether, the depictions of futuristic worlds in a noir atmosphere, the potentials of virtual spaces, the digital transcendence of the body and media-saturated urban landscapes—together with the complex social, political and economic ramifications of such advancements—have been some of the most important subjects scrutinized by cyberpunk. With its intricate plot, powerful noir atmosphere and hologram-enhanced cityscape, *Altered Carbon* clearly possesses a number of visual and textual characteristics of the cyberpunk genre. The concept of technologically enhanced human life, the digitization of the mind, and the meditations on dis and re-embodiment of human beings across virtual and physical realities are equally decisive in the narration of the show, which reflects upon these issues in their wider sociopolitical, economic and psychological contexts.

The primary objective of this essay is to critically engage with the futuristic depictions of human subjectivity as it is enmeshed with technological advancements in *Altered Carbon*. Particular attention is paid to how embodiment and consciousness—the two dimensions of human subjectivity—are affected and altered by their intersections with various biogenetic, cybernetic and digital technologies. In order to facilitate this analysis, this essay draws upon two interconnected theoretical frameworks: Donna Haraway's formulations on the cyborg subjectivity (1991) and N. Katherine Hayles' understanding of posthumanism (1999). On the first level, it investigates the technologically modified human subjects in *Altered Carbon* through the lens of Haraway's cyborg imagery, which consists of various man-machine amalgamations. By examining the narrative and the main characters of the show, the essay analyzes how multiple human and non-human agents interact to form a cyborgian subjectivity, which complicates naturalized and essentialized constructs of identity.

As said earlier, *Altered Carbon* also illustrates the ways in which sophisticated digital technologies allow the human mind to separate itself from the body. Although this separation is a widespread practice in the series, where virtual reality becomes a sphere in which human consciousness can exist, the corporeal human form is still the preferred medium to connect to material reality. In this light, it is suggested that the Cartesian dualism, which considers the mind as the core constituent of human subjectivity, becomes increasingly paradoxical within the context of *Altered Carbon*. Hence, on the second level, the current essay explicates the material aspect of subjectivity in the light of Hayles' vision of posthumanism, which is concerned with technologically connected yet physically embodied forms of existence. It is argued that Hayles' insistence on re-situating the posthuman identity in its material contexts has powerful resonances with the imagined realms of *Altered Carbon*, which problematize the primacy of the mind by re-asserting the importance of the body for the constitution of subjectivity and humanity's quest for enhanced longevity. But before embarking on such analysis, the essay first delves deeper into the complexities of *Altered Carbon*, exploring the themes, characters and the world of the show in greater detail. It then proceeds to discuss the implications of the entangled relationships between biological and digital spheres, as well as between the conscious mind and the physical body for the construction of the human self in the series.

Inside the World of Altered Carbon

The TV series *Altered Carbon* is set more than 300 years in the future, where Earth is not the only planet inhabited by humans. The colonies on other planets are referred to as the "Settled Worlds," while the narrative primarily takes place in the futuristic Bay City. In this far-future world, a person's thoughts, memories and experiences can be encapsulated into a digital device called a "cortical stack," which is inserted in the spinal cord at the base of the skull. Every one-year-old is fitted with a cortical stack, which in essence is a microchip that records and collects data comprising the human consciousness. As mentioned in the show's opening episode "Out of the Past," inside the stack is "pure human mind, coded and stored as DHF: Digital Human Freight" (*AC* 1, "Out of the Past"). These stacks can be removed, placed into advanced computer systems and reinserted into new "sleeves"—the human bodies that act as hosts to the stacks inserted into them. This means that when someone dies, his/her entire cognitive history can be uploaded either into storage, or resleeved into a new body, transferring every past memory, feeling and experience into a new physical embodiment. Thus, humans are intertwined with specialized hardware that allows their consciousness to be digitized. People have the ability to transfer their minds from one body to another, rendering death a temporary state of being. Real death can still occur, yet only in one of the following ways: either one's cortical stack is destroyed physically; or one requests to be granted a real death when his/her "birth sleeve" dies.

While the repeated uploading into new sleeves theoretically makes immortality attainable for all, it is only the wealthiest, referred to as "Meths," who possess the finances to obtain it. This rich and powerful class is able to remotely store the back-ups of their minds in satellites, ensuring that even if their stack is damaged, they can still be resleeved. The chosen few also have the means to engage in technologies that allow them to clone their birth sleeves. Hence, by being resleeved in their clone replacements on a continual basis, they can live an eternal life. Meanwhile the less wealthy, who do not have access to such expensive technological solutions, have to buy or rent other bodies from the State; whereas the truly poor, who cannot even afford an ordinary sleeve, continue to remain in storage without much hope of returning to life.

In addition, the legal system no longer punishes live criminals, only their digitized minds. When a person has to serve a prison sentence, his/her stack is removed and placed in storage. This storage, acting as a digital prison, does not allow the consciousness to engage in daily human activities; but rather it is described as a "dark place" (*AC* 1, "Out of the Past"). In this manner, *Altered Carbon* creates a future world where the bodiless minds—DHF—are put in storage during their prison sentence, while the mindless bodies—sleeves of prisoners—become commodities from which the State profits by selling or leasing them.

Takeshi Kovacs, the protagonist of *Altered Carbon*, is an ex–Envoy with mercenary skills who is awakened in a new sleeve in Bay City, following several hundred years of digital imprisonment. Previously imprisoned for insurgency against the UN Protectorate—which rules Earth and the other Settled Worlds—his stack remained in storage until he got a new shot at life. Having Japanese-Hungarian origins, Kovacs finds himself resleeved in the body of a white detective Elias Ryker, in order to solve a crime. Bancroft, a prominent Meth, pulls Kovacs' stack out of storage in order to investigate what he believes to be his "sleeve murder." If Kovacs succeeds, he will win his freedom and keep his newly found body; if he fails, he will return to the digital prison to serve the rest of his sentence. Given an offer he cannot refuse, Kovacs sets out to solve the murder of the world's richest man.

Altered Carbon provokes fundamental philosophical and ontological questions regarding the nature of human existence, its limitations and borders. It opens up spaces to examine what constitutes being human in a technologized future, by exploring the intersections among the mind, machine, body and identity. When digital implants like cortical stacks are inserted into biological organisms, and the organic bodies are opened to the intrusions of technological apparatuses, how can we begin to understand the human self? Amidst this profound intermixture of the body and technology, what happens to the boundaries of human species and identity? Further questions emerge when considering the advanced stack technology that enables the presence of different realities—virtual and physical—and the separation of the consciousness from the embodiment. In a world where the human mind can be turned into a downloadable, copiable and transferable digital file, what is the role of the body and its physical materiality? Do physical bodies or sleeves become mere disposable or interchangeable vessels for this digital mind? Finally, if our consciousness is permitted to inhabit computers or the bodies of others, what makes us who we really are? While this part of the essay introduces the elaborate world of *Altered Carbon*, the next two sections critically review Haraway's conception of cyborg subjectivity and Hayles' articulations on posthumanism, which provide the theoretical backdrop for addressing the important questions touched upon by the show.

Haraway's Cyborg Subjectivity

In her influential essay "A Cyborg Manifesto: Science, Technology, and Socialist-Feminism in the Late Twentieth Century" (1991), science and technology scholar Haraway contests the liberal human subject which depends on binary logic and fixed identity politics. For Haraway, this liberal humanist view, which assumes a stable, self-sufficient, unified and essentialized subject, is inherently problematic, as it rests on several "antagonistic dualisms" (1991, p. 180) and questionable taxonomies between self/other, nature/culture, and man/machine, among others. However, high-tech culture offers possibilities for breaking down this traditional humanist notion of the subject, as well as its attendant antagonistic dualisms, which entail an exclusion, opposition and separation among different ontological categories. Hence in her "Cyborg Manifesto" (1991), Haraway analyzes and anticipates the shifts occurring in the socio-cultural sphere due to the rapidly evolving technologies of the late 20th century. For her, contemporary technological advances have become an indispensable part of everyday life, making "thoroughly ambiguous the difference between natural and artificial, mind and body, self-developing and externally designed, and many other distinctions that used to apply to organisms and machines" (1991, p. 152). In high-tech contexts, it is no longer clear "who makes and who is made in the relation between human and machine" (1991, p. 177). In this way, Haraway reflects on the irrevocable changes happening to the human subjects due to their intimate interactions with the increasingly advanced technologies.

Accordingly, Haraway introduces the conceptual figure cyborg—"a cybernetic organism" (1991, p. 149)—in order to address and theorize these ongoing entanglements of the human and the technological universe. The concept of cyborg emerges as a rejection of the notions of essentialism and naturalism, as well as the rigid ontological boundaries, notably those separating human from non-human, living from mechanical, natural from artificial. In so doing, it proposes a chimerical, monstrous world full of unnatural couplings between diverse organisms and machines. Thus, not concerned with any pure origins or essences, the cyborg is the impure mingling of man and machine; in Haraway's words, it represents "transgressed boundaries, potent fusions, and dangerous possibilities" (1991, p. 154).

Following Haraway's argument, the cyborg is also described as "the melding of the organic and the machinic, or the engineering of a union between separate organic systems" (Gray, Mentor, & Figueroa-Sarriera, 1995, p. 2), while for Anne Balsamo, it entails a "boundary figure belonging simultaneously to at least two previously incompatible systems of meaning—the 'organic/natural' and the 'technological/ cultural'" (1996, p. 5). In this respect, the concept of cyborg calls for a non-essentialist, mutable and malleable self, capable of uniting heterogeneous orders, rather than a homogeneous, unified identity based on antagonistic locations and conventional binary categorizations. It conceives a new version of subjectivity that constitutes a progressive challenge to the humanist accounts of individuality and the fixed notions of human identity with a biological unity or organic wholeness. This new version of subjectivity is further characterized by Haraway herself as a "disassembled and reassembled, postmodern collective and personal self" (1991, p. 163). As such—neither sufficiently human nor machine, organic nor technological—the cyborg always strives toward becoming at once fragmented and multiple, fractured and complex, as a means to account for the postmodern idea of partial selfhood. It stresses the subject as a multiplicity—whether this is a multiplicity of different bodies, or disparate components of a singular body. Correlatively, Haraway envisions "a cyborg world" which is about "lived social and bodily realities" wherein people are "not afraid of permanently partial identities and contradictory standpoints" (1991, p. 154). All things considered, the basic premise of her manifesto is the continual co-existence of humans and machines, in which neither one nor the other is left out when contemplating the body and identity in contemporary and coming age.

Hayles' Posthumanism

Haraway's iconic figure of the cyborg is in many ways the precursor of what philosopher Hayles calls "posthuman" in her seminal book *How We Became Posthuman: Virtual Bodies in Cybernetics, Literature, and Informatics* (1999). Indeed, Hayles' work on posthumanism is informed and motivated by the work of Haraway and has a theoretical alignment with her cyborg ontology in terms of the co-existence of humans with machines. Thus, this section moves the discussion from the figure of cyborg to the posthuman model.

In her book Hayles, once again, provides a framework for understanding the intersections of biology and technology through a rigorous critique of the liberal humanist subject of the Enlightenment, which is defined by "rationality," "free will" and "autonomous agency" (The University of Chicago, 1999). However, this liberal humanist notion of selfhood, which argues for a fixed, sovereign, coherent and fully-centered human self, is contested in the light of the information technology advancements of the late 20th and 21st centuries. Hayles discusses how a range of developments in such fields as "computer science, cognitive sciences, artificial life and artificial intelligence" brought about a new vision of the human so different from the liberal humanist subject that "it can appropriately be called 'posthuman'" (The University of Chicago, 1999). Thus, like Haraway, Hayles creates a vision of contemporary subjectivity that deconstructs the notion of a natural, singular and individual self—one that emerges when humankind is hybridized, mixed and enmeshed with the technology it creates. In her discussion of the subject, Hayles suggests that "the posthuman view configures human beings so that it can be seamlessly articulated with intelligent machines"; and in the posthuman subject, "there are no essential differences or absolute demarcations between bodily existence and computer simulation, cybernetic mechanism and biological organism, robot teleology and human goals" (1999, p. 3). Thus, the posthuman model continues to denaturalize and blur the assumed boundaries between human and non-human, man and machine, nature and artifice, facilitating the seamless integration of human beings with their digital environments. More specifically, it does so by enabling a linkage between the human cognition and the man-made cognition of machines. As such, implicit in the idea of the posthuman is the fact that there is a "distributed cognition" (1999, p. 3) dispersed among the human body, computers and the environment. This distributed cognitive environment across various human and non-human agents, in turn, complicates "individual agency" (1999, p. 4), and entails a shift from "an 'I'" into "the 'we' of autonomous agents operating together to make a self" (1999, p. 6). The posthuman subject, therefore, emerges as a collective, de-centered, heterogeneous entity located in divergent parts, beyond the centrality of the liberal humanist subject.

Besides contemplating on how the idea of posthuman may disrupt the purely humanist portrayals of subjectivity, Hayles is also cautious about the previous approaches to posthumanism which lead to the erasure of embodiment from subjectivity. Despite articulating the various interactions between humans and information technologies, for Hayles, these other perspectives tend to privilege information and digitization over substance and materiality. More precisely, they equate posthumanism with disembodied information—

patterns of data that can be digitally transferred from humans to intelligent machines. In her text *How We Became Posthuman*, Hayles asserts that these versions of posthumanism privilege "informational pattern over material instantiation" to the extent that "embodiment in a biological substrate is seen as an accident of history rather than an inevitability of life" (1999, p. 2). Thus, throughout her analysis, she criticizes these approaches for belittling the significance of the physical body for the survival of humanity, and failing to remember that it is embodied in the first place.

To ground her argument, Hayles traces the emergence of cybernetics research after the Second World War, which for her created "the cultural perception that information and materiality are conceptually distinct and that information is in some sense more essential, more important and more fundamental than materiality" (1999, p. 18). Hayles remarks that the popular media, literature and cybernetic theory of the late 20th century viewed information as disembodied, "stripped of context ... not tied down to bodies or material instantiations" (1999, p. 56), as something that "lost its body" (p. 2). Because information is abstracted from its material base, in the context of such discourses "embodiment is not essential to human being" (1999, p. 4), rather it has been "systematically downplayed or erased in the cybernetic construction of the posthuman" (p. 4). Hayles discusses how the translation of human minds into machines—as suggested by cyber-theorists like Hans Moravec—signifies contempt for the flesh and compromises the embodied aspect of our identity in the current age (1999, p. 1). This perspective argues for a future in which, through interfacing with a computer, humans can be uploaded into a complete virtual existence, breaking free from the limitations of corporeality and achieving a bodiless immortality in cyberspace. As a result, Hayles astutely observes that these popular conceptions of the cybernetic posthuman are characterized by a disregard for physicality and an emphasis instead on disembodiment associated with virtual reality.

This disembodied conception of posthumanism inevitably invokes a sense of Cartesian duality, which regards the mind as a distinct and detachable entity that can continue to exist independently from the physical body. It sets up a dichotomy between the mind and the body, portraying the former as superior to embodied existence and the true source of personal identity. Within such an approach, the body is clearly of minimal significance to the constitution of subjectivity. It is denigrated into the status of a mere vessel or container for the mind—and not much else. In an analysis consonant with this perspective, Allison Muri states that one of the main thrusts of the cyberculture theories of the past decades has been that "the human body is vanishing, irrelevant or, interfaced with the machine, an empty shell robbed of what is variously called spirit, consciousness or identity" (2003, p. 73).

In her book, Hayles takes up the challenge of dismantling this disembodied vision of posthumanity, which she associates with a nightmare:

> If my nightmare is a culture inhabited by posthumans who regard their bodies as fashion accessories rather than the ground of being, my dream is a version of the posthuman that embraces the possibilities of information technologies without being seduced by fantasies of unlimited power and disembodied immortality ... and that understands human life is embedded in a material world of great complexity, one on which we depend for our continued survival [1999, p. 5].

Said another way, Hayles attempts to amend the liberationist fantasies of cybernetic discourse which advocates the separation of the informational mind from the material body, and in her own words, "put back into the picture the flesh that continues to be erased in contemporary discussions about cybernetic subjects" (1999, p. 5). For her, subjects in a potential posthuman future must essentially remain embodied, as embodiment is an equally important aspect of our sense of being. In this manner, Hayles re-conceives the encounter between human beings and intelligent machines through an insistence on the embodied reality of the body. Accordingly, what she promotes is an embodied vision of posthumanism whereby the subject becomes an "amalgam, a collection of heterogeneous components, a material-informational entity whose boundaries undergo continuous construction and reconstruction" (1999, p. 3). Ultimately, much of Hayles' emphasis remains upon the multiplicity, plurality and collectivity of material experience—as diverse interpenetrations of organisms and machines—in the configuration of posthuman subjectivity. Having detailed Hayles' posthumanism and Haraway's cyborg ontology, which constitute two key conceptualizations of the human/technology interface in postmodernity, the task of the following section is to pursue a closer analysis of technologically modified humanity in *Altered Carbon* in conversation with these conceptual resources.

Embodied Reality in Altered Carbon

As a theory that foregrounds the conjunctions of varied human and non-human elements in the creation of a heterogeneous subjectivity, Haraway's cyborg serves as a productive entry point into the rich variety of human-technology mixtures in the speculative futures of *Altered Carbon*, as well as the various degrees of bodily transformations resulting from such admixtures. Much like the hybridized figure of "machine and organism" (1991, p. 149) described by Haraway, many of the characters presented in the series embody a malleable, changeable and composite self in their intimate exchanges with the achievements of futuristic technoscience.

The first and most crucial form of these bodily alterations takes place via the stack and sleeve technology. As discussed at the onset of this essay, a storage device—cortical stack—is installed in everyone as an infant that records their informatics knowledge, including memories and thoughts. This stack, which contains DHF, is surgically implanted into the vertebrae at the back of the neck. During this process, cutting-edge inorganic implants fuse and fold into the organic human flesh, destabilizing the clear-cut separations between self and non-self, human and non-human, biology and technology, hence the idea of stable, unified and autonomous subjects. The natural body is penetrated and modified by artificial components; it incorporates them into itself and merges with external devices, leading to unfixed corporeal territories. This embodied reconfiguration of humans through the installment of cortical stacks, in turn, provides the foundation for the growth of the cyborg subjectivity. Indeed, partly biological, partly mechanical, the characters of the show are pointing toward a more complex, multi-dimensional and cyborgian form of humanity, confounding easy dualisms through which "we have explained our bodies and our tools to ourselves" (Haraway, 1991, p. 181). Furthermore, since the stacks can be repeatedly removed and uploaded into new sleeves, *Altered Carbon* portrays the progressive fusion of multiple organisms and digital entities, displaying the impure mingling of "organic and technological flesh" (Haraway, 2008, p. 12) at stake in Haraway's cyborg ontology.

Besides the stack technology, the show presents a series of other sophisticated technologies that have the capacity to physically alter and modify human beings. However, these additional technological upgrades and alterations are strictly dependent on financial status; if individuals have the required money, they can further enhance their sleeves. One of these enhancements occurs through ONI: a product of advanced communication technology commonly used in the show. ONI (Optical Neural Interface) is an enhanced version of a smart phone. This device is installed into the brain to connect the optical system to the neural system. Through ONI one can make phone calls or look up information on the web.

Human beings in the world of *Altered Carbon* can be equipped with other kinds of high-tech features, including biotechnologically engineered drugs. In the first episode, the central character Kovacs spontaneously buys himself a number of narcotics. One of these drugs, which he takes in through his eye, augments his vision, enabling him to see a digital dimension on top of what he normally sees. As a result, an apparently normal street becomes an entirely new environment with the introduction of virtual elements, including advertisements for whorehouses, hotels, casinos and fighting rings. Another prominent way in which a sleeve can be enhanced or modified is through neurochemical conditioning. The new body (Ryker's body) Kovacs is sleeved into at the beginning of the show, comes equipped with military-grade "neurachem," providing him with ultra-fast reflexes and enhanced sensory perception. Haraway states that "communications technologies and biotechnologies are the crucial tools recrafting our bodies" (1991, p. 164). Indeed, whether through surgical, mechanical, digital or biochemical interventions, the bodies in *Altered Carbon* are radically recrafted and reconfigured. In incorporating divergent technological tools into their physical selves, they become a compilation of disparate parts without recourse to a biological unity, hence delineating a partial, multiple and contradictory standpoint on embodiment and identity. This multiple ontology, which bridges the gap between the conventionally dichotomous categories of biology and technology, closely aligns them with the cyborg Haraway imagines in her manifesto.

While the cyborg imagery provides a fruitful means for conceptualizing the alternate futures of humanity in *Altered Carbon*, it is not the only possibility. Through the cortical stacks grafted into them, Kovacs and others also become part of a digital environment that allows their consciousness to be uploaded into computers and transferred to different bodies—a process which implies the seamless melding of human intelligence and intelligent machines. As such, the series' depiction of resleeving technology propels humanity into a decidedly posthuman state, by seamlessly integrating cybernetic technology and corporeality.

However, besides this seamless biological and mechanical integration, another recurring motif in *Altered Carbon* is the detachment of human consciousness from the biological body that houses it. Through the realization of the hypothetical stack technology, the human mind can be condensed and reduced into a downloadable information pattern in the context of the show. At first glance, this vision of the human future in *Altered Carbon* seems to resemble the nightmarish posthuman scenario outlined by Hayles: the blatant affirmation of the separation of the informational mind from the material body, and the corresponding denigration of embodiment in favor of consciousness, which is perceived as the real ground of being. Contrary to this initial view, the vision of posthumanity portrayed in the show is not an immaterial one; *Altered Carbon* places a high degree of importance on the biologically embodied and embedded existence of its characters in the real world. Despite the prevalence of revolutionary technologies, which have the capacity to separate the mind from the body, the mind still needs a functioning embodiment in order to maintain a connection to reality. The stacks as the repositories of human consciousness are only meaningful and effective when they are planted back into a new human body/sleeve. In other words, the disembodied information that exists on hard drives only makes sense when re-embedded in embodied experience. It is important to remember that the prolonged longevity of humanity in the imagined futures of *Altered Carbon* is not guaranteed by the mind coded and stored in the stacks, but rather by its ability to later return to a physical body. Even in the age of radically advanced technologies, life is impossible outside the confines of the flesh. In this regard, the series reclaims the importance of embodiment as a vital signifier of existence, while simultaneously displacing the centrality and superiority of the mind for subjective selfhood. In so doing, it strongly resonates with Hayles' insistence on resituating the posthuman subjectivity in its material contexts, envisioning posthumans "as embodied creatures living within and through embodied worlds" (1999, p. 24).

The importance assigned to embodied forms of existence in the show is also evident in its characters' constant desire to be incarnated into the tangible world, regardless of what sleeve they happen to possess. As mentioned earlier, resleeving in the world of *Altered Carbon* is not something everyone can afford; and there is a huge difference between the sleeve options available to the rich and the poor. However, when economic factors are left aside, it becomes evident that the most preferred option is to live through one's own biological body, or birth sleeve. In case the birth sleeve is harmed or damaged, then the next preferred option is to be resleeved into a clone replacement. However, only the ultra-wealthy Meths have access to cloning facilities that can biologically grow clones of their birth sleeves. The third and most commonly used option is to buy a sleeve. Yet, the good sleeves are highly expensive and come with qualities that are valued in society, while the cheap ones might be of really bad quality. The poor who cannot afford high quality sleeves may have to rely upon bodies that are of different age, sex, ethnicity or race than the person inhabiting them.

This is poignantly exemplified in the show through the case of a small child named Cindy, who is resleeved into the body of an old woman after she is murdered in a hit-and-run. Kristin Ortega, a Bay City police detective, explains that this is a common procedure in "victim restitution," where the State gives whatever is on hand for free. Shocked and afflicted, Cindy's father cries out: "What have you done to our daughter? Cindy is seven years old!" (*AC* 1, "Out of the Past"). The guard tells him that this sleeve is provided for free, and this is all they get unless they have the money to upgrade to a more appropriate sleeve. Not having the required finances, her family has no other option than to accept this sleeve. Otherwise, they have to put her back into storage, where she would remain disembodied and disconnected from reality. In another scene that confirms this difficult situation, Gus, an employee of the cloning-facility for Meths, remarks that "folks resleeve in whatever they can find, if they can afford it" (*AC* 2, "Fallen Angel"). In this way, the narrative insists on a teleological return to the tangible realm through a fleshy existence, and thus departs from the theorization of the body as an irrelevant or superfluous entity. Indeed, the aim is always to revert to a carnal state through resleeving and interact with the world through an embodied interface—even if this entails losing all physical markers that influence a large part of one's identity. The body—whatever form it may take—is still the preferred agent to connect to material reality in the future worlds of *Altered Carbon*.

Technology in the context of the show has so evolved that it also includes virtual worlds. However, as the narration suggests, virtual reality is never a desirable alternative to corporeal reality; but rather it appears as a tool that can be used for two different purposes. The first and most frequent use of virtual reality is as an interrogation and torture chamber. The torture takes place on the level of one's consciousness, but its psychological impacts are making the experience feel real. Although the physical body does not get hurt, the person is severely traumatized psychologically. In the fourth episode "Force of Evil," Quell, the leader of Envoys, describes the torture in virtual environment as follows: "DHF made it possible to put someone in virtual, torture them to death and then start again. To the mind, pain is pain. Torture, die, repeat. Eventually, you'll break. And if it doesn't stop, you'll go insane" (*AC* 4, "Force of Evil"). In this respect, the series predominantly focuses on the punitive aspects of virtual and computer-generated realities, presenting them as convoluted disembodied platforms to be avoided if possible. This is aptly reflected in the same episode, when Kovacs is captured and brought to Wei Clinic—a facility specialized in virtual torture—after he starts investigating Bancroft's sleeve death. At the clinic, his stack is uploaded into a virtual construct where he is interrogated and tortured gruesomely. Thanks to his envoy training, Kovacs eventually manages to escape the constructed virtual environment.

Besides torture, virtual reality in the series is depicted to have a rehabilitative function. Lizzie Elliot, who has been traumatized by the torture she underwent at Wei Clinic, is later rehabilitated by artificial intelligence (AI) Poe in virtual reality. Once Lizzie is convinced that her rehabilitation is over, she expresses her wish to be resleeved and return to physical reality to be with her family. As such, virtual reality in the show is not presented as a utopian place in which individuals can continue to exist as pure minds by getting rid of their embodiment and leaving their fleshly reality behind. In this regard, the narrative of *Altered Carbon* places further focus on an ontology based upon corporeality and visualizes a potential posthuman future "grounded in embodied actuality rather than disembodied information" (Hayles, 1999, p. 287). Correlatively, it works against the earlier discourse on cybernetics, which was primarily concerned with processes of bodily erasure, while deviating from traditional cyberpunk's celebration of immaterial modes of existence in cyberspace.

This focus upon body and physicality, not only highlights the embodied nature of the posthuman identity in the show, but also complicates the Cartesian paradigm which creates a hierarchy between the mind and the body, by treating the latter as an arbitrary shell with only minimal implications for the construction of personality and identity. Indeed, there are some compelling scenes and moments in *Altered Carbon* which demonstrate that bodies are, in fact, essential to the thinking and being of the individuals inhabiting them. One of them is when Kovacs awakes in a new body in the first episode and asks for a mirror. Upon seeing an unfamiliar face staring back at him, he screams and feels betrayed. This indicates that one's outer image is more than a shell to live through; it plays an inevitable role in the subject's formation and subsequent self-perception. In his new sleeve, Kovacs is also shown to experience the urge to smoke cigarettes. Even though he did not have the habit of smoking before, he notices that he craves nicotine, as Ryker, the previous owner of his sleeve, was a smoker. Similarly, when Ortega connects the cortical stack of her grandmother to the sleeve of a criminal for the special occasion of *Dia de Los Muertos*, her grandmother drinks a lot more alcohol than she used to—a scene implying that she inherited this urge from the criminal's body. As both of these examples powerfully suggest, it is impossible to think human consciousness apart from the sleeves it occupies; they are connected the moment the cortical stack is uploaded into a new sleeve.

Each sleeve has its own body chemistry and contains the traces of previous use; it thus undeniably affects the cognition, behavior and perception of the person currently residing in it. This is not to suggest that the characters' past experiences, thoughts and memories—which amount to their digitized consciousness in the stacks—are overcome by simply putting them into different sleeves. Instead, whenever a new body is inhabited, this digitized consciousness is obliged to integrate with its unique biological and chemical compounds. This arguably accords with Hayles' project of postulating posthuman identity as a corporeal experience. In that sense, *Altered Carbon* captures the influence of corporeality upon subjectivity, and in the process, demonstrates that identity cannot be located solely within consciousness. Physicality does influence personal identity in the show; and individuality is not reducible to the information pattern in the digitized mind. Accordingly, the narrative of *Altered Carbon* works to diminish the hierarchical gap between the mind and the body, delineating the body not as an inconsequential vessel containing the transcendent mind, but rather an integral component of selfhood.

A final important aspect regarding the mind/body relationship in the show is related to the complications of resleeving. This process does not come without challenges: when individuals are resleeved, they get "sleeve sick," indicating that an adjustment period is needed in order to get used to their new skin. As stated in the narrative, it is normal to go through "disorientation, visual and auditory hallucinations, and even low-grade amnesia" (*AC* 1, "Out of the Past") when a person is resleeved. Additionally, if people are resleeved repeatedly, they experience a "personality frag," which indicates that they lose grasp on reality. As Kovacs says, if "you resleeve too many times, eventually you go nuts" (*AC* 2, "Fallen Angel"). The emphasis here is that resleeving is not merely an act of changing clothes, but rather has further implications for the subjectivity. Indeed, the body, in the context of *Altered Carbon*, cannot be regarded as a piece of clothing that can be easily switched, replaced or discarded, as each resleeving has its own consequences, creating a sense of doubt or confusion about one's sense of self. In other words, resleeving into a body that is not one's birth sleeve does affect identity. Consequently, the idea that future technological advances will allow the human mind to be transplanted from one body to the other without any challenges is also problematized in the show.

Conclusion

This essay probes into the technologically altered human subjectivity in the context of the Netflix series *Altered Carbon*. It specifically looks at how the body and the mind—the two components of human subjectivity—are negotiated, changed and altered in their conjunctions with various futuristic technologies. For this aim, this essay adopts the interlinked frameworks of Haraway and Hayles, which locate technologically modified humanity as one of their primary concerns. Haraway's theory on cyborg subjectivity enables an analysis of the various enmeshments of the organic and digital, biological and technological spheres in the series, which propel humans into a multiple, assembled and heterogeneous state of being. Through an analysis of the character portrayals of the show, it is recognized how this new version of being signals a dissolution of the humanist conceptions of personhood and the fixed organizations of the subject based on dualistic structures, and thus becomes an inevitable manifestation of Haraway's cyborg ontology.

This essay further argues that the world of *Altered Carbon* features a blend of cyborgian and posthuman elements. As such, the characters of the show become so technologically sophisticated that they are no longer confined to the parameters of humanness; but rather extend toward a posthuman condition in their seamless interfacing with advanced stack technology. On the one hand, *Altered Carbon* demonstrates that the mind can be separable from its original body through this hypothetical stack technology, while, on the other, the mind is still dependent on another body in order to enact its experiences of the world. Said another way, the series conceptualizes the human consciousness as a floating data or information pattern that can hover between different bodies and realities (virtual and physical), however, it is emphasized that this floating consciousness needs to be attached to a physical embodiment in order to connect to material reality and ensure the enhanced longevity of humanity. This attachment, to a certain extent, overturns the Cartesian tradition that privileges or prioritizes the mind over the body—assuming the former as the true essence of an individual's identity. Hence, by turning toward Hayles' understanding of posthumanism, which argues for an embodied subjectivity extended by technology, this essay posits that *Altered Carbon* delineates a model of posthuman subjectivity built on the informational mind and the material body, which constantly interact and coalesce with one another. Indeed, the posthuman vision advocated in the show is a collusion between information and materiality, digitized consciousness and embodied corporeality, cybernetic technologies and the biological flesh, echoing what Hayles has suggested elsewhere: "the posthuman subject is an amalgam, a collection of heterogeneous components, a material-informational entity" (1999, p. 3). In this respect, *Altered Carbon* points toward a potential posthuman future wherein identity continues to reside in the amalgamation of the conscious mind and the physical body, suggesting that both play an indelible role in the constitution of subjectivity.

REFERENCES

Balsamo, A. (1996). *Technologies of the Gendered Body: Reading Cyborg Women*. Durham: Duke University Press.
Frelik, P. (2010). Woken Carbon: The Return of the Human in Richard K. Morgan's Takeshi Kovacs Trilogy. In *Beyond Cyberpunk: New Critical Perspectives*. Murphy, G., & Vint, S. (Eds.). New York: Routledge, pp. 173–190.
Gray, C.H., Mentor, S., & Figueroa-Sarriera, H. (1995). Cyborgology. In *The Cyborg Handbook*. Gray, C.H., Mentor, S., & Figueroa-Sarriera, H. (Eds). London: Routledge, pp. 1–14.
Haraway, D. (1991). *Simians, Cyborgs and Women: The Reinvention of Nature*. New York: Routledge.
Haraway, D. (2008). *When Species Meet*. Minneapolis: University of Minnesota Press.
Hayles, N.K. (1999). *How We Became Posthuman: Virtual Bodies in Cybernetics, Literature and Informatics*. Chicago: University of Chicago Press.
Hollinger, V. (1990). Cybernetic Deconstructions: Cyberpunk and Postmodernism. *Mosaic: An Interdisciplinary Critical Journal* 23, no. 2 (Spring): 29–44. http://www.jstor.org/stable/24780626.
Lenic, J.G. (Producer) & Kalogridis, L. (Creator). *Altered Carbon*. (2018–). [Series]. United States: Netflix.
Morgan, R.K. (2002). *Altered Carbon*. London: Gollancz.
Muri, Allison. (2003). "Of Shit and the Soul: Tropes of Cybernetic Disembodiment in Contemporary Culture." *Body & Society* 9, no. 3 (September): 73–92. https://doi.org/10.1177/1357034X030093005.
University of Chicago Press. 1999. An Interview/dialogue with Albert Borgmann and N. Katherine Hayles on humans and machines. http://www.press.uchicago.edu/Misc/Chicago/borghayl.html.

Embodiment in *Altered Carbon*

Lars Schmeink

Introduction

In her seminal book, *How We Became Posthuman* (1999), N. Katherine Hayles discusses the connection of subjectivity and embodiment and warns her readers that "my nightmare is a culture inhabited by posthumans who regard their bodies as fashion accessories rather than the ground of being" (p. 5). What propels this nightmare is a view of the posthuman privileging "informational pattern over material instantiation, so that embodiment in a biological substrate is seen as an accident of history rather than an inevitability of life" (p. 2). In some forms of posthuman thinking, the body thus becomes malleable, interchangeable, and ultimately superfluous to posthuman subjectivity—and by extension a possible site for commodification and the whims of fashion. But Hayles' warning is clear: this form of the "cybernetic posthuman" (p. 4) is deeply entrenched in conceptions of liberal humanism, of the universality of the human and the self-possession of the individual, "a claim that depends on erasing markers of bodily difference, including sex, race, and ethnicity" (pp. 4–5), and identifies the body not as (part of) the self, but as "an object for control and mastery" (p. 5).

In opposition to the cybernetic posthuman, critics such as Hayles or Sherryl Vint posit a different view of the posthuman as embodied and relational. In her book *Bodies of Tomorrow* (2007), Vint argues that subjectivity is constructed both from material embodiment and social community: "subjectivity is as much material as it is abstract, about the body as well as about the mind, and subjectivity is shaped by cultural forces that produce the sense of an interior" (p. 6). Technologies, especially those that define the posthuman in their intervention on the body, have influence on the way we culturally construct the human: "The human body, like the human subject, is a product of both culture and nature" (p. 17). Vint argues that body and subjectivity are intertwined through material and cultural construction: "The material and the discursive body are mutually productive: the material body is read by discourses, and the conclusions produced by these readings structure practices which influence the ways bodies come into being" (p. 18). How we represent bodies and subjectivity in our discourses, be they political, economical, or cultural, is thus ideologically loaded and reveals the positions available in dealing with the posthuman.

The Netflix series *Altered Carbon* (Lenic & Kalogridis, 2018–), based on the novel of the same name by Richard Morgan (2002), is a valuable case study to explore the representation of posthuman subjectivity, as it propagates exactly the kind of commodification nightmare that Hayles warns against, while at the same time complicating this concept through representations of embodiment and material entanglement. While the premise of the show—that human consciousness can be transferred via cortical stacks and either "spun up" in virtual worlds or "sleeved" in a variety of biological and synthetic bodies—fully adheres to conceptions of the cybernetic posthuman, the representation of posthuman bodies in the series nevertheless reveals a complex material and communal grounding for subjectivity.

Commodification of Bodies

In its depiction of downloading the human mind/consciousness into a "stack," *Altered Carbon* represents the specific form of the cybernetic posthuman that is embraced by classic cyberpunk and transhumanist thought alike—the idea, as Hans Moravec puts it that "a human mind might be freed from its brain" (1990, p. 4). According to transhumanism, the physical body is flawed and humans should be transcending its limitations into a "postbiological" (p. 1) age through the use of technology. Moravec sees the best option to become posthuman in the "idea that a human mind can be transferred to a new body" (p. 110), at best a machinic body to circumvent biological limitations. In terms of subjectivity, he argues for "*pattern-identity*," assuming the "essence of a person" is not defined by "the stuff of which a body is made" but rather "the *pattern* and the *process* going on in my head" (p. 177, emphasis in original).

A similar fixation on the "pattern" rather than the bodily "stuff" is at the heart of cyberpunk, which as a genre propagates the idea of the body as meat and the mind as data that can escape bodily limitations. As Vint has pointed out, in its depictions of posthuman existence, cyberpunk is "best known for its rejection of embodiment and embrace of an existence in cyberspace" (2007, p. 102). Analyzing William Gibson's emblematic novel *Neuromancer* (1984), Vint makes the point that cyberpunk "appeals to the (impossible) desire to escape the vicissitudes of the body and occupy the place of selfmastery" (p. 104), while in its representation of embodiment it simultaneously reveals a strong critique of an "extremely commodified world" in which the material body is at risk (to be controlled, harmed, sold), thus justifying the desire "to escape the consequences of having a body" (p. 108).

Altered Carbon is ripe for a similar analysis, depicting a world in which bodies have become exchangeable commodities and the stack (i.e. the mind) of a person can be transferred into many different forms of embodiment: naturally born, resleeved in a different body, vat grown in a cloning facility, illegally bio-printed from sampled DNA, synthetically created, or spun up in any kind of virtual environment. The choice of body/bodies is only limited by one's economic means, as each option comes with a price tag—in the show, "flesh is just another kind of economy," as Julie Muncy (2018) has succinctly put it. Bodies, then, are the ultimate commodities through which power differentials are expressed. As Mark Bould has pointed out, cyberpunk "inaugurated the SF of multinational capital and corporate globalization, its depiction of information circulating in cyberspace a potent metaphor for the global circulation of capital" (2005, p. 220). In cyberpunk everything is subsumed by capitalist power, and in *Altered Carbon* even human bodies become the object of biopolitical control through the abilities granted by the stack-technology. Karen Cadora has argued that technology itself is the divisive instrument to uphold such hierarchies of control: "cyberpunk imagines a world where technology is a tool of both oppression and liberation. Poverty is pervasive in cyberpunk, and technological resources are expensive luxuries. Those without access to [...them] are effectively kept in the underclass" (1995, p. 359).

Altered Carbon drives this inequality to the extreme, sending "socioeconomic stratification into overdrive, creating dire new realities for the poor ... while simultaneously producing an elite upper-class," as Devon Maloney has argued (2018). The upper-class, simply called Meths (in reference to the biblical Methuselah, hinting at their unnaturally long life-span) in the show, treats bodies as a resource to be used for their personal entertainment and gain. Laurens Bancroft (James Purefoy) and his wife Miriam (Kristin Lehman) keep a number of grown clone bodies at hand, should their current body fail and need to be replaced. Bancroft regularly visits a camp of survivors of a "contagion bomb" attack, touching and hugging them, thus contaminating his own body and dying a slow death. In a religiously connoted scene, surrounded by the plagued carriers reveling in his touch, presenting himself in a messianic fashion, he argues that the visits and his "deaths" are "my sacrifice to help them feel noticed" (*AC* 5, "The Wrong Man"). But Takeshi Kovacs

(Joel Kinnaman), the protagonist of the show, is not fooled by the theatrics, calling out the Meth's (and, one could argue, the Christian churches') bigotry: "If you care so much, why don't you buy them new sleeves?" As one of the richest people alive, Laurens would have enough money to provide the camp with synthetic sleeves, but his own egomania of being revered and symbolically dying for (one of) humanity's sins is more valuable to him. His body becomes a commodity to be handed out for the return of a unique experience and the power it grants him.

Miriam Bancroft has also commodified her body for unique experiences. She wants to feel "irresistible": "Have you heard of Empathin? Merge9 [...] It's a biochemical pheromone. Puts bodies in touch with one other. This sleeve is state-of-the-art biochemtech from Nakamura Labs. I secrete Merge9 when I'm aroused. It's in my saliva, in my sweat, in my cunt." (*AC* 2, "Fallen Angel"). She uses made-to-order sleeves to play the role of irresistible witch, a bioengineered Circe, complete with her own pleasure island full of her own clones able to engage in sexual play at the same time. Her clones are so well made and tempting that her own daughter uses one to seduce men and experience the sensation—borrowing the sleeve as if it were a car: "Why wouldn't I want to take 'em for a spin? I have fun, okay?" (*AC* 3, "In a Lonely Place").

But sleeves are not just used for pleasure; they also facilitate business interests, and can be operated for special tasks. Kovacs himself has been given the sleeve of ex-cop Elias Ryker, because it "came equipped with military-grade neurachem and combat muscle memory" (*AC* 1, "Out of the Past"), making it perfect for soldiers and law-enforcement. When the fight club proprietor Carnage (Matt Frewer) discusses his next fight for which he "stocked up on inventory," he shows Kovacs and Ortega Kovacs's old sleeve (Will Yun Lee), praising it for its "hot rod envoy flesh, with all the modern accouterments" (*AC* 5, "The Wrong Man"). Kovacs's sister, Reileen Kawahara (Dichen Lachman), similarly uses genetically modified sleeves for her fights, as well as a variety of different bodies for her covert-actions, among them that of a young child so as to better manipulate those around her (*AC* 9, "Rage in Heaven").

When you have the money, biomedicine is able to provide any kind of specialized body you wish for or require. In a hypercapitalist society, though, technology and resources also produce a divide and entrench systems of inequality. As James Caccamo argues, "the digital divide will no longer be a social reality but will be written into our bodies and minds" (2018, p. 209). Caccamo points out that "radical inequality results from the posthuman development process" and that it will entrench or even accelerate "the injustices that characterize our contemporary society" (p. 209). For the poor and disenfranchised, the body they are born with becomes one of the few, if not the only commodity to trade with. Within the subject matter of *Altered Car-*

bon this is most poignantly demonstrated by the penal system. In reality already a form of biopower that is used to generate revenue for private owners, the series makes literal what is currently only figurative: convicted criminals become the property of the penal system, their stacks are stripped from their bodies and "put on ice," while their sleeves are reused and available for sale: "Now that you have paid your debt to society, you have been resleeved from our available inventory of prisoners" (*AC* 1, "Out of the Past"). When prisoners are released, or when victims of crime get a free sleeve as "restitution," the state pays for the body, providing "what they have on hand. Broken down crap [...] Prisons lease out the good sleeves for profit" (*AC* 1, "Out of the Past").

In the first episode, when Kovacs is picked-up by Lt. Kristin Ortega (Martha Higareda) at one of the resleeving facilities, we see a middle-aged woman looking around the room, frightened, then moving over to a couple in their thirties: it is their daughter. The father confronts the guard: "What have you done to our daughter? Cindy's seven years old.... She was murdered in a hit-and-run. The law says she gets a free sleeve" (*AC* 1, "Out of the Past"). But the guards (and the law) are blind to the needs of the child or the parents, arguing that a free sleeve is any that is available in the inventory of the prison, "if you don't like it, pay for an upgrade or put her back in storage" (*AC* 1, "Out of the Past"). What is meant as "victim restitution" is thus cruelly adding insult to injury of those that cannot afford the upgrade; the family is left with the traumatic experience of a child in an older woman's body.

Another group that is presented as disenfranchised in the sleeve-economy are sex workers, who provide their bodies to the wants and needs of their clientele. Whereas virtual reality could provide an outlet for sexual fantasies, in the world of *Altered Carbon*, physical sex is seen as more desirable and is thus a better-paid service. Here again, the desires of the Meths are the most extreme. At "Jack It Off," the low-end club that Bancroft regularly frequents, he is known to be violent and sometimes kill the (biological) sleeves of the girls he stays with. But, as one sex worker argues: "He's one of the good ones. If he breaks it, he buys it. ... You know, if he accidentally kills a girl he buys her an upgraded sleeve" (*AC* 1, "Fallen Angel"). The sex workers see their bodies as commodities to trade with, most of the time the only commodity they have to offer. Lizzie Elliot (Hayley Law), Lauren's favorite at "Jack It Off," for example, is selling her body in order to pay for her mother's sleeve, to get her back once she is released from prison. She is even willing to sacrifice her own bodily integrity (on Bancroft's violent tendencies), in order to restore the unity of her family.

Even more extreme are the actions at the high-end bordello "Head in the Clouds," which makes use of synthetic as well as biological sleeves. The TV show never really discusses the synthetic sleeves and, except for Carnage and Lizzie in the final episode, no one uses them. This is noteworthy, especially since synths feature the ability to restructure the outer shell of the sleeve to any wishes (within seconds), making them ideal for sex work. An explanation as to why they feature so little in the show might be found in the original novel, where Morgan discusses a sort of "uncanny valley" feeling of being inside a synthetic sleeve: "Cheap, but it's too much like living alone in a draughty house, they never seem to get the flavor circuits right. Everything you eat ends up tasting like curried sawdust" (2002, p. 13). That the show fails to discuss the more practical option of synthetic bodies hints at an ideological point about the primacy of the biological. One could argue that the show, by omission, promotes a similar "uncanny valley" feeling for those dealing with synths. Carnage, for example, looks grotesquely unreal in his sleeve, "human, but not quite," and Ortega makes a quip about the sleeve's ability to alter its face to what is desired.[1] As Shahizah Ismail Hamdan has pointed out (for the novel, but relevant here, too): "Resleeving in a non-organic body fails to capture the finer details of an organic body" (2011, p. 128). Lizzie, echoes this, arguing that she is keeping the synth, because "it's not real. And she doesn't know if she is either" (AC 10, "The Killers"). Dealing with and being in a synth might thus not be seen as authentic or natural human experience, embodiment in a biological sleeve is proposed as central to feeling human.

In fact, a biological body of a sex worker is a prerequisite for the most exclusive service at "Head in the Clouds," as it deals with hurting, torturing, and killing human beings for sexual, sadistic pleasure. Clients can pay for any sort of mistreatment of bodies and the sex workers[2] believe to be repaid by new sleeves: "I am all yours.... You could cut holes in me anywhere. Fuck me in them. Tear me apart, General. Rip me open with that big dick" (AC 9, "Rage in Heaven"). The thrill of killing is an experience so unique that wealthy Meth clients pay extraordinary sums for it. The so-called "Iridium Experience," though, does not provide a resleeving, as the girl hopes in her naiveté:

> VERNON: How many times have you done this?
> GIRL: It's my first.
> VERNON: Do you know of any other girls that come back?
> GIRL: Well, turnover's pretty high and we don't, you know, socialize. But you have to kill me. If you don't, they're gonna fire me [AC 9, "Rage in Heaven"].

Unbeknownst to the sex workers, Reileen has found a way to manipulate "religious coding" and mark them as Neo-Catholic believers in one-body-incarnations, thus denying them the possibility of resleeving or any form of after-death testimony in virtual reality. This life is the only one they will ever have; their death will be permanent. The show never makes explicit whether Reileen does this due to some social taboos around killing a sleeve or some sexual practices, strict regulations on and supervision of permission by law to damage sleeves (see below), or because she can market the service to the Meths as even more exclusive. Either way, the practice of providing the experience of torture and killing is what Anya Heise-von der Lippe describes as the worst form of "technologically enhanced, neoliberal late capitalism and its necropolitical exploitation of human bodies" (2020, p. 268). Meths see bodies as mere objects to be used and discarded in any way they see fit, no matter the actual cost to the person inhabiting it.

This view of bodies as mere objects has even found its way into law practice and policy, where Meths can apply for a permit of "Extreme Organic Damage," which basically equates killing a human to property damage—as long as it is monitored by police, you simply sign a waiver of permission and the damaged party will get reimbursed. Bancroft uses this practice to stage a fight to the sleeve death between a married couple: "The winner gets an upgraded combat sleeve. The loser gets a downgraded one" (*AC* 3, "In a Lonely Place"). Interestingly, the show implies the communal consequences of this practice, as Kovacs highlights the emotional distress that the couple's children will be subject to—their parents continuously appearing in different bodies. Heise-von der Lippe argues that the show propagates a "negligent position towards death: the prospect of resleeving undermines death as a meaningful category for humanity" (2019, p. 7). But as we have seen, this is not equally true for everyone—death does have meaning to those that cannot afford this hypercapitalist fantasy of the cybernetic posthuman and it has communal consequences for loved ones that have to deal with new forms of embodiment and identity.

The Corporeality of Existence

Meths value unique experiences, especially if these are connected to bodily sensations—which the show foregrounds by its emphasis on sex, drugs, and violence. Obviously, there is a dissonance here with the concept of disembodied "pattern-identity," which rejects the importance of that "stuff of which a body is made" (Moravec, 1990, p. 177). In this, *Altered Carbon*, makes explicit what Allison Muri has pointed out—that the "rhetoric of disembodied cyborgs" (2003, p. 74) is flawed, as the body cannot simply be made to vanish into non-corporeality, but demands attention regardless of our technological level:

> If we are going to be talking about the living human body …, we need also to emphasize that human consciousness is inalienably enmeshed with its corporeality, with the everyday actualities of its flesh, its giving-birth, its growths and excrescences, the regularities or indignities of its secretions; our consciousness is mediated by hunger

pangs roiling beneath the rib cage, by dripping and oozing mucal secretions, by the insistence of that imperative erectile tissue in our genitalia, by the sometimes pleasurable and urgent necessity to shit. These undignified aspects of human life sharply contrast the supposed dematerialization of flesh into data that have continued to be a powerful metaphor in literary and cultural studies for decades [Muri, p. 77].

Underneath the shiny possibilities of the transfer of human consciousness and endlessly perfected clone bodies, *Altered Carbon* nonetheless presents a future very much grounded in the carnality of the body. And in fact, mixed in with its glossy visual, the show does not hide the biological workings of the body. After seeing the murdered family of Ortega, hardened cop Tanaka (Hiro Kanagawa) breaks down and vomits, while a funny scene with Ortega's grandmother cross-sleeved in a big, male gang member's body has her peeing standing-up and joking about the biological difference. The "actualities of the flesh" cannot be erased in the show.

But more than just bodily functions, the show highlights the threat that every body is under from the techno-capitalist system it is living in. As Vint has argued for Case in *Neuromancer*, the same is true for Kovacs: "In a world where everything has become a commodity, even body parts risk being harvested by the more powerful. The cyberspace elite stance begins to look more like a defence mechanism to prevent the subject from realizing how little control it has" (2007, p. 108). Indeed, after having been resleeved by Bancroft, thus literally having been bought, and discovering his servitude to the Meth, Kovacs escapes into bodily cravings, first getting high on a variety of drugs ("some brain grease," "some epic shit") and then soliciting prostitutes ("Well, I got money and he's got girls, so I think we will be good"), but essentially denying any responsibility for the world around him ("I'll take eternity on ice," "This isn't my world" [AC 1, "Out of the Past"]).

In fact, Kovacs's reaction to being controlled in the first episode is exemplary of how the show itself revels in corporeality and bodily dysfunction—highlighting embodiment in its visual focus on the breaking-down of the human. As seen above, the show presents the moral break-down of the elite, underscoring this with vivid imagery of their depravity and opulence. Miriam Bancroft collects "Elder civilization artifacts," among them "the only Songspire tree on Earth" (AC 1, "Out of the Past"), which, as Kovacs remarks, should be in a museum (accessible to the community) and not a private home. Later, Miriam even manages to secure "the fossil of an actual Elder," the bones of a creature with angelic wings, displayed in her home to her friends as her latest prize (AC 10, "The Killers")—monopolizing the access to such cultural artifacts gives her social capital and power. The show pushes this need for a display of power further: one scene depicts the elite gathering for a theme party under the motto "unique," one person bringing a human being illegally sleeved into a snake ("Turns out you go quite mad"), the "rare dish" of the evening consists of tiger meat, and Bancroft displays Kovacs as his unique item: "Something no one owns in the entire Protectorate but me. Ladies and gentlemen, I give you the last Envoy" (*AC* 3, "In a Lonely Place"). Meths, the show makes clear, know no ethics in how they interact with their surroundings; pleasure and power drive their self-interests.

Even more expressive than the moral decay, is the shows visual repertoire of breaking bodies, as Heise–von der Lippe points out, "a number of scenes highlighting fights, injuries, and torture in a manner verging on body horror" (2020, p. 268). Bancroft's body decays with blisters and peeling skin during the camp scene; the married-couple-fight is presented in vivid detail in a low-gravity environment, so as to highlight the dark red blood spatter as the bodies are slashed open; when Kovacs is ambushed by armed mercenaries in The Raven Hotel, the automated guns of the hotel rip through their bodies in slow-motion, the chaos tracked by CGI displays of blood spattering and bodies torn; when Kovacs and Ortega are forced to fight genetically enhanced warriors at Fightdrome, Reileen shows up wielding a katana, slaughtering an army of fighters, while the camera tracks a circling motion, recording the falling bodies, pierced and sliced, around her; and as Ortega takes out a dozen or more versions of Reileen in the clone facility, the camera lingers on the repetition of naked bodies (slashed, shot, broken) that accrue in the chamber. In all of these scenes (and many others), the visual focuses on the broken bodies, showing slashed and battered skin, broken bones and projectiles piercing flesh, blood, guts and brain spattering the scene.

Moreover, a whole episode is devoted to vivid expressions of torture in virtual reality, visually foregrounding this as bodily harm is done to Kovacs (though simulated), including severe burns, amputation, scarring, and body intrusions. In this episode (*AC* 4, "Force of Evil"), Kovacs is brought into a clinic that specializes in torture and information extraction. Intercut with the torture scenes, the clinic technicians are shown. In the background, presented only in snippets, the camera keeps glossing over the dissection of the sex worker that Kovacs dealt with at "Jack It Off"—her body is splayed open and her organs are harvested, she is being systematically emptied of any "reusable" material. The shots are gruesome and qualify as some of the most disgusting displays of violence against female bodies in the show, though they are by far not the only ones. In fact, as Heise–von der Lippe points out, the show "reiterates gendered differences to the point of presenting stereotypical heteronormative patriarchal violence as the norm" (2020, p. 269) and in its visuality foregrounds female bodies as abused and mistreated through sexual and non-sexual violence. Furthermore, the show goes out of its way to sexualize female bodies, showing nudity of almost all female characters and using sexual desire as a means of manipulation. The female body, in *Altered Carbon*, is an object to be desired, viewed, manipulated, and discarded by the powerful.[3]

Resistance in Community and Materiality

In its depiction of Meths and their hypercapitalist commodification of bodies, the show firmly positions itself in the cybernetic posthuman that Hayles warns about. Nonetheless, there is a form of resistance to this concept in the visual representation of bodily harm and the focus on bodily abuse that allows for a different stance on the posthuman. Heise–von der Lippe notes, that while Meths advocate a "cavalier stance towards damaging" bodies, other characters, including Kovacs and Ortega, are "repeatedly presented as adverse to gratuitous violence and prone to preserve a person's sleeve" (2020, p. 268). While I do not see a stance against gratuitous violence, both Kovacs and Ortega argue for keeping intact a sleeve that holds an emotional connection for them. The previous relationship between Ortega and Ryker emotionally ties her to his sleeve—now inhabited by Kovacs—and informs her interactions with Kovacs. When Kovacs threatens damage to his sleeve, Ortega gives in and declares her feelings for Ryker and her motives for caring for the sleeve (*AC* 5, "The Wrong Man"). Later in the episode, Ortega and Kovacs get close to each other, tellingly by her tending to his wounds and discussing the old scars that literally mark history on his/Ryker's body. At one point Kovacs asks about a scar and Ortega begins to mix the two persons present (body/mind) together:

> KOVACS: When you look in my eyes what do you see?
> ORTEGA: They're not your eyes.
> KOVACS: What about this?
> ORTEGA: That one's from me. I forget why, but you deserved it. This is a mistake. [SIGHS]
> When I look into his eyes, I see you looking back at me, and it's been a long time since someone looked at me like that.
> KOVACS: I'm sorry I'm not Elias.
> ORTEGA: Just shut the fuck up [*AC* 5, "The Wrong Man"].

The combination of Ryker's sleeve (which echoes the physical relationship they had) and Kovacs's feelings for Ortega (reflected in his look, reminding her that Ryker no longer feels this way) conflates Ryker and Kovacs in her view, making it impossible to ignore the embodied reality of her relationship with Kovacs. Meaningful human connection is only possible in its embodied form.

Kovacs reacts similarly when the Ryker sleeve is damaged in a fight and Reileen wants to let it die, "You're gonna wake up in a new body, something more durable and a little less gaijin and with better hair." Kovacs is adamant, though, fighting hard against Reileen's casual dismissal of the body: "You have to save this sleeve" (*AC* 7, "Nora Inu"). Knowing of his complex and embodied relationship to Ortega and not wanting to loose it, Kovacs insists on being sleeved in Ryker. He also holds on to Ortega after Leung (Trieu Tran) attacks her and she almost dies. Kovacs does everything to save her, rushes her to the hospital, pays for "specialized treatment," and when her arm needs amputation and replacement, chooses a "seamless interface" design so that it blends in with Ortega's body. He is aggravated by the casualness of the doctor's capitalist interest in the body as a product: "Offer me one more thing and I'll put your head through the wall. ... Just fix her" (*AC* 6, "Man with my Face"). For both Ortega and Kovacs, their bodies are connected and essential to their emotional involvement; they cannot see their relationship without this specific embodiment.

This does not only hold true for lovers, but also for family relationships, though it is more complicated. As we have seen before, resleeving a loved one in a body perceived to be "wrong" can cause harm to the social and communal bonds—parents now physically younger then their seven-year old daughter will have to face social dissonance. The same is true for resleeving those that died, as the already mentioned scene with Ortega's family on *Dia de Los Muertos* (*AC* 4, "Force of Evil") shows. When Abuela returns to the family dinner in the body of a tattooed, male gang member, everyone reacts in shock ("that sleeve you gave her, my god!") and has trouble accepting the loving grandmother. Her physical presence as a large man is not to be ignored, especially since she pushes the issue in conversation ("Maybe we should only get one body. But then you have to enjoy it, huh? Not feel trapped every minute of your life"; "This is a miracle, right here") and through action ("I'm peeing standing up!"). Recognition of the loved one in a different sleeve, especially if they are present as a totally opposite body image, takes working against an innate sense of an embodied human existence. A communal and social dissonance has to be actively overcome.

In the show, this idea is transported in many instances: Kovacs being mistaken for Ryker by criminals bent on revenge, the Bancroft children sleeving their parent's clones and assuming their roles, Kovacs not recognizing Reileen in Ortega's body. When Kovacs needs a hacker and gets Ava Elliot out of prison, she is cross-sleeved into a man (Cliff Chamberlain) and her husband Vernon (Ato Essandhoh) at first reacts with irritation and disgust: "Whoa, whoa! Back off, buddy! What are you, drunk?" (*AC* 8, "Clash by Night"). It takes a while for them to adjust and in the end, Ava resleeves in her original body for the family to be reunited. The only one not needing adjustment is their daughter Lizzie, who (in virtual) recognizes her mother immediately: "Sometimes, belief isn't about what we can see. It's about what we can't" (*AC* 8, "Clash by Night"). For the already strained cognitive ability of Lizzie's broken psyche, stuck in virtual and rescued from the brink of insanity, there is no guarantee that any data received by the senses is real anyway. Seeing her parent is a matter of belief, relation is confirmed by communal consensus.

In fact, the show points out the unreliability of physical recognition when Kovacs and Ortega discover an illegally cloned Bancroft at his son's house: "How do I know you are who you are? Before stacks, yeah. A face is a face. But now, could be anyone in there" (AC 5, "The Wrong Man"). That community and social consensus determine identity when physical recognition is impossible is even more present in the novel, where the ritual of "Ascertainment" takes the place of recognizing your loved ones: it is described as "a deeply respected underlying aspect of social relations. Outside of expensive hi-tech psychographic procedures, it's the only way we have to prove to our friends and family that, regardless of what flesh we may be wearing, we are who we say we are. Ascertainment is the core social function that defines ongoing identity in the modern age" (Morgan, 2002, pp. 335–36). The TV show only hints at these social/communal functions of identity construction, but overtly reveals the consequences of dissolving the connection of subjectivity and embodiment.

Conclusion: The Politics of the Posthuman

In its depiction of posthumanity, *Altered Carbon* can be understood as "an attempt to intervene in and diversify what posthumanism can mean" (Morgan, 2002, p. xiii) or as an intervention into posthuman discourse, as Thomas Foster has posited for cyberpunk as a cultural formation (Foster, 2005, p. xiii). The show's premise of stack-technology promises the transhumanist fantasy of the cybernetic posthuman that Hayles has warned against and which sees the complete embrace of capitalist, neoliberal notions of human ownership and mastery of the body, as much as humanist notions of essential human nature based in the primacy of the mind over the body: "Liberal humanism severs the subject from his or her embeddedness in material circumstances, just as mind/body dualism severs the mind from its relation to the body. The politics of each suggest that the individual has a constant essence or identity regardless of circumstances, and that there is something universal about this essence of being human" (Vint, 2007, p. 90). This view on the posthuman brings with it a culture that "advocates both individual freedom and individual responsibility, and the absence of government constraints and controls" (p. 90).

Technically then, as with any form of the disembodied posthuman, markers of "embodied difference" (p. 88), such as race, gender, or disability, should be eliminated and discrimination ended. But, as Vint remarks for a similar scenario in Ian M. Banks Culture-novels, "the concrete specificity of living in differently raced or gendered or sexed bodies is effectively erased" (p. 88) from the experiences portrayed in this kind of fiction. The "mind/body dualism has historically allowed some subjects—male, white, heterosexual—

to construct themselves as unmarked by the body" (p. 89), thus foregrounding the mind as essential to their subjectivity. In terms of those subjects that do not have efficient means of moving between bodies, they are thus anchored in their limited embodied existence, meaning they will "not [be] able to attain true subject status, since subjectivity has been equated with the mind alone" (p. 89). *Altered Carbon* propagates a view of Meth subjectivity as the "natural" state of human existence, and confirms this by portraying foremost Laurens Bancroft (white, male, able-bodied, wealthy) as the ideal of the stack-technology influenced world. Embodied human existence to the Meths are "fireflies, each a tiny spark whose beauty lies in how quickly it's extinguished" (*AC* 8, "Clash by Night").

This view, though, to adapt Vint's argument, detaches the Meths from those fireflies, "those body-subjects who do not matter in the current ideological configuration.... This type of posthumanism so distances the subject from his embodied life that he feels that the 'long run' perspective of millions of years of evolution is the appropriate model upon which to base his relationship to other subjects in the contemporary world" (2007, p. 180). It ignores the social constructions and institutions that ground the human in embodied and material existence.

In the end, the Meths' actions catch up to them and the show sides with Kovacs and Ortega, who foreground a specific embodied existence and realize "that [they] must continue to live in a material world of other subjects and ethical responsibilities" (p. 183). The show concludes with a policy passing that allows victims of murder to be spun up and provide a testimony on their own murder—giving voice and subjectivity to those unheard. Lastly, Kovacs returns Ryker's sleeve: "He deserves his life back. Everything he lost" (*AC* 10, "The Killers"). In restoring Ryker to his community, his relationship with Ortega, as much as his position as a cop, Kovacs acknowledges the subjectivity of the other, and his own fluid posthuman existence. In this, the show gestures toward the potential of the posthuman technology, to right the wrongs of systemic discrimination and restore a view of the human as part of a network of social relations; a view of an embodied, material, and connected subjectivity.

Notes

1. It is no coincidence that Carnage looks synthetic. He is portrayed by Matt Frewer, the original actor to star in the cyberpunk TV show *Max Headroom* (1987–88). In *Max Headroom*, Frewer plays a double role, that of Edison Carter, a journalist, and of that Max Headroom, a virtual being created by scanning Carter's mind. Digital imaging in the 1980s was not very sophisticated and Max's appearance in the TV show is rather synthetic—similar to that of Carnage in *Altered Carbon*. What is ironic, though, is that within the diegesis of *Max Headroom*, Max and Carter are supposed to look "the same" (see Rogers for more on the show), whereas in *Altered Carbon*, Carnage's "uncanny valley" appearance is commented upon and joked about.

2. Technically sex workers can be of any gender and sexual orientation, though the show almost exclusively focuses on females with a heterosexual orientation. As Julie Muncy has pointed out in her review for Wired.com, the show pushes aside any "provocative questions" of the stack-technology, including those regarding homosexual, non-binary, or transgender issues.
3. Unfortunately, the gender politics of the show are questionable at best and would need further extensive commentary, which this chapter cannot provide. Suffice it to point out that the show "falls victim to the same critiques about conservatism and masculinist heteronormative tendencies" (Heise–von der Lippe 8) that plagued original cyberpunk fiction (for more on gender in cyberpunk see the articles/chapters by Cadora, Nixon, Gillis and Melzer).

References

Bould, M. (2005). Cyberpunk. In *A Companion to Science Fiction*. Seed, D. (Ed.) Hoboken, NJ: Wiley, pp. 217–31.
Caccamo, J. (2018). The Catholic Tradition and Posthumanism: A Matter of How to Be Human. In *Posthumanism: The Future of Homo Sapiens*. Bess, M., & Walsh Pasulka, D (Eds.). London: Macmillan Reference.
Cadora, K. (1995). Feminist Cyberpunk. *Science Fiction Studies*, vol. 22, no. 3, pp. 357–72.
Foster, T. (2005). *The Souls of Cyberfolk: Posthumanism as Vernacular Theorty*. Minneapolis: U of Minnesota. p. 200.
Gillis, S. (2007). The (Post)Feminist Politics of Cyberpunk. *Gothic Studies* vol. 9 no. 2, pp. 7–19.
Hamdan, S.I. (2011). Human Subjectivity and Technology in Richard Morgan's *Altered Carbon*. In *3L: Language, Linguistics, Literature. The Southeast Asian Journal of English Language Studies*, vol. 17, pp. 121–32.
Hayles, N.K. (1999). *How We Became Posthuman: Virtual Bodies in Cybernetics, Literatre, and Informatics*. Chicago: U of Chicago P.
Heise–von der Lippe, A. (2020). Gothicism. In: *The Routledge Companion to Cyberpunk Culture*, McFarlane A., Murphy, G.J., & Schmeink, L. (Eds.). New York: Routledge, 2020. pp. 264–72.
Lenic, J.G. (Producer) & Kalogridis, L. (Creator). Altered Carbon. (2018–). [Series]. United States: Netflix.
Maloney, D. (2018, September 2). Invasion of the Body Snatchers: Transhumanism is Dominating Sci-Fi TV. *Wired*. Retrieved from wired.com/.
Melzer, P. (2020). Cyborg Feminism. In: *The Routledge Companion to Cyberpunk Culture*. McFarlane A., Murphy, G.J., & Schmeink, L. (Eds.). New York: Routledge, 2020. pp. 291–99.
Moravec, H. (1990). *Mind Children: The Future of Robot and Human Intelligence*. Cambridge: Harvard UP.
Morgan, R.K. (2002). *Altered Carbon*. London: Gollancz.
Muncy, J. (2018, February 2) Altered Carbon May Not be the Cyberpunk Show You're Looking For. *Wired*. Retrieved from wired.com/.
Muri, A (2003). Of Shit and the Soul: Tropes of Cybernetic Disembodiment in Contemporary Culture. *Body & Society*, vol. 9, no. 73, pp. 73–92.
Nixon, N. (1992). Cyberpunk: Preparing the Ground for Revolution or Keeping the Boys Satisfied." *Science Fiction Studies*, vol.19, no. 2, pp. 219–35.
Rogers, S. *Max Headroom: Twenty Minutes into the Future*. In: *The Routledge Companion to Cyberpunk Culture*. McFarlane A., Murphy, G.J., & Schmeink, L. (Eds.). New York: Routledge, 2020. pp. 178–83.
Vint, S. (2007). *Bodies of Tomorrow: Technology, Subjectivity, Science Fiction*. Toronto: U of Toronto P.

Wearing Wellness on Your Sleeve

On Meths, Self-Control and Capitalism

Łukasz Muniowski

Introduction

In the world of *Altered Carbon* bodies and stacks are kept separately. Whereas stacks are simply placed in storage, bodies remain in flotation gel. While this may serve as a prime example of the mind-body dualism, most notably described by René Descartes, there is another cause for such division. The reason for their parting is very simple and based solely on wealth, as those better off can purchase, or rather upgrade, sleeves that are more to their liking, whereas the poor are somewhat stuck with what the government has to offer.

In one of the first scenes in the series, a middle-aged couple waits in Download Central for their daughter, who was killed in a car accident. Thanks to what is referred to as "victim restitution," the seven-year-old girl has the right to a free sleeve. The parents do not recognize her because she has been put into a body of a middle-aged woman, looking a bit older than the parents. Confusion seems to be a common occurrence in Download Central, where it is the person placed in the new sleeve that is somewhat obliged to recognize her relatives. The biggest issue that she can encounter is that they might be in different sleeves as well.

This is partially dependent on how long a given person/stack has spent in storage, but more so on the material status of the family. The "good," appropriate sleeve, which in this particular case refers to the one looking like a seven-year-old girl, is reserved for the rich or, as they are called in the series, Meths. Their name comes from the biblical character of Methuselah, who supposedly lived for 960 years. Because of their resources, the Meths are able to avoid aging, despite being, like Laurens Bancroft, even 360 years old.

Uncertainty, which is the central topic of a collection of essays devoted to health and wellness edited by Donald C. Wood (2008, p. 2), is never a factor in the oversimplified world of *Altered Carbon*. At least not for Meths, who are able to sustain islands filled with clones of themselves, while keeping them secret from their spouses—a truly ridiculous representation of ridiculous wealth. Wood attributes uncertainty to everyday situations, over which we have no influence, yet in this world it seems that money can influence reality to the point that it simply prevents unwanted events from happening.

I mention wellness not without merit, as the idea of sleeves coming in all shapes and sizes is the extension of the present-day wellness culture, which forces individuals to be the best versions of themselves. According to a definition by Charles B. Corbin, William R. Corbin, Gregory J. Welk and Karen A. Welk:

> Wellness has been recognized as the positive component of optimal health. It is characterized by a sense of well-being reflected in optimal functioning, health-related quality of life, meaningful work, and a contribution to society. Wellness allows the expansion of one's potential to live and work effectively and to make a significant contribution to society [2008, p. 4].

So wellness goes well beyond egotism, as caring for oneself is supposed to serve others, even though it is not specified how that is supposed to work in practice. Wellness is also more than an idea or a mind-state. Ari-Veikko Anttroiko characterizes it as "a genuinely heterogeneous group of interrelated industries that, as a development concept, comprises diverse forms of activities, from wellness products to services, events, micro environments, full-service destinations and urban design" (2018, p. 153). To put things short, wellness is *everything*, and because of its pervasive presence, its influence over our daily lives cannot be disputed.

Today, in order to upgrade our "sleeves," we need to go to the gym five days a week and follow a restrictive diet, whereas the Meths just go to PsychaSec and buy the sleeves they "deserve," as one of the holograms encountered by Kovacs advertises. Initially they move their cortical stacks to different sleeves, and after they get the look they ultimately want, they make clones of themselves in order to avoid personality frags. These occur when one often resleeves to different bodies. This implies that the lower classes fall victim to glitches precisely because of their inability to afford clones. The division between the rich and the poor is therefore very physical and visible. As observed by Barbara Ehreinreich in *Natural Causes*: "the gap between rich and poor ... has widened to such an extent that a single word, 'health,' no longer suffices to describe what was once a universally desirable biological status" (2018, p. 109).

Whereas one might describe this urge to obtain the newest version of a sleeve as a direct influence of materialism, in this essay I will show how it is actually the consequence of wellness culture. In the world of *Altered Carbon* one no longer buys gym memberships or meal plans. Instead, all the hard work put into obtaining the perfect body is replaced by hard work at the office or any other location one is employed at.

The society of *Altered Carbon* has reached a capitalist ideal, as the body, the biggest obstacle in keeping one productive 24/7, has become an actual goal for the employee. The best way to look how one wants is by going to work and earning as much as possible. However, since, as observed by Henri Lefebvre, "all self-realization … appears to be, and becomes, total alienation" (1958, p. 100), the results of this over-reliance on good looks are as futile as those experienced by today's fitness addicts.

You Deserve This Sleeve

Jonathan Crary writes that "an illuminated 24/7 world without shadows is the final capitalist mirage of post-history" (2013, p. 9). Whereas actual events have proven Francis Fukuyama's famous assumption wrong, *Altered Carbon*'s reality can be characterized as the actual "end of history" (Fukuyama, 1992, p. 288). The fact that the most powerful citizens are able to accumulate wealth and power over the span of centuries is a testament to capitalism's durability. According to Fukuyama "Universal History," a term by which he understands a pattern of development of human societies, culminates with capitalist liberal democracy (1992, p. 289).

Crary states that nowadays "most of the seemingly irreducible necessities of human life—hunger, thirst, sexual desire, and recently the need for friendship—have been remade into commodified or financialized forms" (2013, p. 10). This is exactly what Laurens Bancroft alludes to, when he says that "in this world the only choice is between being the purchaser and the purchased" (*AC* 5, "The Wrong Man"). Meths are clearly the purchasers, as they can afford anything they please. This obviously includes healthy-looking, beautiful and handsome sleeves. Meths can obtain their desired look without putting any physical effort into taking care of their bodies, which makes wellness a case of class rather than strong-will or genetics. Ehrenreich writes that "wellness is mainly the domain of the rich, described in the fitness industry as a 'luxury pursuit'" (2018, p. 109), but the luxurious, slim and muscular body becomes a commodity in its purest form only when it can actually be paid for.

In *The Wellness Syndrome* (2015) Carl Cedeström and Andre Spicer show how the fit employee has also become the productive employee. It is not so much that an athletic worker is somewhat better at his position, but his discipline signifies a supreme work ethic and enormous devotion to the tasks he is assigned. Many companies present their employees with the possibilities of self-improvement by creating training facilities, providing the workers with information about health, etc., but the main thing wrong with the transformation they promise is that it will never be complete (Cedeström & Spicer, 2015, p. 39). After all, reaching, but more so sustaining wellness is a daily struggle.

The pursuit of healthy-looking bodies is omnipresent in *Altered Carbon*, where everybody is in need of new, upgraded sleeves. The futility of this pursuit is best presented at Bancroft's party, where a married couple are about to face each other in a duel to the death. Sleeve-death of course, as their stacks, barring some unfortunate event, will remain untouched. The winner gets an upgraded sleeve, whereas the loser is downgraded. The absurdity of the situation is observed by Kovacs and Ortega, but the couple are so focused on one of them reaching a higher class, that the observations of the detectives fall on deaf ears. It is evident that if one spouse gets one class higher while the other falls a class lower, the result is always zero. Still, in a society which pressurizes its citizens to aspire to great things, losers are inevitable. Even if they are members of one's closest family.

The lower classes are clearly not forgotten though, as they also serve a purpose in the societal system. Criminals like Kovacs are kept in storage for ages. The main hero of the story has been there for 250 years which is not that bad, considering how some of the poor are stuck there for much longer. They are there until their relatives can find a "free" sleeve, or it is just their turn to come back to life. In *Altered Carbon*, the novel on which the series is based, Kovacs gives the example of Murakami, "one guy in the Corps," who was supposed to pick up his great-grandfather from Download Central. The man has been put away over a century back, before Murakami was even born (Morgan, 2002, p. 16). Why is the consciousness of such citizens kept alive for so long, if they are about to enter a reality that is decades or centuries removed from the one they knew? After all, they do not stand a chance in adapting to new conditions.

Meths need the poor to reinforce the norm. They can remain rich if the poor remain poor, maintaining the *status quo*. In order for things to stay the same, the poor need to continue to work for those above their class and aspire to unattainable things. Once they are put into an unknown world, they are more likely to fail at reaching a higher status. Note that this does not apply to Kovacs, who is an Envoy—their main talent was instantly absorbing and understanding the present situation. So despite 250 years "on ice," Kovacs quickly becomes aware of the workings of the system, whereas the poor who come back to life do not possess such skills. It must also be stressed that the workings themselves have not changed as much as one would expect in the span of 250 years—capitalism and wellness are still the main ingredients of the social order.

Ehrenreich characterizes the lower classes as "willfully unhealthy," a new stereotype which "quickly fused with their old stereotype as semiliterate louts" (2018, p. 98). According to those better off, the poor remain at the bottom because they want to. Seeing them in person is like taking a trip to the amusement park during which one can exhibit one's power, or playing a video game and dominating NPCs (non-playable characters) on easy mode. Case in point, Bancroft's visit to the camp of those infected by a contagion bomb (*AC 5*, "The Wrong Man"). He goes there to spend time with the sick and allow his sleeve (not himself) to become infected as well. He brings various gifts and touches people who are not supposed to be touched by anyone. When Bancroft's sleeve dies, as the virus is devouring his body, the inhabitants of the camp are moved to tears.

Kovacs rightfully points out that this is all a spectacle, because if the Meth actually cared about the infected, he would just buy them new sleeves. To this Bancroft replies that he gives them something to believe in. That something is Bancroft himself, the "City Father," as they refer to him. The whole routine—because this is not the first nor the last time the Meth does this—is reminiscent of the Native American ceremony of potlatch. The participants were urged to either give away or destroy their goods in order to exhibit their power. The more goods one destroyed, the more powerful one seemed.

These people are hopeless, their disease is incurable, so they are stuck forever—they mate and have children which are also infected since birth—at this place, controlled by government forces. If they perceive something as simple as human touch as a luxury, Bancroft's (in)action is actually reinforcing their oppression. By observing their reactions to him, a man from the outside who allows them the "privilege" of touch, Bancroft sustains the idea that they are at the bottom of the social ladder, whereas he himself keeps up the illusion that he is a god among men.

Just a Bunch of Rich Assholes Who Don't Look Their Age

That Meths consider themselves gods is also a consequence of wellness culture, and its extraordinary focus on the self. Health is nowadays considered a choice, as "every death can now be understood as suicide" (Ehreinreich,

2018, p. 96). When one abstains from taking care of one's body, one is embarking on a path to slow death. According to Jenepher P. Shilingford and Anne Shilingford Mackin "the concept of wellness espouses self-responsibility for a healthy lifestyle" (1991, pp. 457–458). *Self*-responsibility is crucial here, since one is alienated, left to oneself, almost put in opposition to some mysterious outside forces. In his attempts to conceptualize wellness Anttiroiko also points out that wellness is a concept based around personal choice and individual responsibility for well-being (2018, p. 8).

Carol-Ann Farkas makes a similar observation in her analysis of self-help magazines' coverage of wellness, when she writes that "the very nature of the self-help magazine ensures a focus on the self over the group: one's problems are one's own, and often brought out by one's own deficiency; the only solution is to recognize—constantly, every month—one's flaws, confess them, and perform elaborate rites of penance through vigilantly dieting, exercising, and shopping" (2010, p. 127). Even though the author sees here potential for cooperation, since according to her the focus on self can be redirected to the group, there is no such lesson learned in the thousands years which separate our present and the future of *Altered Carbon*.

"I" takes center stage whenever the matter of personal experience arises. Because of their esteemed position, Meths feel that society owes them something. Robert C. Solomon writes that "all too often we approach death with the self-indulgent thought that my death is a bad thing because it deprives the universe of me" (*Spirituality of the Skeptic*, 2006, p. 120). Since Meths are able to continue living for hundreds of years, maybe even forever, they will never come to that realisation. Because the Meths have conquered death, they consider themselves to be gods, and present themselves as such. Bancroft is not the creator of Bay City, yet the people in the camp call him "City Father" because for them he personifies god-like qualities. He is the one that touches them when others do not dare, implying he is more powerful than everyone else. He dies and comes back to life only to die again, all in front of their eyes.

The Meths are allowed to shape and mold reality as they please, just as they do with their sleeves. The sleeve turns into a body once a stack is inserted into it. It is only then that the body can either become a place of conflict or a unified whole. The results of the former are glitches, most often resulting from too much resleeving. However, "if the body ... somehow 'wants' to act as a unified whole, then it should be easy enough to bring it under our conscious control. All we have to do is use the mind to encourage this natural urge toward wholeness, and inevitably ... wellness will follow" (Ehrenreich, 2018, p. 112).

In a world where wealth determines if one lives or dies, branding of the self is crucial. Everything has been commodified, hence the self must constantly reaffirm his or her status as a brand. Cedeström and Spicer stress how important sales and product development are when job seeking: "sales in the sense that you need to come up with new ways to market, brand and sell yourself. Product development in the sense that you need to find new ways to refine, enhance and change yourself" (2015, p. 94). The Bancrofts know that all too well; that is why they need to mean so many things to so many people. Some see them as gods, others consider them assholes, but there is no denying the influence that they have on everybody around them.

That influence is gained precisely by their ability to modify themselves. Consider Miriam's sleeve, which produces Merge Nine or Empathin, a powerful chemical enhancing the sexual pleasure of both partners. As Miriam reacts to what her partner is feeling, he in turn reacts to her pleasure. This creates a physical (and sensual) co-dependence during the sexual act.

The purely sexual nature of the modifications of her sleeve is a direct representation of the patriarchal society of the future. Whereas the holograms of male sleeves from PsychaSec urge Kovacs to buy them because he deserves them, the female ones tell him: "put your wife in me." (*AC* 2, "Fallen Angel"). The husband buys the sleeve for his wife, however he does not really purchase it *for* her, but for himself. It becomes clear that wellness means different things to men and women. Whereas for men a new sleeve is a symbol of status and power, for women it only means that they will bring more pleasure to their husbands/partners.

Still, female Meths are in a better position than the grounders, who have little to no control over their lives. The rich can transgress, but their crimes must be contained and concealed so that the public will not learn about them. Bancroft's affinity for violent intercourse with prostitutes, which often ends in their sleeve-death, is nothing more than a departure from norm. Murdering these girls' sleeves allows him to act accordingly in other situations, while rewarding them with upgrades for participation in said acts silences his consciousness. Clearly referring to other, less horrific deviations, Ehrenreich writes that "the wealthiest can be out-of-control from time to time, but after these brim organized moments of chaos, they must return to control and self-mastery" (2018, p. xiii).

The moments of chaos are organized, even planned, as Bancroft strikes a deal with his lovers that he will not harm their stacks and buy them better sleeves if they allow him to murder them. The fact that no one goes to the police or the local press to report him is a sign of his enormous power. If the public would find out that Bancroft does not control his urges, that his mind does not work as well as his sleeves do, he would not be as highly regarded as he is now.

Bancroft is genuinely surprised that he committed suicide. He thinks he could not have done it not because he had no reason to take his own life. His death has more to do with the fact that gods simply cannot die. Their existence is uninterrupted, their power limitless. Even his closest family is under Bancroft's control. His children are way older than they look, but he keeps them in younger-looking sleeves in order for them to be frozen in a state of permanent adolescence. They resort to mishaps, like borrowing their mother's sleeves for sex or heavy drinking, because they are not able to rebel in any other way.

The Bancrofts have the best sleeves money can buy, they actually look rich. They are reminiscent of today's fitness enthusiasts, who sculpture their bodies in gyms all over the world. However, the Bancrofts are a dysfunctional family, who hide their vices from regular citizens not only behind the clouds, in the Aerium where they live, but more so behind perfect-looking sleeves. The same can be said of wellness fanatics, whose minds and bodies are also not always in sync.

Conclusion

Shilingford and Mackin write that "the wellness movement is here to stay because it (1) meets the needs of the individual, (2) recognizes that the locus of control for a healthy life-style is within each individual, and (3) provides some systems whereby an individual may gain control of his or her life" (1991, p. 458). The attractive, healthy-looking body is primarily a statement of control and the same can be said of a new sleeve. Both are paragons of narcissism, permeating today's capitalist culture.

"It is easier to imagine the end of the world than it is to imagine the end of capitalism" is a famous phrase, which Mark Fisher attributes to both Frederic Jameson and Slavoj Zizek (2009, p. 2). Series (and books) like *Altered Carbon* reinforce the myth that this economic system can go on forever, which would somewhat stand in agreement with the thesis that we live in a time of post-history put forth by Francis Fukuyama. It seems that as long as capitalism will prevail, wellness will be its vital element, as both form a symbiotic relationship. One reinforces the other, creating a viscous circle of working to remain healthy in order to remain working. Adam Smith, father of capitalism and the free market, established self-love and justice as the two poles of his moral psychology (Solomon, "Beyond Selfishness," 1993, p. 455). And what is more just than having the body one really loves? After all, "you deserve this sleeve."

REFERENCES

Anttiroiko, A.-V. (2018). *Wellness City*. London: Palgrave Macmillan.
Cedestrom, C., & Spicer, A. (2015). *The Wellness Syndrome*. Cambridge: Polity Press.
Corbin, C.B., Corbin, W.R., Welk, G.J., & Welk, K.A. (2008). *Concepts of Physical Fitness: Active Lifestyle for Wellness*. Boston: McGraw-Hill, 2008.

Crary, J. (2013). *24/7: Late Capitalism and the Ends of Sleep.* London: Verso.
Descartes, R. (1641; 2010). *Meditations on First Philosophy.* Ocean Shores: Watchmaker Publishing.
Ehrenreich, B. (2018). *Natural Causes. Life, Death and the Illusion of Control.* London: Granta Publications.
Farkas, C.-A. Tons of Useful Stuff': Defining Wellness in Popular Magazines. *Studies in Popular Culture.* Vol. 33, No. 1 (Fall 2010), 113–132.
Fisher, M. (2009). *Capitalist Realism: Is There No Alternative?* London: Zero Books.
Fukuyama, F. (1992; 2006) *The End of History and the Last Man.* 1992. New York: Free Press.
Lefebvre, H. (1958; 2014) *Critique of Everyday Life. The One-Volume Edition.* London: Verso.
Lenic, J.G. (Producer) & Kalogridis, L. (Creator). *Altered Carbon.* (2018–). [Series]. United States: Netflix.
Morgan, R.K. (2002). *Altered Carbon.* London: Gollancz.
Shillingford, J.P., & Mackin Shillingford, A. Enhancing Self-Esteem Through Wellness Programs. *The Elementary School Journal* Vol. 91, No. 5. Special Issue: Sports and Physical Education (May, 1991), pp. 457–466.
Solomon, R.C. "Beyond Selfishness: Adam Smith and the Limits of the Market." *Business Ethics Quarterly.* Vol. 3, No. 4 (Oct., 1993), pp. 453–460.
_____. (2006). *Spirituality of the Skeptic: The Thoughtful Love of Life.* Oxford: Oxford University Press.
Wood, D.C. (Ed.) (2008). *The Economics of Health and Wellness: Anthropological Perspectives.* Series: Research in Economic Anthropology. Volume 26. Boston: Elsevier.

New (Cloned) Bodies for the Old

Biopolitics in Altered Carbon

ALINE FERREIRA

Altered Carbon (Lenic & Kalogridis, 2018–) is centrally about the fantasy of eradicating death, as well as the survival and negotiation of identity in a new body. This fantasy, coupled to that of extending the human life span, has been a long-standing, persistent dream, given recurrent expression in mythological and biblical accounts, in early epic narratives and in art. A considerable number of recent works, both literary[1] and cinematic,[2] engage with the possibility of almost infinite life extension, usually by being reborn in a new body. This lengthy list of visual and fictional narratives dealing with the age-old ambition of quasi-immortality bears witness to a genetic, transhumanist imaginary that is taking the goal of progressively abolishing death more seriously. *Altered Carbon* can be inscribed in this increasingly emphatic thematic cluster that envisages novel ways of prolonging life, offering its own solutions to the inevitability of death, including new (cloned) bodies for the extremely wealthy. The premise of erasing death is not new, of course, neither is the concept of body hopping or body swapping,[3] but the extent to which it is applied in *Altered Carbon*, where it is valid for everybody, is unprecedented.[4]

These fantasies have been updated by envisaging the possibility of avoiding or postponing death by being reincarnated into a new body or, more radically, by always having cloned versions of one's body ready to receive one's memories, kept in a "cortical stack," as is the case in *Altered Carbon*. These cloned versions can only be afforded by the extremely rich, which yet again introduces dystopian capitalist hierarchy and selection into this transhumanist scenario where death has been all but eliminated. While *Altered Carbon* has given articulation to that ancient dream of quasi-immortality, it also points out some considerable drawbacks of the realization of that dream.

Altered Carbon revises radical life extension scenarios by taking them to the next level, that is, by almost completely eliminating not only death but also the fear of death. The series takes place in the year 2384, in a futuristic version of San Francisco named Bay City, whose atmosphere, cityscape and weather are reminiscent of *Blade Runner* and *Blade Runner 2049*, probably due to the effects of global warming. Although babies are still being born, the series predominantly shows alternative birthing scenes consisting mostly of adult bodies either being "resleeved" or emerging from cryonic preservation or a type of suspended animation. We first see Takeshi Kovacs, the main character, floating in an amniotic-like fluid and then emerging from a womb-like tank, covered in slime, a (re)birth called decanting, as in Aldous Huxley's *Brave New World*. This is a scene reminiscent of many other birthing scenes where people come out fully formed as adults from an artificial womb, as in Kenneth Branagh's *Mary Shelley's Frankenstein* (1994), Lily and Lana Wachowski's *The Matrix* (1999) and Dennis Villeneuve's *Blade Runner 2049* (2017). It has been 250 years and Kovacs has been given a new "sleeve." At first, when he looks at himself in the mirror, he sees his last sleeve's face and then his new one gradually takes over in an uncanny fusion, while a mixture of panic and fury mingle and are reflected in his expression. He soon learns that he is now the property of Laurens Bancroft, who has hired him to solve his own murder.

"Guaranteed immortality"

Laurens Bancroft is one of the founding "Meths," the New Methuselahs, with a virtually endless lifespan given the availability of ever new clones. He is over 360 years old and fully intends to reach and surpass the biblical Methuselah who reputedly lived for 969 years. His wife, Miriam Bancroft, who is also over three centuries old,[5] has a secret island with a clone tank and resleeving facilities, apart from those in the Bancroft family vault.

In this society, every citizen has a cortical stack, a small device that contains one's consciousness, coded and stored as DHF: Digital Human Freight, implanted when they are one year old. As a technician explains: "Your consciousness can be downloaded into any stack, in any sleeve. ... A sleeve is replaceable but if your stack is destroyed you die. There's no coming back from real death" (*AC* 1, "Out of the Past"). In his introduction to the novel *Altered Carbon*, on which the series is based, Richard Morgan explains he wanted to explore the notion of "digitised human consciousness" (Morgan,

2002, p. vi).⁶ The altered carbon technologies in this future world mean that death was rendered "if not wholly obsolete, then certainly negotiable" (p. vii), while people with greater wealth have at their disposal better bodies to be resleeved into. In the novel and also in the series, Laurens Bancroft's cortical stacks are stored remotely and updated every forty-eight hours at the PsychaSec installation at Alcatraz, while his clones are kept on ice in the same facility, which means that he has virtually "guaranteed immortality" (p. 37).

Cloned Bodies

What if you could have a clone that was built from your own cells and then rapidly grown and kept in a type of suspended animation, ready to serve as your new body and receive your cortical stack? This is what PsychaSec, a powerful biotech corporation, promises to do for those clients with enough money, providing designer-enhanced sleeves to an elite clientele. Their primary business, however, is the creation of clones, costing more than an average person would earn in their lifetime. The major retrieval and resleeving insurance companies, like PsychaSec, have clone banks of their very wealthy customers, where they can download the cortical stacks into the waiting sleeves. When Kovacs visits the Bancroft family vault where their clones are kept, a huge space, the size of a "temple" (p. 80), lit by a "womb light" (p. 81), he is in awe, as the novel states:

> The clone sacs were everywhere, veined translucent pods ... suspended from the ceiling by cables and nutrient tubes. The clones were vaguely discernible within, foetal bundles of arms and legs, but fully grown. Or at least, most were; towards the top of the dome I could see smaller sacs where new additions to the stock were being cultured. The sacs were organic, a toughened analogue of womb lining, and they would grow with the foetus within to become like the metre and a half lozenges in the lower half of the vault [p. 80].

The clones are grown in organic versions of an external, artificial womb. There are also sophisticated metallic cylinders that function as "full life support suspension chambers" (p. 82) with basically the same "environment as the pods ... where all the resleeving is done" (p. 81). The process is described as follows: "We bring fresh clones through, still in the pod, and load them here. The tank nutrients have an enzyme to break down the pod wall, so the transition is completely trauma-free" (p. 82). In addition, PsychaSec has been instructed by Mr Bancroft to always "hold a spare clone of himself and his immediate family ready for decanting" (p. 82).⁷ Reileen Kawahara, another Meth, also keeps her clones in similar vaults, in womb-like sacs.⁸

(Un)Ethical New Bodies for Old

Can all these cloned bodies, built purposefully to become hosts for the cortical stacks and neural nets of other people, ever be regarded as ethical? In the recent film *Replicas* (Jeffrey Nachmanoff, 2018) the process is still in an experimental phase and in *Altered Carbon*, although not illegal, only those who can afford the very expensive procedure, as well as the upkeep of the clones in a closely guarded and regulated environment, have access to it. This question, however, may be at the forefront of the bioethical discussion that will precede the possibility of neural uploading and transfer, since transplanting a brain to a cloned body, with chemicals accelerating its growth, seems medically more feasible in the not too distant future than the former method. Opinions will differ, but shopping for new bodies to move into when one no longer feels comfortable in one's original body, a vision dramatized in Hanif Kureishi's *The Body* (2002), or indeed having a cloned body-in-waiting like the elite in *Altered Carbon*, may become a reality sooner than we think. The protagonist of Kureishi's novella chooses a new, young body to become the receptacle of his brain by going to a shop where he can select and buy his favourite body, a scenario that might become common practice in the not too distant future. The Newbodies, as they are called in Kureishi's novella, will constitute "a new class, an elite, a superclass of superbodies" (Kureishi, 2002, p. 97), like the Meths in *Altered Carbon*. As is explained by a character in the series, the clones, kept in cryopreservation, "are not aware. Their brains are blanked, stacks are empty. The bodies are electrically stimulated periodically so they don't lose muscle tone" (*AC* 2, "Fallen Angel"). If no harm is done to these insentient bodies, which will only be revivified with the transference of neural information from the deceased or the living person wishing to abandon their body, then it can be argued that they did not suffer from not being fully alive before.

The world of *Altered Carbon* can be broadly described as having moved to a version of posthumanism or transhumanism. As *Altered Carbon* makes abundantly clear, however, class structures still mean that it is the very wealthy who get all the privileges and the best bodies. If you are not wealthy you get "what is available in the inventory" and cannot choose a sleeve either for yourself or members of your family. As detective Kristin Ortega explains, "prisons lease out the good sleeves for profit" (*AC* 1, "Out of the Past"). Class and socioeconomic forces are still very much at play in this future society.

Although the almost complete eradication of death brings numerous benefits to countless people and erases the perennial death anxiety present in human societies, it also introduces numerous further complexities to the social fabric, as well as huge class divisions between the Meths and the non–Meths, the Catholics and the Neo-Catholics. Indeed, religion still shapes the decisions of many citizens, with Catholics in particular resisting or refusing the elimination of death by resleeving, especially when there is often no choice regarding the body.[9] After all, the world in *Altered Carbon* is only giving visual and speculative expression to widespread religious views such as the Christian faith in an afterlife where the dead will be resurrected and reunited, or the Hindu and Buddhist belief in reincarnation. In this respect the refusal of many Catholics to be resleeved, choosing "real death," contrasts with John G. Messerly's confident assertion that "technologically guaranteed immortality will end most people's opposition ... when immortality is real, most will choose it rather than dying and hoping for a heavenly reward" (2013, p. 278).

In this future society Catholics often get killed because their murderers know their victims will not be able to testify against them since they do not believe in resleeving. However, if a new law were to be passed, Proposition 653, then being considered in the UN Courts, which would allow victims of violent crime to be brought back to life in order to give evidence against those who murdered them, even if they have Neo-C (Neo-Catholic) coding, many would be brought to justice and their victims vindicated. This is precisely what Reileen, the owner of Head in the Clouds, an elite sex club, fears most, since some very unorthodox practices perpetrated by a few of her clients, such as killing sex workers, might become known under the new law. Reileen, who has illegally changed some of her workers' codes to Neo-C, is particularly worried about the death of a young woman with Neo-C coding who was murdered by Bancroft under the influence of a drug; if Proposition 653 became legal, she would be resurrected and accuse Bancroft, who does not know he was the perpetrator, since those crucial hours were erased from his stack, of her own murder.[10] Reileen needs her brother to solve Bancroft's murder so that he can remember what he did and use his influence to stop Proposition 653 from going ahead. This is the mystery that drives the plot.

"Your body is not who you are"

Altered Carbon also centrally engages with the question of identity, intimately associated with the cortical stack, enshrined as the recipient and container of an individual's consciousness. Indeed, only the destruction of the cortical stack would result in "real" death, since otherwise it can always be transferred to another "sleeve." In a world where death is not the end and rebirth in a new sleeve is practically taken for granted, the question of what makes us who we are, as unique individuals, is crucial. Toward the beginning of the first episode we are unequivocally told: "Your body is not who you are. You shed it like a snake sheds its skin. Leave it, forgotten, behind you" (*AC* 1, "Out of the Past").¹¹ In this society, your body is indeed not who you are, since you can change bodies as many times as you die. As Kovacs puts it: "How do I know you are who you are? Before stacks, yeah, a face is a face, but now it could be anyone in there" (*AC* 5, "The Wrong Man"). It is your cortical stack, where your memories are stored, that contains who you are. So are you your brain, where your memories are stored? But your body is an integral part of who you are and of how your brain functions, since a disembodied brain cannot work. In the world of *Altered Carbon* you are your cortical stack, where your memories are stored. Thus the idea is that when your cortical stack is implanted in another body your consciousness will also have been transferred.

This concept can be inscribed in a long line of philosophical discussion of the mind/body dualism question. Seemingly in *Altered Carbon* mind and body are separated, since the cortical stack is moved across different bodies that will house one's mind. This procedure partially reinstates or reinvents Descartes's dualistic separation of mind and body, questioned by many philosophers and neuroscientists, such as António Damásio, who argues that emotions are a necessary part of rational thought and that the former are inextricably bound up with the body (Damásio, 1994).

Will whole brain emulation ever be possible? It is very unlikely. Asked whether it will ever be feasible to upload our minds into other bodies, Anders Sandberg (2018), a Research Fellow at the Future of Humanity Institute at Oxford University, is very skeptical:

> Scanning a living brain is likely much harder than scanning a neatly frozen brain since everything is moving about, there is an active immune system that tries to interfere, and the scanning method better not interfere with function. I think it is physically possible but likely much harder. We need not just great nanotechnology but also a fine understanding of how to interface brains to electronics on a truly vast scale: it is going to take much longer than getting the first uploads to work from frozen scans [2018].

Clone duplicates, on the other hand, will probably be created, even some that can grow extremely fast, given the use of growth hormones and other stimulants. Kovacs himself is double-sleeved at a particular point in the narrative, where a fully-grown clone of himself, with a copy of his stack, is developed as we watch, with recourse to Bancroft's son Isaac's illegal portable 3-D bio-organic printer, which he keeps hidden at home, as well as a 3-D printed sleeve of his own father, to pass as his progenitor when convenient.

Transhumanist Zoltan Istvan (2018) believes that it will be possible to bring back people from the dead with recourse to 3-D printing technologies. After all, entire organs are already being printed, so why not whole bodies? The field of quantum archaeology is progressing apace and technological resurrection seems possible in the not too distant future. But Istvan goes even further, suggesting that with quantum archaeology the humanitarian aim of overcoming death could be extended so that it might be feasible to bring back those who have died, especially those whose death was premature. As Istvan points out, however, some people might not want to be resurrected and have to cope with a very different world than they were used to,[12] not to mention overpopulation and the sustainability of social security.

Altered Carbon also effectively disrupts entrenched ideas about gender by having poorer people resleeve into new bodies that may be of a different sex, as when Ortega's grandmother is resleeved into the body of a young man covered in tattoos or when Lizzie's mother reappears as a man. This enforced gender fluidity will presumably have had some impact on sexual politics and may have changed stereotypical perceptions about gender roles by making people more accepting of the characteristics of the other sex, since they may be resleeved into a differently sexed body, but the general narrative drift belies these assumptions. Holograms of near naked women in seductive poses are scattered around the cityscape, strongly reminiscent of *Blade Runner* and *Blade Runner 2049*. Head in the Clouds, an upscale brothel, even though it is run by a very powerful woman, Reileen, caters to an elite, mostly male, clientele. At PsychaSec, the biotech corporation that provides sleeves for the rich and powerful, the advertisements are mostly directed to men. While a naked woman behind glass seductively advertises her body as the "Best sleeve money can buy. Put your wife in me" (*AC* 2, "Fallen Angel"), there is no young male enticingly and persuasively suggesting to (potentially a woman) to place her husband in that sleeve! Another sleeve, a young man, advertises sleeves saying: "You deserve to feel on the outside the way you feel on the inside. You deserve this sleeve" (*AC* 2, "Fallen Angel"). Male and female stereotypes thus continue to operate in this society.

The Meaning of Life and Death

How does the almost radical abolition of death impact human existence? Is a life that is no longer finite still considered meaningful? *Altered Carbon* crucially revolves around these questions. Even though the traditional philosophical view has been that the inevitability of death precludes rational speculation on "what if" scenarios, advances in medicine and longer lifespans, as well as transhumanist visions of ways of postponing or even reverting physical death, such as cryonics, have meant that pondering the very possibility of avoiding death has been receiving increased attention. Indeed, Michael Cholbi argues that we are now living through a renaissance of philosophical inquiry into death (2015, p. viii), a second "golden age" in probing the meaning of death after some Greek and Roman philosophers like Plato,

Epicurus and Lucretius. Until relatively recently, very few studies in philosophy had been devoted to the topic of immortality or the prolongation of life, a theme, in Gerald Joseph Gruman's words, "relegated to a limbo reserved for impractical projects or eccentric whims not quite worthy of serious scientific or philosophical consideration" (2003, p. 2). In addition, the predominant view in these commentaries has tended to be critical of the prospect of life extension.

According to John G. Messerly, the issue of life's meaning is the "*most important philosophical question*, and possibly the most important question of any kind" (2013, p. 6) (emphasis in the original). Sigmund Freud famously states that "the aim of all life is death" (1991, p. 311), while Martin Heidegger similarly maintains that since life is finite and we are "Being-towards-death" (1962, p. 243), it is essential to be prepared for death as the fact that leads to authentic, meaningful existence. Deprived of this sense of the unavoidable finitude of life, the citizens in *Altered Carbon* develop a different attitude toward interactions with others, apparently more selfish and egocentric, since there is always more life and time to redeem past mistakes.

For Bernard Williams in related vein to Freud, "immortality, or a state without death, would be meaningless ... in a sense, death gives the meaning to life" (1973, p. 82). He goes on to clarify that given the facts of human desire and happiness, "it follows both that immortality would be, where conceivable at all, intolerable, and that [other things being equal] death is reasonably regarded as an evil" (1973, p. 82); an "eternal life would be unliveable" (1973, p. 100), since the individual would be assailed by the tedium of immortality. Mark Rowlands, in turn, argues that we are "essentially *beings-towards-a-future*. But death is the ultimate horizon against which the things in our life that make us what we are stand out. We are *beings-towards-a-future*, but we are also, even more fundamentally, *beings-towards-death*," since death is "what gives our life meaning" (2004, p. 258).

I take issue with this view for I do not think many of us would be at a loss to supply meaning for our lives if we had much longer lifespans, provided we could stay reasonably healthy. New projects would keep presenting themselves, demanding our attention and offering physical and mental stimulation. Grace Jantzen, for instance, addresses the fear of perpetual and unassuageable boredom that some critics believe would make the prospect of eternal existence unbearably tedious, suggesting that since "one enterprise leads to another, and provided endless progress were possible, we might pursue an endless series of challenging and absorbing tasks, each one developing into another, without any risk of boredom" (1994, p. 267). In related vein, Adam Buben (2015) defends the proposition that greatly extended life spans can be a source of fulfilment. In Messerly's summary, "we may become bored with eternal consciousness, but as long as we can end our lives if we want, as long as we can opt out of immortality, who wouldn't want the option to live forever?" (2013, p. 241).

Indeed, most commentators argue that death can be regarded as a harm to the person who passes away. For Nick Bostrom death is evil and all efforts should be made to extend the "human *healthspan*" (2005, p. 277) (emphasis in the original) as long as possible. Jack Li finds the Epicurean argument that death cannot harm someone who has passed away to be defective and concedes that death can be a harm to the person who dies (2010, p. 131). Messerly, in turn, summarizes this issue by stating that "almost everyone does think that death is an unmitigated disaster, and the Epicurean argument is of limited value" (2013, p. 238).

John K. Davis extends this inquiry by asking whether prolonging life can harm others, arguing that life extension is "*on balance*, a good thing and that we should fund life extension aggressively" (2018, p. 4) (emphasis in original)[13] if there is equal access to it and measures are taken to prevent a Malthusian crisis. What Davis finds more worrisome in the whole inquiry into the ethics of life extension is not whether it is desirable or not, but the question of unequal access to the technologies necessary to achieve it, which could divide society into "castes of mortals and near-immortals, making inequality worse, allowing dictators to live forever" (2018, p. 3) and other, related concerns. Questions of distributive justice are also crucial in *Altered Carbon*, where only the wealthiest have access to the best sleeves, which are often their own, cloned bodies. There seem to be drawbacks to practically every model of immortality depicted in fantasy and fiction, which suggests that the utopian dream and desire for immortality might indeed turn out for many to be a dystopian nightmare.

"The Darkest Angels of Our Nature"

In *Altered Carbon* Quellcrist Falconer (formerly known as Nadia Makita), a leader of the Envoys and the inventor of the cortical stack, also reflects at great length on the consequences, practical and philosophical, of her discovery. She considers that the creation of stacks was a miracle but also the beginning of the destruction of the human species. She believes humanity will become a new class of people, so wealthy and powerful "they answer to no one and cannot die" (*AC* 7, "Nora Inu"). As she remarks during her conversation with Kovacs, in his former body: "Now the monsters among us will own everything, consume everything, control everything. They will make themselves gods and us slaves" (*AC* 7, "Nora Inu"). Significantly for Quell, to die is to be human. She considers that humans are not created to live forever, since that possibility would corrupt even those with the highest moral standards. As she observes: "If we do not stop the curse of eternal life in our realm our children will inherit despair. The ebb and flow of life is what makes all equal in the end" (*AC* 7, "Nora Inu"). Quell has written a program, called Acheron, which allows every person to live 100 years, making death no longer optional. She defends that the Uprising must end immortality, since "eternal life for those who can afford it means eternal control over those who can't."

Quell's connections to the Bible and Abraham Lincoln are also revealing. She tells Kovacs that death was the "ultimate safeguard against the darkest angels of our nature" (*AC* 7, "Nora Inu"), a phrase she partially borrowed from Lincoln in his inaugural speech, where he refers to the "better angels of our nature,"[14] stating that "We are not enemies, but friends. We must not be enemies. Though passion may have strained, it must not break our bonds of affection. The mystic chords of memory will swell when again touched, as surely they will be, by the better angels of our nature" (1991), an exhortation to life in harmony and egalitarianism, unlike the selfish, narcissistic society in *Altered Carbon*.

The reference to the biblical Enoch is also meaningful. It appears in Episode 7, where Kovacs is seen writing a poem in Quell's diary, above which is visible the following passage from *Genesis* 5:23: "And all the days of Enoch were three hundred sixty and five years." Not only did Enoch, Methuselah's father according to the Old Testament, live for three hundred and sixty-five years, but he never died, according to some interpretations of *Genesis*, for he was taken by God and entered Heaven alive: Enoch "walked with God: and he was no more; for God took him" (*Genesis* 5: 21–24).[15] Quell can be described as the "mother" of the New Methuselahs in *Altered Carbon*, a situation she now regrets and wishes to change with the Acheron program.[16]

Quell's vision is a lot closer to Hayles's (1999), Braidotti's (2006) or Vint's (2007) beliefs in the importance of an embodied, ethical existence, rather than an indefinitely long or virtual life. For Braidotti "thinking through the body, and not in flight from it, means confronting boundaries and limitations and living with and through pain" (2006, p. 216). Jeff Noonan, in related vein, argues that the limits to our existence and to the realization of all desires, which he calls "frames of finitude" (2018, p. xii), are actually fundamental to the "good it is possible to realize in life" (p. xii), a view Quell would certainly endorse. It is against this vision that the transhumanists defend the concept of a potentially immortal posthuman being, like the Meths in *Altered Carbon*.

Conclusion

Altered Carbon is centrally about death and identity. It taps into the widespread human desire to avoid dying, given added impetus by biotechnological breakthroughs. It also crucially addresses questions of distributive justice and access to the resleeving and cloning technology, which allows only the Meths to pay for an almost endless life in an identical, younger body. For the others, the sleeve they are assigned after death basically depends on what is available, without consideration to matching sex or age. This is far from a utopian posthuman, transhumanist scenario of an egalitarian, highly advanced society, but one with appalling inequalities. *Altered Carbon* is then a cautionary tale about fair access to medical technologies and the desirability of almost indefinite life extension, as well as whether building cloned bodies to have at one's disposal could ever be legal and ethical.

For philosopher and transhumanist John G. Messerly, death should be optional (2014), a state of affairs basically achieved in *Altered Carbon*, even though society is profoundly asymmetrical. Messerly argues that eliminating death is "perhaps the fundamental imperative for our species" (2013, p. 241). The huge social impact of such a massive paradigm change is hard to envisage. The way it was implemented leaves a lot to be desired in the future world of *Altered Carbon*, which can serve as a forewarning to ensure that future medical advances will be introduced and implemented gradually and justly.

Altered Carbon also implicitly addresses the philosophical idea of freedom. I would argue that there can be no complete freedom without immortality, freedom from death, or at least the prospect of a very long life span. There exists a fundamental contradiction in the belief in human freedom, or at least a measure of human freedom, and the unavoidable limit which is imposed on human life, that is, death. In that sense, human beings can never be totally free because their lives are always already curtailed by death. Freedom is the will to live, and it is also the freedom to choose to die, but there is no freedom to carry on living if you wish to postpone death beyond what medical science can now achieve, and it is precisely that *unfreedom* that goes against the traditional philosophical concept of freedom and removes the possibility of a wholly fulfilled life, a point also made by Messerly who states that "death eradicates the possibility of complete meaning for individuals," while also maintaining, as I have argued, that "only if we can choose whether to live or die are we really free" (2013, p. 241).

As suggested at the beginning, *Altered Carbon* can be placed alongside a substantial list of recent films, television series and fiction that address the perennial fantasy of a longer life, achieved with recourse to medical advances, whose sizeable number is strongly indicative of the increased attention and visibility of this ambition, fueled by a genetic, medical imaginary. The cloned bodies in *Altered Carbon*, peacefully waiting to be awakened from their cryogenic, suspended animation are quickly becoming cultural, bioethical icons, with their heightened promise of continuity and infinitely longer, healthier lifespans. After all, provided all bioethical advice and care is followed through, why not? These fantasies are only anticipating and engaging with the multiple facets and ramifications of a future where death no longer rules and *Altered Carbon* constitutes an integral part of in this thought-provoking conversation.

NOTES

1. An early example of a novel in which the brain of a person can be duplicated and stored as a backup in a "restoration bank," so that that person can then be restored when they die is *Altered Ego* (1954) by Jerry Sohl, a novelist and scriptwriter for *The Twilight Zone, The Outer Limits, Star Trek* and other shows. In the event of death, their biological body is healed and rejuvenated, with their mind and memories restored to the last moment when they had a backup. The hope is that eventually technological advances will enable a person's "brain record" or duplicate to be installed in a different body. Another version of this scenario is also present in Arthur C. Clarke's *The City and the Stars* (1956), where memories are transferred to new bodies.

Recent versions of this scientific imaginary where dead bodies are brought back to life or their consciousness is transferred into cloned bodies include Lois McMaster Bujold's *Mirror Dance* (1994) where the brains of the very wealthy are transferred to cloned bodies which allow them to start again, as in *Altered Carbon*. Iain M. Banks's Culture series, in turn, provides an interesting counterpart to the world in *Altered Carbon* since it portrays a society in the far future of very long-lived people, where death is an option. In Banks's *Feersum Endjinn* (1995), for instance, the minds of the citizens are uploaded into a computer network, a procedure that enables them to be reincarnated. They appear to lead fulfilled lives in an egalitarian, post-scarcity society, described by Banks (1994) as space socialism, unlike in *Altered Carbon*, which seems to be predicated on rampant capitalism exacerbated by environmental decay and ecocide, probably due to global warming. Indeed the ethical and moral questions surrounding who has access to the better bodies ("sleeves") permeate *Altered Carbon*.

Jenna Black's *Replica* (2013) is another representative instance of this trope. In Black's novel, in a future dystopian society, a very sophisticated AI program has developed the skills to replicate people, so that a Replica can be created in a few hours when the original dies. The AI, called Thea, is now working on creating backups of a person's brain separate from the body, a feat which has been eluding it. However, if Thea manages to develop that technology, then "she can create the Replica of a human mind in any body she wants" (2013, 329). Jessica Chiarella's *And Again: A Novel* (2016) dramatizes the trials and tribulations of waking up in a new cloned body and memory transfer after life-threatening diseases, being granted a second chance at life.

2. This fantasy has also been abundantly addressed in filmic representations, such as Roger Spottiswood's *The 6th Day* (2000), where consciousness can be downloaded through the optic nerves and transferred to cloned bodies. In Damir Lukacevic's *Transfer* (Germany, 2010), an elderly couple arranges to have their minds transferred into the young bodies of two African-Americans paid to go through this metamorphosis. The latter, however, can regain their own consciousness for a few hours every night. An interesting comparison could be established here with an episode of *The Twilight Zone* "The Trade-Ins" (Season 3, Episode 31, 1962), where an elderly couple is also offered the possibility of trading their bodies for younger models.

Questions of identity, romantic love, distributive justice and human rights are at the core of the movie *Get Out* (Jordan Peele; 2017), which can be watched as a companion film to Lukacevic's *Transfer*. Jennifer Phang's *Advantageous* (2015) is another instance of the trope of having a person's consciousness transferred to a new, cloned body. In this case, however, the technology is still at the experimental stage and the transfer does not work out as planned. In John Frankenheimer's *Seconds* (U.S., 1966) a man is given a new body and a new chance of life. Tarsem Singh's *Self/less* (2015) provides a related instantiation of this topic, where a wealthy man near death is given the chance to have his consciousness transferred to another, genetically engineered body, through a medical procedure named "shredding," with unpredictable consequences. In *Transferts* (TV series, France, 2017–), in turn, a man who was in a coma for five years has his mind transferred to the body of another man, thanks to new technology that, despite being illegal, is used by wealthy and influential people to prolong their lives or their loved ones.' Ironically, however, his new body belonged to an officer of the BATI, the unit that fought against transfers. Significantly, in both *Transferts* and *Altered Carbon* there are effusive demonstrations against bringing back the dead. In the latter, demonstrators outside the Bay Area prison hold banners stating "Spirits not Sleeves," "No resleeving," telling the resleeved people "Shouldn't have come back!," shouting "Justice! Let the dead speak!," and calling for Resolution 653 to be passed. Analogously, in Jeffrey Nachmanoff's *Replicas* (U.S., 2018), a neuroscientist who has been working on neural transfer to an android, devastated by the loss of his family in a car accident, decides to try and bring them back with recourse to copies of their neural maps and new cloned bodies, grown in seventeen days, that would replace their dead ones.

3. A whole body transplant, or transferring the contents of the brain to a different body, are other variants on this persistent dream of a longer life and/or immortality.

4. While Robert Louis Stevenson's *The Strange Case of Dr. Jekyll and Mr. Hyde* (1886) portrays Mr. Hyde as a younger, more energetic and alive version of Dr. Jekyll, albeit uncannily repulsive, H.G. Wells's "The Story of the Late Mr Elvesham" (1896) and Kureishi's *The Body* (2002) more specifically describe the fantasy of moving into a younger body, articulating a desire for a reversal of time, of rejuvenation.

5. In the novel she is in her eleventh body (p. 49).

6. See Huberman's (2018) discussion of digital immortality with recourse to mind cloning.

7. The term decanting is also used in Aldous Huxley's *Brave New World* to refer to the process of "birth," where the clone babies are extracted from their "bottles."

8. In the novel they are described as having bullet-proof, impact resistant lining (286).

9. As for the Catholics in *Altered Carbon*, Dickson (2018) ponders to what extent "Can, or should, Christians endorse pursuing the sorts of technologies that are proposed by transhumanists" (99); in his view, "from a traditional Christian perspective, the *value* of a human life does not depend on its length" (100).

10. In this particular context *Altered Carbon* can be aptly compared with another American TV series, *Westworld*, where the guests in a kind of theme park can do what they please, including killing the hosts, since they are androids whose memories are erased every day so that they can start anew the following day.

11. The symbol of the Ouroboros that appears during the credits, a snake biting its tongue, may suggest that the end is a new beginning.

12. Some of these issues are addressed in the recent Australian TV series *Glitch* (2015–), where a group of people inexplicably rise from their tombs, seemingly healthy, even though some have been dead for decades or even centuries.

13. Zoltan Istvan, who ran for president of the U.S. in 2016, also believes that as much money as possible should be channeled to extend life and find cures for diseases.

14. This quote also prompts a reference to Pinker (2011), which does not seem to apply to the future society in *Altered Carbon*, depicted as very violent.

15. Like Enoch, the prophet Elijah is also described as not having died but having ascended to Heaven alive in his chariot of fire.

16. In ancient Greek mythology Acheron was a river in Hades, across which the dead would be ferried to enter the Underworld. It is fitting then that the program with the same name created by Quell is associated with death, since its purpose is to limit the human life span to 100 years.

REFERENCES

Ayres, T., & Fox, L. (Creators). *Glitch* (2015–). [Series]. Australia: Netflix, ABC.
Banks, I.M. (1994). A Few Notes on the Culture. Retrieved from https://web.archive.org/web/20120322183158/http://www.futurehi.net/phlebas/text/cultnote.html.
_____. 1995. *Feersum Endjinn*. London: Orbit.

Black, J. (2013). *Replica*. New York: Tor Teen.
Bostrom, N. (2005). The Fable of the Dragon-Tyrant. *Journal of Medical Ethics*, 31, no. 5: 273–277.
Braidotti, R. (2006). *Transpositions: On Nomadic Ethics*. Cambridge: Polity Press.
Branagh, K. (Director) (1994). *Mary Shelley's Frankenstein* [Motion picture]. United States: TriStar Pictures.
Buben, A. (2015). Resources for Overcoming the Boredom of Immortality in Fischer and Kierkegaard. In *Immortality and the Philosophy of Death*. Cholbi, M. (Ed.) Lanham, MD: Rowman and Littlefield, pp. 205–219
Chiarella, J. (2016). *And Again: A Novel*. New York: Touchstone.
Cholbi, M. (Ed.). (2015). *Immortality and the Philosophy of Death*. Lanham, MD: Rowman and Littlefield.
Clarke, A.C. (1956, 2001). *The City and the Stars*. Southlake, TX: Gateway.
Damásio, A. (1994). *Descartes' Error: Emotion, Reason, and the Human Brain*. New York: G.P. Putnam's Sons.
Davis, J.K. (2018). *New Methuselahs: The Ethics of Life Extension*. Cambridge, MA: MIT Press.
Dickson, M. (2018). The *Imago Dei* and the *Imago Mundi*. In *Christian Perspectives on Transhumanism and the Church*, Donaldson, S. and Cole-Turner, R. (Eds.). Cham (Switzerland): Palgrave Macmillan, pp. 97–115.
Frankenheimer, J. (Director) (1966) *Seconds* [Motion picture]. United States: Paramount Pictures.
Freud. S. (1920, 1991). Beyond the Pleasure Principle. *On Metapsychology: The Theory of Psychoanalysis*, Strachey, J. (Trans.) Harmondsworth: Penguin.
Gruman, G.J. (2003). *A History of Ideas about the Prolongation of Life*. New York: Springer.
Hayles, N.K. (1999). *How We Became Posthuman: Virtual Bodies in Cybernetics, Literature, and Informatics*. Chicago: University of Chicago Press.
Heidegger, M. (1962). *Being and Time*. Macquarrie, J., & Robinson, E. (Trans.) New York: HarperCollins.
Huberman, J. (2018). Immortality transformed: Mind cloning, transhumanism and the quest for digital immortality. *Mortality* 23, no. 1: 50–64.
Huxley, A. (1932, 1998). *Brave New World*. New York: Perennial Classics.
Istvan, Z. (2018). Quantum Archaeology: The Quest to 3d-Bioprint Every Dead Person Back to Life. *Newsweek*. Retrieved from https://www.newsweek.com/.
Jantzen, G. (1994). Do We Need Immortality? In *Language, Metaphysics, and Death*. Donnelly, J. (Ed.). New York: Fordham University Press, pp. 265–277
Kureishi, H. (2002). *The Body and Seven Stories*. London: Faber & Faber.
Lenic, J.G. (Producer) & Kalogridis, L. (Creator). *Altered Carbon*. (2018–). [Series]. United States: Netflix.
Li, J. (2010). *Can Death Be a Harm to the Person Who Dies?* London: Springer.
Lincoln, A. (1991). *Great Speeches*. Appelbaum, S. (Ed.). NY: Dover Publications.
Lukacevic, D. (Director). (2010). *Transfer* [Motion picture]. Germany: Schiwago Film.
Messerly, J.G. (2013). *The Meaning of Life: Religious, Philosophical, Transhumanist, and Scientific Perspectives*. Darwin & Hume.
_____. (2014). Death Should Be Optional. *Salon*. Retrieved from https://www.salon.com/.
Morgan, R.K. (2002). *Altered Carbon*. London: Gollancz.
Nachmanoff, J. (Director). (2018). *Replicas* [Motion picture]. United States: Company Films.
Nolan, J., & Joy, L. (Creators and Producers). *Westworld*. (2016–). [Series]. United States: HBO.
Noonan, J. (2018). *Embodiment and the Meaning of Life*. Montreal, Quebec: McGill–Queen's University Press.
Peele, J. (Director). (2017). *Get Out* [Motion picture]. United States: Blumhouse Productions.
Phang, J. (Director). (2017). *Advantageous* [Motion picture]. United States:Good Neighbors Media.
Pinker, S. (2011). *The Better Angels of Our Nature: Why Violence Has Declined*. New York: Viking Books.

Sandberg, A. (2018). "Will We Ever Be Able to Upload a Mind to a New Body?" *Gizmodo*. Retrieved from https://gizmodo.com/.
Scasso, C., & Benedek, P. (Creators) & Khamlichi, N. (Producer). *Transferts* (2017-). [TV Series]. France: Arte France.
Scott, R. (Director) (1982). *Blade Runner* [Motion picture]. United States: Warner Bros.
Serling, R. (Creator). *The Twilight Zone* (1958-1964) [Series]. United States: CBS Productions.
Singh, T. (Director). (2015). *Self/less* [Motion picture]. United States: Endgame Entertainment.
Sohl, J. (1954). *The Alter Ego*. London: Pennant Books.
Spottiswood, R. (Director) (2000). *The 6th Day* [Motion picture]. United States: Phoenix Pictures.
Stevenson, R.L. (1886, 2003). *The Strange Case of Dr Jekyll and Mr Hyde*. Harmondsworth: Penguin Classics.
Villeneuve, D. (Director). (2017). *Blade Runner 2049* [Motion picture]. United States: Warner Bros.
Vint, S. (2007). *Bodies of Tomorrow: Technology, Subjectivity, Science Fiction*. Toronto: University of Toronto Press.
Wachowski, L & L. (Directors) (1999). *The Matrix* [Motion picture]. United States: Warner Bros.
Wells, H.G. (1998). "The Story of Mr Elvesham." In *Thirty Strange Stories*. New York: Carroll & Graf, pp. 67-87.
Williams, B. (1973). The Makropulos Case: Reflections on the Tedium of Immortality. In *Problems of the Self*. Cambridge: Cambridge University Press, pp. 82-100.

"Meths" versus "Quellists"
Altered Carbon *as the Battleground of Two Ideologies*

Damla Pehlivan

The realm of *Altered Carbon* presents us with a future which has been granted to the human race by modern science's stunningly new and advanced innovations, yet, it still seems not so remotely different from today's imagination, if not today's reality. *Altered Carbon* may be a few hundred years further in our new millennium, however, we, too, see the total reign of technology along with the idea of "information" and a vital change in our perception of the world in our age. The "information" flooding us at the speed of light from our "smart" and "digital" innovations is enabling us to have a more intangible existence and a unique sense of limitlessness; life seems liquefied and running into every direction trough our technologically advanced gadgets. Our identities are multiple and our technology's characteristic instantaneity is abolishing distances and divisions, in return constructing artificial connections. Also, because these gadgets are so deeply ingrained in our everyday life, the significance of terms like cyborg, transhuman, and even posthuman is increasing with every technological development.

In *Altered Carbon* the innovations are even smarter and through them humans are really embodying the above-mentioned terms. Firstly, equipped with "cortical stacks" they are all cyborgs. These stacks also turn them into transhumans who have conquered death with the use of "Digital Human Freight" technology. And with enough money, neither stacks nor sleeves can confine a human being to a singular and limited existence any longer. The new millennium has truly changed our perception, and for *Altered Carbon*, it has "altered" even the definition of a human being. Whether the significance of this change, however, is understood as a successful step toward the perfection of the human race or the continuation of the "contemporary process of self-dehumanizing," is open to debate (Kroeber, 1988, p. 23). *Altered Carbon* constructs an environment proper for this discussion to take place via presenting the representatives of both sides of the argument, and through a multilayered narration, places them in a metaphorical battleground. Opposed to each other at every front, Meths' and Quellists' ideologies fight for their perception of humanness to prevail. Yet, at the core of both ideologies lingers the question which is relevant today as well: if we are modifying the qualifications for "humanness" via technology, what does this change in definition indicate? Or in *Altered Carbon*'s words, "Are we even God's creatures any longer?" and if we are not, whose creatures are we? (*AC* 4, "Force of Evil"). This inquiry will be the main subject of this essay.

Firstly, this question, although posed in a new way, is not actually new in its essence. A complete transcendence from human constraints and the world as we know it recalls an old debate from our first millennium. Another group of people called Gnostics, after their perception of the world had changed, arrived at a conclusion for the same question which is still relevant and important today. Accordingly, this world had nothing to offer but agony and the only way to improve existence was opening a new way out through *gnosis* (knowledge). Similarly, our "information society," in Dorien Zandbergen's words, can be understood "as both a society that is obsessed with speed and acceleration, as well as one that celebrates gnostic, timeless, universal interconnections between all that exists" (2012, p. 45). However, how exactly this ancient system is relevant to our world and to *Altered Carbon*'s debate remains a question that needs answering.

The Altered Carbon: Gnostic Brush Strokes on the Modern Canvas

The need for transcendence is an ingrained drive for human beings which we have carried with us throughout our history. "We are meaning-seeking creatures," explains Karen Armstrong (2005, p. 2), and "one of the essential yearnings of humanity is the desire to get 'above' the human state" (p. 27). Those *new* definitions of humanness, our modern science and modern technology, our obsession with information and digitality recall this archaic need for transcendence which we feel fading away from our world more intensely in the harsh light of millennial information. "The age of adventurers is over" and our cosmos does not have many secrets into which we can attribute meaning anymore (*AC* 1, "Out of the Past"). Neither we nor anything we used to believe seems to have the power for eliminating the universal, and timeless limits of our existence alone. To recall Max Weber's famous phrase, "the disenchantment of the world ... which aimed at producing the climate of rationalization and efficiency in which technology could do its proper salvific work" is what characterizes millennial human beings and their idea of transcendence (Ferkiss, 1980, p. 18). Erik Davis (2004, p. 6) explains this situation as follows: "For well over a century, the dominant images of technology have been industrial ... this myth of an engineered utopia still propels the ideology of technological progress, with its perennial promises of freedom, prosperity, and release from disease and want." Therefore, our efforts of "enchantment" seem to have turned toward its source: "the mark of the modern scientific mind is a disenchanted attitude to the natural realm and an enchanted attitude to the human realm, as epitomized by the belief in 'progress'" (Fuller, 2006, p. 124). Because once we exhaust the possibilities offered by our surrounding universe, we feel the threat of getting confined in a non-transcendental and non-transgressive existence which would put the individual in the position of its sole exceeder.

In its essence, Gnosticism, too, does not offer a system of thought which is primarily concerned with the improvement of the present that is fundamentally destructive, painful and deceptive; it is more about the individual achieving an "unknown" and "new" existence. The meaning which we are looking for, according to Gnostics, has never existed in this non-transgressive world; the true "knowledge" belongs to an all-transcendent God: "The deity is absolutely transmundane, its nature alien to that of the universe, which it neither created nor governs and to which it is the complete antithesis: to the divine realm of light, self-contained and remote, the cosmos is opposed as the realm of darkness" (Jonas, 2001, p. 42). In this perception, *gnosis* is not bounded with acquired information, but with the acknowledgment that such a state actually exists. This proves to the Gnostic that the universe, and everything in it, works like a series of tests to endure on the path to transcendence: "Enclosed in the soul is the spirit, or 'pneuma' (called also the 'spark'), a portion of the divine substance from beyond which has fallen into the world" (Jonas, 2001, p. 44). The "humanness" in this sense is in an ultimate state of dispute: the parts constructing the being are in a whirl which is defined by the alternating pull of "light" and "darkness." Therefore, as the flesh and other physical restrictions become the greatest restrictions on the path to salvation, the soul becomes the ultimate transcendental force. Freedom from all the restrictions with the strength of the unrestrainable inner "spark" is in the foundations of the Gnostic system which through the "knowledge" of an existence unrelated to present experience promises an all-comprehensive transcendence.

These characteristics of the Gnostic system correlate with our ways of "enchanting" our universe because at the core of both perceptions of transcendence there is the idea of exceeding the hostility of existence. "Gnostic myth is precisely concerned with translating the brute factuality experienced in the gnostic vision of existence," explains Hans Jonas, "and directly expressed in those queries and their negative answers, into terms of an explanatory scheme which derives the given state from its origins and at the same time holds out the promise of overcoming it" (2001, 65). And taking its source from this millennial perception, *Altered Carbon* displays a Gnostic-ornamented realm in which a technologic transcendence is combined with Gnostic symbolism. For this realm, the need for transcendence is literally bred-in-the-bone; the cortical stacks can be considered as the Gnostic spark translated into millennial digitality, enabling the humans to acquire new kinds of possibilities. Via the "altered carbon" the stacks release the mind from the flesh the same way that sleeves release the identity from the body. DHF technology and multiple life spans cancel the limitations of time and memory upon the knowledge and experience. And through needle-casting, distances become irrelevant. The figure of "Alien" as a representation of the light has an important place in the Gnostic understanding; as the person feels "alien" within this world because of the part that he or she brought from the ultimate existence in light, the god is "alien" to this cosmos (Jonas, 2001, pp. 49–50). Like the manifestations of this idea, these ground-breaking "alien" technologies are intersecting on a brightly "engineered utopia" which enables acceleration from all the delusions of flesh, time and space, which are the very reasons of our sleepiness and stagnancy in the Gnostic point of view (Jonas, 2001, pp. 68–69). Both in form and appearance, they give out the feeling that they are the perfect combination of machinery and light, which does not only back the idea that science and technology pave the way for a modern transcendence but also this transcendence's construct circles back to the Gnostic thought. Like the "Alien God" figure at the foundation of technological transcendence, the "tree" symbol which tells about the interconnection of life with the light—both as sparks' connection to each other and to the realm of light—is presented by the magnificent Songspire Trees (Jonas, 2001, pp. 93–94).

They also have a strong relation with the female characters, emphasizing their role as the revealers of knowledge in correlation with the Holy Spirit or "Sophia" in Gnosticism (Jonas, 2001, p. 93). Moreover, because the "eternal sleep" is replaced by a constant waking-up until the "real death," the millennial technologic existence seems to be in correlation with the belief that in most of the Gnostic sects, the spark reincarnates and passes through multiple spares of the world, leading toward either salvation in the light or annihilation in the darkness (Jonas, 2001, p. 44). And as it is in Gnosticism, everything earth-related and mundane in the show is opposed to this path of transcendence, as well as placed in correlation with the dark and gloomy atmosphere of the Earth. Society, economy, politics and all other intuitions, legal or illegal, act like the *Archon*s, the malevolent guardians of the spares of the earth, who get strength from the pain they caused, as their only purpose is to keep the spark in captivity (Jonas, 2001, pp. 44–45).

However, for the ancient world the distinction between the earthly and transcendental, was simpler than it is for the modern world. The apocryphal texts' main warning was to distinguish the real, all-comprehensive, alien god from its arrogant earthly impersonators, or the *demiurge* (the creator) "who reigns as king and lord, who acts as a military commander, who gives the law and judges those who violate it..." (Pagels, 1989, p. 36). The technology's transcendental role in the modern world should be approached with the same caution, as expressed by one of the characters, Dimitri the Twin: "Where is the voice that said altered carbon would free us from the cells of our flesh? The visions that said we would be angels. Instead, we became hungry for things that reality could no longer offer. The lines blurred" (*AC* 5, "The Wrong Man"). Although technology is our most powerful weapon in the war with our limitations and the greatest generator of new possibilities, it also adds incomparably new ways to our suffering. Therefore, even the Gnostic innovations seem to be shaping and enhancing *Altered Carbon*'s universe, the question that begs posing is: toward what end?

Meths: Practicing Gnosticism in a "Disenchanted" World

The commitment to technology as a tool for perfecting the human race and possessing the long-lost transcendence is the cornerstone of the Meths' ideology. Correlatively, the ones who are enjoying the technology's enhancing and enchanting power the most seem to be Meths as well. Living in the air, over the clouds, in a place called "*Aerium*" (aerial), they seem removed from anything earthly: "Our quick and messy little lives are so small for them. They build their homes up here so the clutter of our existence is out of their sight" (*AC* 1, "Out of the Past"). These perfect post-humans make use of every opportunity that their world can offer: endless life-spans, numerous clones, the most valuable artifacts, extremities of every kind of experience, but most importantly, influence, dominance and power. They are the ones who really built for themselves an "engineered utopia" and are currently living in the wildest dreams of humanity. It is crucial to take one important question into consideration while looking at this privileged group of people: are Meths the practitioners of Gnostic ideology in the new millennium or a new generation of demiurges of the Earth?

Immortality seems to be the defining force of the Meths' lifestyle; their way of life abounds with endless possibilities resulting from the perfect combination of money, technology and freedom from restrictions. Even the word

"Meth" is connoting immortality, as it has been indicated by Ortega when the term is first introduced in the series. Meth is short for Methuselah who, according to the Bible, lived almost a thousand years (*AC* 1, "Out of the Past"). However, Meths' ideology is not only about living *like* they were immortal but living in a completely transcendental way, enhancing and accelerating every aspect of human life while denying the limitations regarding their experiences and entertainment options. This lifestyle can be seen as an advanced phase of the enchantment of the world through improving the human realm via technology and "[a]s a result," explains Ihab Hasan (1973, p. 560), "matter intervenes less and less in the transactions of mankind. And mind is free to pursue its destiny: to become the antientropic, or syntropic, force in the universe, gathering knowledge, expanding consciousness, regenerating *metaphysically* a *physically* decaying universe." Therefore, it can be said that this kind of opportunity provides a lifestyle perfect for the Gnostic system of thought to be practiced because even though most of the people can and do feel the Gnostic alienation from the universe, only a few are capable of realizing the entrance into the path of *gnosis*. Not everyone can become a Meth because pursuing immortality not only requires a certain amount of money and power, but also complete isolation from mortal perception. Gnosticism as well is considered to be an elitist system which also corresponds with Gnostic sects' tradition of distancing the self from social or institutional bounds and rules, in order to build an identity which is free from any obligations and liberate the self. This could even mean having no morals, friendships or familial bounds in the traditional sense, which is best encapsulated by this sentence from the series, in a way serving as a catch phrase of the Meth ideology: "Laws don't apply to people like us" (*AC* 3, "In a Lonely Place").

However, these features are not ways of manifesting a simple rebellion but a reasonable conclusion: in both Meths' and Gnostics' immortal lifestyle those kinds of interactions with the world are weightless because if the world is disenchanted and deprived of meaning, to abide by any of its rules becomes pointless. Thus, explains M. Roger Lundin (1993, p. 83), "[h]aving grown into their enlightened adulthood men and women have come to recognize that the source of all divinity lies within." Accordingly, any system of thought can offer guidance for transcendence but the ones that are self-constructed cannot be accepted because every other creation within the cosmos becomes inferior to the self as the self becomes superior to the cosmos. Therefore, all the other forces can only serve as disturbances on the path to transcendence.

This view enables us to re-mystify the existence as well as secularize any dogmatic, captivating establishment so it is not surprising that technology has become the medium for this process as it steadily changes, alters and transgresses every limitation. Science, which once deemed the world non-transcendental, is reestablishing the sense of transcendence in a different manner and it is, in its essence, Gnostic:

> For the modern scientistic gnostic, science saves because it puts the human person in a right relationship to the perceived grounds of its being. It is a way to achieve harmony between the self and some ultimate reality, not a supernatural reality that would promise an eternal destiny, but merely what is left as ultimate once such beliefs are discarded—namely the knowing self that transcends material nature [Lessl, 2002, p. 134].

The modern Gnostic science—which demystified the cosmos, disenchanted the world, secularized the establishments of society and culture, and enchanted the human—is reappointing all of these fundamental elements of the life, for them to end in humanity. In other words, "observed from the lens of the sociology of religion, it has all the trappings of secularization-only in this case, science is itself the target rather than the agent of secularization" (Fuller, 2006, p. 123). According to this point of view Meths, whose ideology is constructed upon the modern role of science, argue that the only divine beings in the world are the few humans who have realized their true nature; or in Bancroft's words, who know that "God is dead," and "[w]e have taken his place" (*AC* 3, "In a Lonely Place"). Science has yet to provide the tools allowing for the perfection of human beings; however, if we are becoming gods, does not that mean that we are also losing what makes us human, or, if we are both merely human and our own gods, what does this change signify?

These aspects of Gnosticism were the underlying reason for the main criticism against apocryphal texts. The antipathy toward this system revolved around the idea that believing in this heresy was the greatest infidelity one could commit, because Gnostics believed in a false god while blaspheming all the others. For our modern world, it can be said that the situation is reversed for the Gnostic science and technology; not to believe in the power of science and technology seems to be a bigger sin. However, the criticism reserves its ground for both: "The gnostic program ... retains for itself the name 'philosophy,' and the speculative system in which the gnostic unfolds his will to make himself master of being insists on calling itself 'science'" (Voegelin, 2012, p. 36). Whatever name and value are attributed to this "program," it seems to have annihilative power on either transcendence or humanness.

At this point it seems reasonable to consider another meaning of the word "Meth": in Hebrew "meth" means "death" and this term is especially bound with a myth which tells about the murder of god as truth. According to Voegelin's (2012, p. 42) narration of the myth, two adepts make a man who wears the name of *emeth* (truth) on his forehead. However, as the man comes to life, it erases the first syllable from *emeth*, leaving only *meth* (dead) "to warn the adepts that the truth is God's; the second truth is death," so the golem dies (Voegelin, 2012, p. 43). Deprived from "death," in *Altered Carbon*'s universe the same golem seems to be replaced by the "Patchwork Man" (*AC* 4, "In a Lonely Place"). Indeed, the modern cyborgian post-humans are living like this monster, looking for the elements of life, "to cut up, and to sew into [themselves]" (*AC* 4, "In a Lonely Place"). In other words, Meths act like both gods and monsters, Gnostics and demiurges. Yet, before these monster/gods there stands another ideology that we must consider before establishing the place of Gnosticism in the new millennium.

"Quellism": To Think Like a Gnostic

Embraced by the Envoys, Quellism can be defined as the counter-ideology to Meths but not to Gnosticism: loyal to their millennial roots, Quellists' aims echo the fundamentals of Gnostic thought of the second century. Molded by the idea of the divine as the foundation of the self, Meths' methods indicate that "truth" is bound with the power of the individual as opposed to any outer divinity, while showing that this process has only one possible conclusion. On the contrary, Quellism's teachings are about taking "what is offered," therefore their understanding of "truth" is highly different from the definition enforced by Meths. For them, "the truth is a weapon" because "finding truth is more than a search for data. It's an excavation of self. You have to keep going no matter where it takes you" and at that point, the conclusions can be various (*AC* 5, "The Wrong Man"). The truth, according to this view, is not about discovering a god who can make everything possible; it is more about simultaneously embracing ability and power as well inability and powerlessness. Because the search for truth is an inward journey which reveals that nothing is free from light and dark forces of life, "first thing you'll learn is that nothing is what it seems. Ignore your assumptions. Don't trust anything. What you see, what you hear, what people tell you, what you think you remember" (*AC* 1, "Out of the Past").

Not becoming the master of the whole existence, which is where the Meths' execution of Gnosticism took them, but "mastering the self" is the backbone of this ideology. And like Quellism, the ancient Gnosticism never overlooks the fact that even if elevation of self through "the truth" were possible, it could not be reached by means of ignorance: "God created humanity; [but now human beings] create God. That is the way it is in the world—human beings make gods, and worship their creation. It would be appropriate for the gods to worship human beings!" (from the *Gospel of Philip*, as quoted by Pagels, 1989, p. 122). Thus fighting for mortality is a return to the bases of the Gnostic thought, not as infidelity but as a reinforcement of a system whose primary concern is to question the whole "construct."

As much as ancient, Quellism is also millennially Gnostic, albeit not in a modernized, behavioral manner. Rather it is such in thought as it seeks to question the real source of this promising transcendence. Therefore, the Uprising can be seen as an effort of expressing the main values of Gnosticism: "It tries, not to demonstrate agreement, but to shock by blatantly subverting the meaning of the most firmly established, and preferably also the most revered, elements of tradition" (Jonas, 2001, p. 92). Quellcrist explains the real tenets at stake in the millennial enthusiasm toward transcendence with these words: "The creation of stacks was a miracle and the beginning of the destruction of our species. A hundred years from now, a thousand, I can see what we will become. And it's not human. ... Death was the ultimate safeguard against the darkest angels of our nature. Now the monsters among us will own everything, consume everything, control everything.... The Uprising must end immortality" (*AC* 7, "Nora Inu"). Modern Gnosticism is driven away from its core values: the second century Gnostics were not seeking information about how they could become gods of the kingdom of falsehood, but how to accelerate to a whole other existence through intuition. The combination of Gnosticism with science is valid as long as one believes that this new existence can be achieved through mundane means. From this perspective, however, this combination seems rather ironic because Gnosticism's essence is to acknowledge the existence of the unknowable, not to discover the unknown:

> On the one hand it is closely bound up with revelationary experience, so that *reception* of the truth either through sacred and secret lore or through inner illumination replaces rational argument and theory...; on the other hand, being concerned with the secrets of salvation, "knowledge" is not just theoretical information about certain things but is itself, as a modification of the human condition, charged with performing a function in the bringing about of salvation [Jonas, 2001, pp. 34–35].

Moreover, to eliminate suffering from this world would not be reasonable because this world is based upon suffering. And the biggest suffering, "death," is not something to be avoided; rather, it is treasured by the Gnostic system. Without death, one cannot proceed on one's path toward knowledge if he has not completed the circle of life and suffered throughout it from birth until death: "The recollection of his own alienness, the recognition of his place of exile for what it is," states Jonas (2001, p. 50), "is the first step back; the awakened homesickness is the beginning of the return." The aim of Quellism is to resettle the balance after the complication of the definition of humanness, or in Quellist's own words, "they have forgotten who and what we are. Make them remember" (*AC* 1, "Out of the Past").

And for our modern world, to exclude death, which is an inevitable part of life, regardless of the outcome can only be the continuation of the process of disenchantment, reflected also upon the human realm, confining the self in the drug-like enjoyment of a seemingly superior position within the cosmos, without actually accelerating it. Thus, for Quellism as it is for Gnosticism, "salvation" becomes more literate than it is in any other religious system as this salvation does not bring the perfection of the existence but the perfect existence without any trace of the prior one.

Quellism, empowered by the ancient Gnostic thought, tries to acknowledge and evaluate the colliding forces in every aspect of life. The existence is the sum of every detail, similar to "the branches of a tree" spreading far and wide, as it has been used as both a Gnostic and Quellist symbol (AC 10, "The Killers"). Recognizing their interconnectedness offers a transcendence apart from instability, vagueness, and tentativeness of the world. And "if the gnostic impulse finds expression in our time," explains Lasch (1992, p. 40) "…it is because we too, like so many who lived in the fading glow of the Hellenistic civilization, have lost confidence in the world around us." Like Gnosticism, Quellism, too, defines the millennial universe "without an intrinsic hierarchy of being" which "leaves values ontologically unsupported, and the self is thrown back entirely upon itself in its quest for meaning and value. Meaning is no longer found, but is 'given.' Values are no longer beheld in the vision of objective reality, but are posited as feats of valuation.… Will replaces vision; temporality of the act ousts the eternity of the 'good in itself'" (Jonas, 1952, pp. 431–432).

However, constructing a system of thought on this unearthly transcendence brings us back to the start; this understanding provides a world view in which "the idea of an absolute 'without' limits the world to a closed and bounded system, terrifying in its vastness and inclusiveness to those who are lost in it, yet finite within the total scope of being" (Jonas, 2001, p. 51). And as the show demonstrates, the Uprising cannot settle the issue of transcendence nor can the transcended Meths preserve their privileged grounds throughout the eternity. Both of them act like two sides of the same coin, hence the quest for transcendence falls upon the shoulders of another person.

Takeshi Kovacs: The Dilemma of Inbetweenness

After more than two hundred years, Takeshi Kovacs, our protagonist, wakes up to a multilayered mission pushed upon him, which would condemn him to a continuous doubleness, both literally and metaphorically. His doubleness is primarily a way of representing the loss of trust in the world as experienced in the new millennium and it reveals the self-conflict of the modern human: he is divided between a desperate unearthly transcendence and an ignorantly secular transcending self. As the ancient Gnosticism shows us, an objectivity inclusive of every person and all aspects of life was not possible from the very beginning of our history and modern Gnostic science proves that enchantment is a double-sided and always inconclusive process.

Therefore, Kovacs's dilemma, which is the dilemma of the modern individual, is characterized by a feeling of inbetweenness; it is about being painfully aware of all these conflicting and deceptive forces, intersecting upon and equally affecting the self, yet still not being able to bring peace to his condition: "peace is an illusion. And no matter how tranquil the world seems peace doesn't last long. Peace is a struggle against our very nature.... The moments of peace that we find sometimes, they aren't anything but warfare, thinly disguised. And sometimes, surrender can be as savage as any attack" (*AC* 2, "Fallen Angel"). Nevertheless, the real monster, as well as the only source of transcendence is still no one but us.

Kovacs's quest for transcendence is, therefore, primarily a search for an identity among his various incoherent identities with which he should be at peace. He becomes the property of Laurence Bancroft who grants him the power of the immortals through Meth money. His confrontation with Meth ideology and their methods provides an understanding of modern Gnostic science, and demonstrates that this doubleness can be both a weakness (*AC* 5, "The Wrong Man") and a leverage (*AC* 9, "Rage in Heaven"). Prior to all of these, he has already learned to see the pros and cons of sovereign forces, or to put it in Gnostic terms, to see the monster even in the gods (*AC* 3, "In a Lonely Place"). Quellcrist teaches him how to see and evaluate the construct and master himself. This experience has significant effects on his perception. He is thoroughly an Envoy which is originally a Gnostic term meaning "the Messenger" who has been sent to tell about the real "truth," as well as "the Alien Man" who has been deprived from where he belonged (Jonas, 2001, p. 76). His quest is inevitably bounded with Quellism and Meth ideology, ancient and modern Gnosticism, intuition as well as information, and salvation as well as transcendence. He is both a meditative as well as an ideological battleground, as most modern individuals are. However, it will only be possible to discuss whether he is an earthly God, an infidel traitor, a Gnostic Christ, or just another lost soul, as his quest for self-discovery and tranquility continues.

Conclusion

The journey starting with the question of transcendence in the new millennium leads to many more questions and this is precisely where lies the beauty of science fiction. *Altered Carbon* provides us a platform where our inquiries about our place among the continuous transformation of our world and changes in our perception can be uttered. And Gnosticism, whether it seeks an ancient total acceleration of existence or a modern enchantment and enhancement through the transcendence of humanness, seems to be a suitable and significant way of interpreting the complexity of our world, as well as the difficulty of finding our place in it. However, primarily *Altered Carbon*'s Gnosticism teaches us to ask questions in order to learn about our gods as well as our monsters. From this perspective, neither Gnosticism alone, nor the fight between Meths and Quellists over the differences in their ways of understanding and executing this system is enough to explain *Altered Carbon*'s commentary. It leads us to more and more questions and assures that whatever answer we find would be about ourselves. While it is possible that the disenchantment of the world and our search for attaining meaning within these new circumstances has left no place for objectivity or simplicity for the 21st century as well as for other centuries to come, we can still hope for better things in our lives, as *Altered Carbon* shows us. And seeking answers to our questions will be the drive which prevents us from hitting at a harsh limit where we cannot transgress or transcend. Through our questions, *Altered Carbon* assures us, we will never be trapped in an existence without possibilities.

REFERENCES

Armstrong, K. (2005). *A Short History of Myth*. New York: Canongate.
Baudrillard, J. (2012). *The Ecstasy of Communication*. Los Angeles: Semiotext(e).
_____. (2005). Violence of the Virtual and Integral Reality. Lambert-Drache, M. (Trans.). *International Journal of Baudrillard Studies* 2, no. 2.
Bloom, H. (2013). *The American Religion*. New York: Chu Hartley Publishers, 2013.
Davis, E. (2004). *Techgnosis: Myth, Magic and Mysticism in the Age of Information*. London: Serpents Tail.
Ferkiss, V. (1980). Technology and Culture: Gnosticism, Naturalism and Incarnational Integration. *CrossCurrents* 30, no. 1: 13–26.
Fuller, S. (2006). *The Philosophy of Science and Technology Studies*. New York: Routledge.
Grant, E. (2011). *The Foundations of Modern Science in the Middle Ages: Their Religious, Institutional, and Intellectual Contexts*. Cambridge: Cambridge University Press.
Haraway, D. (2001). A Cyborg Manifesto: Science, Technology and Socialist-Feminism in the Late Twentieth Century. In *The Cybercultures Reader*. Bell, D. &. Kennedy, B.M. (Eds.). London: Routledge, pp. 291–324.
Hassan, I. (1973). The New Gnosticism: Speculations on an Aspect of the Postmodern Mind. *Boundary 2* 1, no. 3: 547–570.
Jonas, H. (1952). Gnosticism and Modern Nihilism. *Social Research* 19, no. 4: 430–52.
_____. (2001). *The Gnostic Religion: The Message of the Alien God & The Beginnings of Christianity*. 3rd ed. Boston: Beacon Press.
Keyser, P.T. (1990). Alchemy in the Ancient World: From Science to Magic. *Illinois Classical Studies* 15, no. 2: 353–378.
Kroeber, K. (1988). *Romantic Fantasy and Science Fiction*. London: Yale University Press.
Lasch, C. (1992). Gnosticism, Ancient and Modern: The Religion of the Future? *Salmagundi*, no. 96: 27–42.
Lenic, J.G. (Producer) & Kalogridis, L. (Creator). *Altered Carbon*. (2018–). [Series]. United States: Netflix.

Lessl, T.M. (2002). Gnostic Scientism and the Prohibition of Questions. *Rhetoric & Public Affairs* 5, no. 1: 133–157.
Lundin, R. (1993). *The Culture of Interpretation: Christian Faith and the Postmodern World.* Michigan: William B. Eerdmans Publishing Company,.
McAvan, E. (2012). *The Postmodern Sacred: Popular Culture Spirituality in the Science Fiction, Fantasy and Urban Fantasy Genres.* Jefferson, NC: McFarland.
Mosco, V. (2005). *The Digital Sublime: Myth, Power, and Cyberspace.* Cambridge: MIT Press.
Pagels, E. (1989). *The Gnostic Gospels.* New York: Vintage Books.
Post, S.G. (Ed.) (2004). *Encyclopedia of Bioethics.* 3rd ed. New York: Macmillan Reference USA.
Sheppard, H.J. 1957. Gnosticism and Alchemy. *Ambix* 6, no. 2: 86–101.
Voegelin, E. (2012). *Science, Politics and Gnosticism: Two Essays.* Washington, D.C.: Regnery Publishing.
Zandbergen, D. (2012). Acceleration and Gnostic Timelessness in Silicon Valley: How Gnostic Spirituality Has Come to Matter in the "Information Age." *Etnofoor* 24, no. 1: 29–54.

Look Who's Talking
Haunted Bodies and Uncanny Voices
in Altered Carbon

Dariusz Brzostek

Introduction: The Body of the Other

One of the basic elements of the futuristic universe in which the plot of Richard Morgan's novel and its adaptation, the *Altered Carbon* Netflix series (2002; 2018), takes place is the technological phenomenon of "transferring" the characters' personalities into cloned, artificial, rented, or even stolen bodies. These obviously do not need to be identical to their own biological "source material." This technological innovation evokes a range of problems of political, religious, ethical and criminal nature. Attempting to solve, or at least point out and recognize, some of them falls on the protagonist, entangled in an investigation of an (un)successful murder of a financial mogul who, in theory, cannot be murdered. Religious reservations (Catholic objections toward copying and transferring the soul-personality), political manipulations regarding this very issue (a UN resolution) and moral doubts (guilt and responsibility in the face of one's own-another's body) compose the background for dramatic events, among which the protagonist meets, interrogates, as well as is forced to torture and kill—humans, human personalities in artificial bodies, the dead transferred from data banks into new bodies, and finally, artificial intelligences, be they embodied or not.

The premise, as described above, opens up a number of problematic fields, offering numerous interpretative possibilities, focused on the ideas expressed by the text or on its selected aspects. Without attempting to explain the entirety of the text—its semantic structure and the meanings it generates—I would like to focus on only one issue, directly connected with the notion of identity inscribed in (one's own or another's) body and the voice which becomes a carrier of this identity in situations of social communication, which not infrequently determine the relations between partners in a dialogue (and in life): husband and wife, mother and daughter, etc. Indeed, as Slavoj Žižek has rightly noted, "what is voice if not the medium of pure 'auto-affection' enabling the presence-to-itself of the speaking subject?" (Žižek, 1991, p. 125). After all, it is the voice—coming from my body and belonging to my personality—the voice thanks to which I speak through the body, which confirms my identity in social relations, and thanks to which the agreement between the sound and what it communicates (opinions, views, emotions) is recognized. And thus, a voice coming from another's body, which I am forced to use in order to state my meaning, causes cognitive dissonance and becomes a tool that traumatizes both the speaking subject and the listener. It seems that the author of the novel and the creators of its adaptation are very aware of this issue.

In his novel Morgan relatively frequently characterizes the voices of speaking characters, supplementing them with adjectives referring to gender, emotion ("The voice was smoothly male and devoid of any sales subsonics I could detect." [Morgan, 2006, p. 119]), as well as to the way of articulating words—highlighting, in particular, the opposition between the natural and the artificial voice, the latter potentially being of better or worse quality ("Even through the poor-quality voice, I thought I could hear a soft, sticky delight." [Morgan, 2006, p. 216]). Generally, however, there exist three types of voices in the world of *Altered Carbon*—the novel: male/female/synth voices. The differences between those voices are precisely characterized by the narrator. Indeed, the tensions between those categories are a frequent source of a particular cognitive dissonance for the protagonist, when the voice of the artificial intelligence turns out to be slightly "too human," or a human voice sounds suspiciously "metallic" for him: "'Elias Ryker,' he said, and his voice was not much smoother than the tannoy had been. Someone had done a real cut-rate job on the vocal cords" (Morgan, 2006, p. 212). What raises elementary doubt in the protagonist (Takeshi Kovacs) is his own voice, being, after all, the voice coming from the hired body of Elias Ryker: "When I spoke, Ryker's voice sounded alien in my ears, as if someone or something else was speaking through me" (Morgan 2006, p. 317). That voice—which, according to Kovacs, is not only not his, but also not necessarily "someone's" voice, maybe a voice of "something"—speaks through him, leaving a sense of otherness in the very core of the protagonist's mental identity. How different, in that context, is the sound of a very clear voice of another person (the "other's" voice), when in one of the key scenes Kovacs is haunted by the memory of his father's voice: "The voice jumped into my head, a voice I hadn't heard in nearly a century and a half of objective time" (Morgan, 2006, p. 369). This voice, however, appears in an entirely "natural" manner, due to the power of introspection caused by violent emotions accompanying a fight, and is not a voice inserted into the protagonist's personality due to the power of technological tricks.

It should also be noted that the transfer of one's personality and inhabiting another's body (and, thus, speaking with the voice of the Other) is not an invention of the author of *Altered Carbon* or other science fiction authors, but, essentially, a recurring motif, found in many texts devoted to artificial intelligence, as well as cyborgization and technological modifications of personality. It is worth mentioning here, for example, Charles Stross' novel *Accelerando*, contemporary with Morgan's works, in which a character/a group of characters designated as Bob Franklin/the Franklin Collective appear. This character, whose personality has been partially—since, due to technological reasons, only a fragmentary record of human personality was possible—transferred into a digital environment, exists after the death of his biological body as a particular set of functions (views, opinions, convictions, fancies and aversions—mostly concerning society and politics) in the minds of a group of his disciples. Franklin's mind speaks with their voices as a ghost of a leader haunting the bodies of his followers: "they have partial upload of Bob Franklin. They got it before he died, enough of his personality to reinstantiate it, time-sharing in their own brains" (Stross, 2005, p. 99). This is possible due to biotechnological implants, but leaves the uncanny sensation of haunting in the interlocutors forced to constantly guess who they are talking to: a human carrier of the hive mind called the Franklin Collective or Bob Franklin himself (or, more accurately, "Bob Franklin"—a collection of mental functions) in another's body. This is aided by the quasi-religious dimension of convictions shared by the members of the collective:

> The Franklin Collective believes that you can't get into the future unless it's digitized your neural state vector, or at least acquired as complete a snapshot of your sensory inputs and genome as current technology permits. You don't need to be alive for it to do this. Its society of mind is among the most impressive artifacts of computer science. And it likes to make converts [Stross, 2005, p. 102].

The female character who faces the necessity to choose between her own physical finiteness or the collective immortality of the Franklin Collective exploiting other people's bodies, also needs to confront this sense of cognitive uncertainty that is born out of a meeting with one voice inhabiting different bodies: "'Do you want to live forever?' she intones in Bob Franklin's tone of voice. 'You can live forever in me'" (Stross, 2005, p. 102). What is only a side plot of the story in Stross' novel becomes the main motif of Morgan's novels, as well as the *Altered Carbon* series. A motif which organizes the story and delineates the problematic field of the novel.

Who Is Speaking?

This leads us straight toward a question fundamental from the anthropological perspective: "who is speaking?" And essentially, all available answers are either doubtful or traumatizing. So, who is speaking in *Altered Carbon*? Is it the transferred personality, using available vocal instruments? The body devoid of personality, but haunted by the Other in the shape of a data packet? A dead person returned to life and embodied in a random sleeve? Artificial intelligence in an artificial sleeve? A human in an artificial sleeve or, perhaps, an artificial intelligence in a stolen/rented but human sleeve, which was previously drained of personality? The abovementioned doubts are aptly summarized by Žižek in his film *The Pervert's Guide to Cinema* (Žižek & Fiennes, 2006) when he comments on the case of Regan, the child protagonist of William Friedkin's movie *The Exorcist* (1971). Regan is a girl possessed by a demon who forces her to utter blasphemous and obscene statements with a voice forcefully extracted from the child's body: a male, modulated, unnatural voice. "The voice is not an organic part of a human body," Žižek notes. "It's coming from somewhere in between your body. ... Remember that at the beginning of the film this was a beautiful young girl. How did she become a monster that we see? By being possessed, but who possessed her? A voice. A voice in its obscene dimensions" (Žižek & Fiennes, 2006). According to the Slovenian philosopher, it is nobody else but the voice that possesses the child's body, it is the voice which is the demon. Besides, Žižek generalizes his conclusion, writing that this very case is not a paradoxical, but a model one—which illustrates perfectly the relationship between the body and the voice that inhabits—or possesses—it: "The lesson that we should learn and that the movies try to avoid is that we ourselves are the aliens. Our ego, our psychic agency, is an alien force, distorting, controlling our body" (Žižek & Fiennes, 2006). *Altered Carbon* curtails this situation of the dimension of demonic possession, replacing supernatural horror with a science fiction story, which makes this situation possible due to technological progress, but does it thus make it less traumatic?

However, in order to explore this issue, we should go back to the sources of cognitive anxieties that have been connected with the phenomenon of voice reproduction since its very beginnings—its recording and reproduction, which were inseparably connected with the experience of the aging of the body and its death. As Colin Davis aptly states, "whilst photography made the dead visible once again, moving film and sound recording enabled us also to see and to hear people, to watch their movement and listen to their voices, long after their deaths" (Davis, 2007, p. 20). Summarizing his reflections in this matter, the author of *Haunted Subjects* notes that "by succumbing to the fiction that the dead may speak, we give voice to the haunting within ourselves which ensures that we also are deprived of our own voice" (Davis, 2007, p. 114). Obviously, Davis follows here in the footsteps of Derrida's *Specters of Marx*, referring to the category of haunting, which the French philosopher connected with mourning and the difficulty in demystifying the identity of that which haunts:

> One would have to say: it haunts, it ghosts, it specters, there is some phantom there, it has the feel of the living-dead-manor house, spiritualism, occult science, gothic novel, obscurantism, atmosphere of anonymous threat or imminence. The subject that haunts is not identifiable, one cannot see, localize, fix any form, one cannot decide between hallucination and perception, there are only displacements; one feels oneself looked at by what one cannot see [Derrida, 2006, pp. 169–170].

Davis's observation develops this thought, introducing a directly defined category of loss and the accompanying melancholia:

> Derrida's subject wards off this bitter insight; but it can never entirely suppress it so long as it persists in its endeavour to maintain a dialogue with the dead and thereby positively seeks out the voices of the dead within itself. This position is melancholic because any temporal process leading to recovery is blocked, the subject will never succeed in dissociating itself from the loss or losses by which it is afflicted and constituted [Davis, 2007, p. 145].

Finally, Davis's conclusion is that "the place of the living is displaced and the speaking voice is dispossessed as it endeavors to achieve an exchange with its others" (Davis, 2007, p. 114). The voice which, as the voice of a ghost in a medium's body, haunts the disinherited body—temporarily or irrevocably out of its proper, original identity—invariably traumatizes the listener, regardless of whether they are a witness of such a scene in reality or merely a part of the audience of a movie or a television performance, in which this drama takes place.

How then can this ambivalence of voice in someone else's body be used by an art form comprised of sound and picture such as film? This traumatic potential can be noticed, above all, in movies referring to the supernatural horror convention, and undertaking the subjects of spiritism or mediumism (to mention only classic examples such as *Séance on a Wet Afternoon* [Bryan Forbes, 1964] or *The Treasure of Abbot Thomas* [Clark, 1974]). It appears with almost equal frequency in the context of a mental illness tormenting people haunted by personalities possessing their bodies and speaking with many voices—as in the famous short film *The Ventriloquist's Dummy* (Cavalcanti, 1945), whose protagonist is a ventriloquist dominated by the commanding tone of his dummy's voice. Sometimes both these aspects meet in the motif of characters possessed by another's personality (the ghost of an ancestor, a demonic entity, etc.), driving them to cruel and terrifying acts.

The situation of being possessed by the voice of a person who is dead, lost and returning in the body of a living one, in which their voice becomes a form of a parasite is, indeed, not only traumatic, but straightforwardly psychotic. This is aptly noted by Žižek, who comments on the classic cinematic image of precisely such a situation, found in Alfred Hitchcock's masterpiece, *Psycho*. "In *Psycho*, finally, we reach the level of the real: Norman Bates, who dresses in his mother's clothes, speaks with her voice, etc., wants neither to resuscitate her image nor act in her name; he wants to take her place in the real evidence of a psychotic state" (Žižek, 1991, pp. 98–99). Michel Chion expands on this issue in the context of presenting the so-called "internal voice" in sound cinema, referring also to an example drawn from Hitchcock's *Psycho*: "there's the voice that's called internal but is really a subject-voice-I-voice-that belongs to the mother at the end of the film, superimposed on the images of a silent Norman sitting in his cell" (Chion, 1999, p. 51). Interestingly, Chion follows the path of psychological interpretation to discover an uncanny aspect of this sonic phenomenon haunting the deranged Norman and the cinematic image with which the audience is confronted on the screen:

> the voice of the mother reels off a paranoid monologue. Internal voice of Norman, who we've been told identifies totally with his mother? More than that. The voice is close up, precise, immediate, without echo, it's an I-voice that vampirizes both Norman's body and the entire image, as well as the spectator herself [Chion, 1999, p. 52].

Thus, taking into account the abovementioned contexts and conditions of the traumatic voice of the Other, which our own bodies speak with, let us attempt to examine how this potential is utilized by the *Altered Carbon* series, offering not only a science-fictional rationalization of this phenomenon, but also having at its disposal means to portray all nuances of a cognitive dissonance, trauma and uncanniness accompanying the confrontation with another's voice in an effective and detailed manner.

The Voice of the Other

I would like to focus here on two examples of a voice that haunts the rented body (sleeve), making it—in a specific situation of communication—an uncanny object in the Freudian sense, where "the uncanny [*unheimlich*] is something which is secretly familiar [*heimlich-heimisch*], which has undergone repression and then returned from it" (Freud, 1919, p. 244). This uncanny aspect is revealed when others' bodies, bodies of people unknown to the characters, speak to them in a voice out of which there suddenly and unexpectedly emerges a perfectly well known personality—one belonging to a loved one, embodied in a rented or stolen sleeve.

The first scene takes place in season one, episode four (*AC* 4, "Force of

Evil"), when lieutenant Kristin Ortega brings home, for the *Día de Los Muertos* holiday commemorating the dead ones, her long-dead grandmother. The woman is illegally resleeved into the body of a criminal detained for an interrogation, which the police officer "borrows" from the holding cell for one evening. Ortega forces her mother, a practicing Neo-Catholic—who rejects re-embodying of the consciousness of dead people—to confront her own mother, clothed in the body of a man, a criminal and a person temporarily devoid of personality. Moreover, the technologically resurrected grandmother turns out to be a non-believer who readily makes use of the possibilities offered by returning to this world in the body of a living person.

The second scene takes place in the eighth episode of the series (AC 8, "Clash by Night"), in which Takeshi Kovacs introduces one of the characters, Lizzie, to her supposedly dead mother, Ava, now resleeved into the body of a man. An earlier confrontation between Ava and her husband, Vernon, occurs in the atmosphere of a lack of recognition, suspicion and rejection, when the man cannot reconcile with the fact that his wife is sleeved into a male body. The meeting between Lizzie and Ava, taking place in a virtual environment, is devoid of that traumatic character, as the daughter immediately recognizes her mother, regardless of her bodily representation, noticing only a slight change—which, however, pertains not to the parent's gender, but to her hairstyle. And it is this lack of surprise that constitutes the main source of anxiety in the audience. It is also worth noting that in both cases, these traumatic confrontations pertain to a meeting with a mother in the body of an other—a man, causing the situation to resemble the Lacanian communicative relationship between a child and its mother as an Other. This situation is aptly characterized by Bruce Fink, who writes: "'mother tongue'—is indicative of the fact that it is some Other's tongue first, the mOther's tongue, that is, the mOther's language, and in speaking of childhood experience, Lacan often virtually equates the Other with the mother" (Fink, 1995, p. 7).

Both scenes, expanded and highlighted on the level of the plot, undoubtedly deepen and complicate the psychological relations between the characters. Thus the mother, the model Other of psychoanalysis, turns out to really be an other (person), sleeved in the body of a strange man. It would be difficult to illustrate in a more radical and unambiguous—and essentially, allegoric—manner the key problem of the neurotic's family romance, the necessity to break away from the influence of parental authority and the possibility of seeing the Other in a person that is close and familiar to us. Indeed, from the beginning both sequences are constructed on the basis of confronting expectations (of the characters and of the accompanying audience). The participants of these meetings need to confront reality, which, as it turns out, even in the futuristic world of the possibilities provided by technology exceeds their imagination.

After all, Ortega's grandmother, resurrected in a man's body, speaks in another person's voice expressing views and opinions she was never attributed with before. She is not a devout, well brought up Catholic, but a wanton hedonist. Is that really her, or is she under the influence of a badly matched body?—the family is forced to wonder, appalled by the grandmother's behavior during the holiday. In turn, in the second scene, Lizzie recognizes her mother in a strange man with surprising ease, without betraying any anxiety experienced by the observers of this scene (her father and Kovacs). Does this result from the fact that the meeting takes place in a virtual environment, where everything is possible, or is it the daughter who does not have the slightest doubt that it is not the stranger (other) who is her mother, but that the mother was always the other (mOther)?

This question remains unanswered. What is more important is that the scenes analyzed here perfectly demonstrate that even the most sophisticated scientific rationalization and a showcase of technological powers of personality transfer and sleeving in another's body do not eradicate cognitive doubts, as well as the accompanying anxiety when we are forced to confront a strange voice coming from a well known body, or a well known voice coming from a strange body. This anxiety is perhaps similar to the one we feel when hearing our own voice recorded on a device, removed from our body, when it appears to our ears as someone else's voice (Brzostek, 2014, p. 6). Perhaps at the basis of said anxiety lies a vague sense whose presence has been suggested by Žižek: "Our ego, our psychic agency, is an alien force, distorting, controlling our body" (2006). The ego invariably remains a source of surprise and the trauma that follows.

References

Brzostek, D. (2014). Recorded or Repressed? Towards the Anthropology of the Cassette Tape. *Glissando. Magazyn o muzyce współczesnej*, no. 23: 4–7.

Chion, M. (1994). *Audio-Vision. Sound on Screen.* Translated by Claudia Gorbman, New York, Columbia University Press.

_____. (1999). *The Voice in the Cinema.* Gorbman, C. (Ed. and Trans.), New York, Columbia University,.

Davis, C. (2007).*Haunted Subjects. Deconstruction, Psychoanalysis and the Return of the Dead.* New York, Palgrave Macmillan.

Derrida, J. (2006). *Specters of Marx. The State of the Debt, the Work of Mourning and the New International.* Kamuf, P. (Trans.). New York and London, Routledge.

Fink, B. (1995). *Lacanian Subject: Between Language and Jouissance.* Princeton, Princeton University Press.

Freud, S. (1955). *The Standard Edition of the Complete Psychological Works of Sigmund Freud, Volume XVII (1917-1919): An Infantile Neurosis and Other Works.* London, The Hogarth Press.

Lenic, J.G. (Producer) & Kalogridis, L. (Creator). *Altered Carbon.* (2018–). [Series]. United States: Netflix.

Morgan, R.K. (2006). *Altered Carbon*. New York, Ballantine Books, [e-book].
Stross, C. (2005). *Accelerando*. New York, Ace Books, [e-book].
Žižek S. (1991). *Looking Awry. An Introduction to Jacques Lacan through Popular Culture*. Cambridge, MA: MIT Press.
_____. (Writer) & Fiennes, S. (Director). (2006).*The Pervert's Guide to Cinema* [Motion picture]. United Kingdom: Mischief Film, Amoeba Film.

Cyberpunk

Cyberpunk Resleeved
How Netflix's Altered Carbon *Reformats Its Cyberpunk Ancestry*

Adam Edwards

Pull on the new flesh like borrowed gloves and burn your fingers once again.
—Morgan, 2002

The cyberpunk genre, despite remaining relatively popular since its inception, has often been criticized for refusing to move on. The reception of recent works like *Blade Runner 2049* (Villeneuve, 2017) or the remake of Masamune Shirow's classic *Ghost in the Shell* (Sanders, 2017), is often marred with concerns that they copy earlier works to play on their popularity without deepening any discussion or progressing the detailed social commentary that this specific form of science fiction can provide. This criticism has been explicitly levelled at Netflix's *Altered Carbon* in articles for *The Verge*, *The Guardian*, and *Wired*. While some other works certainly suffer from this flaw, such as Ernest Cline's *Ready Player One* (2011), the inspiration for Spielberg's similarly shallow adaptation, it is the purpose of this essay to highlight the active parodic intention that underlies the familiar cyberpunk aspects recreated in *Altered Carbon*. In so doing, it will reveal the methods with which cyberpunk can update and modify the impact and implications of its features to better fit a contemporary context.

Altered Carbon does not build its world from the ground upwards; it laces itself with aspects of previous cyberpunk works, such as *Blade Runner* (Scott, 1982) and *Max Headroom* (Frewer, 1985), but it does so in order to twist them to suit new purposes. Its connections to *Max Headroom* can be found in its casting of Matt Frewer as Carnage, while similarities with *Blade*

Runner are apparent from both the setting of a futuristic sprawl and the detective's perspective shared by Kovacs and *Blade Runner*'s protagonist Rick Deckard. These similarities, in particular with *Blade Runner*, can often be, for critics, the most damning, drawing a multitude of comments on what they repeatedly see as derivative imagery. However, even those critical of the first season of the show acknowledge the relevance of the cyberpunk genre to contemporary society. Julia Muncy for one, reflects that:

> Cyberpunk, as a specific subset of science fiction, is particularly well suited to our present cultural mindspace. Its focus on the implications of networked, digitized existence, dominated by technocratic regimes that merge economic and technological stratification, is more than a little relevant to where we've found ourselves in 2018 [2018].

Other reviewers have cited academic sources for addressing the relevance of cyberpunk to contemporary audiences. Paul Walker-Emig's (2018) article in *The Guardian* quotes Anna McFarlane's opinion on cyberpunk's "post-national, globalized society" still being "very recognisable to us today." For this reason, as this essay will argue, *Altered Carbon*'s adherence to the established tropes of this genre enables it to tap into the contemporary recognition of its audience and in so doing reflects upon the science-fiction possibilities of real-world technology. Within this genre, however, *Altered Carbon* distinguishes itself in its reimagining of the cyberpunk works upon which it draws, enabling it to build upon the audience's previous engagement with these topics to refresh dialogues about dystopian technology and press such discussions into a distinctly contemporary context.

Parody vs. Pastiche

Cyberpunk literature and media, despite its continued popularity since the 1980s, has received an unfortunately sparse academic consideration for its most recent iterations. Many critics of cyberpunk, e.g., Keith Johnston (2011) or Gregg Rickman (2004), perceive it through its broader membership to science fiction. Others, however, who consider such work within a tighter focus, tend to not analyze contemporary cyberpunk texts, linking the genre to a specific time around three decades ago; Featherstone and Burrows' (1995) collection of essays, for example, or Dani Cavallaro's (2000) discussion of William Gibson's work typify this approach. These analyses also gravitate toward canonical works such as Gibson's *Sprawl* trilogy or Neal Stevenson's *Snow Crash*. The prominent critical engagements with the most recent, and often more mainstream, texts therefore can be found on news sites and in reviews, articles, editorials, and discussion forums. In order to address *Altered*

Carbon's cultural impact, such discourses become incredibly important; they pertain not only to the excitement, production value, or other aspects of viewing pleasure of the show itself, but also capture the thinking that the show can provoke and do so in the absence of sustained academic discussion.

The overall reception of *Altered Carbon* was generally favorable, though it averaged a 64 out of 100 score from critic reviews on *Metacritic* as of January 2019. The mixed response from critical reviews often took a similar shape: *Altered Carbon*'s similarities with earlier works in its genre were acknowledged (and disparaged), only to be followed by the praise it earned for its distinguishing features. Graeme Virtue's brief review (2018) is a good example of this pattern. He notes at the outset that "as cultural consumers, we have been bombarded with variations of this future on and off for more than 25 years ... cyberpunk has become so shopworn that it has become essentially a nostalgic period setting." Following this, however, he highlights how *Altered Carbon* stands out thanks to "pleasingly oddball" aspects. He draws attention to elements such as the inclusion of the AI hotel whose projection takes the appearance of Edgar Allan Poe, and how the series contrasts gruesome torture with a "heartwarming side story" within a single episode. Similarly, Maureen Ryan (2018) of *Variety* concluded her review with the thought that "though 'Altered Carbon' is dependent on a number of the genre's oldest conventions, the casual inclusivity of its cast ... and its ability to shift between worlds and memories becomes impressive over time." Both of these reviews emphasize how *Altered Carbon* is able to distinguish itself, and progress the genre it positions itself within, even while adhering to certain conventions which can feel repetitive at best.

Altered Carbon, then, is typically seen as a show, like other recent iterations of cyberpunk, utilizing the styles of past works from the genre—with *Blade Runner* being far and away the most cited source—without contributing any new perspectives to cyberpunk's exploration of the socio-cultural concerns surrounding technology. Ryan Britt (2018) writes that the series "wants desperately for you to be reminded of the original *Blade Runner* and older Gibson books, rather than challenge the viewer with anything new." While the show does occasionally suffer from unnuanced repetition of established cyberpunk tropes, it is far more than an empty pastiche of older cyberpunk works as it has been denoted in these reviews. It is more appropriate to press analysis of *Altered Carbon* as a parody of not only the transhumanist technology suffusing the cyberpunk genre, but more importantly, as a self-aware and *useful* parody of the wider genre itself. *Altered Carbon* actively seeks to represent, revisit, and reimagine settings, roles, and narrative structures from cyberpunk's history to parodically refresh its messages; it utilizes the familiar elements of cyberpunk history to reignite and update the genre's longstanding fear of a technologically dependent transhumanist future.

In order to analyze *Altered Carbon* as a parody, and so challenge the criticism that it emptily copies a thirty-year-old aesthetic, we can turn to Fredric Jameson's distinction between *parody* and *pastiche*. In *Postmodernism, or The Cultural Logic of Late Capitalism* (1991), Jameson laments the eclipsing of parody by pastiche. In his terminology, *parody* capitalized on the uniqueness of modernist styles to produce mocking imitations; these parodic imitations held elements of respectful sympathy for their sources. What Jameson terms as *pastiche* is instead a negative postmodern phenomenon, an "imitation of dead styles" (1991, p. 18); it is a "blank parody" (p. 17) bereft of the satiric impulse or laughter of its predecessor. Jameson sees this shift as an indication of a downward movement from modernism where "Modernist styles... become postmodernist codes," leaving behind merely "a field of stylistic and discursive heterogeneity without a norm" (p. 17). Our capability to understand the past erodes with this change, restructuring the past as a repository for genres and styles for commodification.

While this distinction in terminology is very useful, this perspective colors approaches to contemporary parody with an assumption that they are worse than their predecessors. *Altered Carbon*'s "copying" of *Blade Runner*'s imagery, after Jameson's critique, is more liable to be viewed as pastiche, and this aligns with the perspective of reviewers outlined above; it is apparent that Jameson's concept informs cultural responses to texts such as *Altered Carbon*, even if it is not invoked by name, and this leads to a silencing of the work that the show does with its recycling of prior art.

Before exploring what *Altered Carbon* achieves with its parody, we can usefully expand on Jameson's concepts by incorporating some terminological distinctions from Linda Hutcheon's *Theory of Parody* (1985). Hutcheon attempts a comprehensive distinction of the range of terms often confused with parody, such as irony, satire, burlesque, and also pastiche. In Hutcheon's definition, "parody is, in another formulation, repetition with critical distance, which marks difference rather than similarity" (p. 6); it is "a method of inscribing continuity while permitting critical distance" (Hutcheon, 1985, p. 20). This aligns with Jameson's perception of the term as an imitation that implies a respect of its source. Neither theorist foregrounds humor as the sole intent of parodic work, and while humor often features in parody, it is not a requisite of the form. The difference between the two is best summarized as follows:

> Parody is bitextual in that it needs the encoder and decoder to superimpose two texts upon one another to incorporate the old into the new, whereas pastiche is more monotextual as it stresses similarity rather than difference [p. 33].

Of particular importance in Hutcheon's definition is the emphasis she places on the "encoder" and "decoder" both actively working to create parody. Parody is designed with intent, and requires engagement and an appropriate cultural awareness to communicate its message. Furthermore, parody strives "to incorporate the old into the new." (p. 33) In this, Hutcheon acknowledges how parody creates new material, and seeks to reshape the messages and traditions of the old into its new context; its "bitextuality" melds two texts rather than simply replicating and glorifying an older work. This resonates, as we will see, with *Altered Carbon*, and how it strives to blend the older texts in its history into new material and the context of its production.

In order to analyse how *Altered Carbon* responds to its parodied material, Hutcheon's definition of "irony" in particular will be of great importance. "Irony," for Hutcheon, is "a strategy used to parodic effect, one which highlights the difference between the parodic and the parodied, and substitutes for the mockery or ridicule of the target text traditionally seen in this area" (pp. 31–32). When irony is seen as a substitute for mockery, it enables the discussion of parodic strategies that seek to highlight the critical difference between the parody and the parodied as a focus of creative intent in itself. While distinguishing between each of these terms, Hutcheon notes that they are not exclusive of each other. She clarifies that "this is not to say that a parody cannot contain (or use to parodic ends) a pastiche" (p. 38). It is therefore not required, here, to establish which single term can best be applied to *Altered Carbon*, but rather to demonstrate how the show utilizes ironic strategies to achieve useful parodic effects, rather than creating an empty pastiche of cyberpunk as the dominant criticisms of the show have repeatedly asserted. To see the show as a simplistic imitator is to miss much of its potential for provoking more nuanced discourse about transhumanism and embodiment in the twenty-first century.

Blade Runner, *Detectives and Critical Distance*

As a cyberpunk text, part of a genre with a high degree of visual and thematic specificity, *Altered Carbon* cannot be detached from the media that precede it. As its critical response so often argues, its visual style and narrative structures do draw heavily from *Blade Runner*. However, Scott's film is hardly the only inspiration for the show which brings together imagery, ideas, and even actors from other cyberpunk work such as *The Matrix* (Wachowskis, 1999) and *Max Headroom: 20 minutes into the future* (Frewer, 1985). *Altered Carbon* embraces its legacy; rather than representing a failure to iterate, it displays a designed commitment to the imagined worlds which stand at the heart of the cultural conception of cyberpunk. *Blade Runner* is a landmark production for the genre and has become its foundational work of visual media; it is almost impossible to uncover discursive pieces on cyberpunk material without mentioning *Blade Runner*. It appears repeatedly, for instance, in both Featherstone and Burrows' edited essay collection, and Cavallaro's discussion of cyberculture, even though her focus is on the work of William Gibson. Brian Baker's study of *Science Fiction* (2014) similarly uses *Blade Runner* a great deal, particularly in the discussion of science fiction and cinema.

Its pervasive presence in cyberpunk is therefore also influenced by the popular cultural resonance of the film in the broader science-fiction and cinematic milieu. Since science fiction films as a whole still invite comparison with *Blade Runner*, *Altered Carbon* would never have been able to escape its legacy. Of similar importance is *Altered Carbon*'s own source text, Richard Morgan's novel (2002). In his own words, Morgan "ransacked the genre and made off with the goods" (quoted in Bullock, 2014) when it came to appropriating concepts that were already embedded in science fiction, so the novel itself was already indebted to classic works, *Blade Runner* very much included. For this reason, *Altered Carbon* had the choice to either deviate significantly from its source material or to embrace the links it had to prior art and to do something different with that same commitment.

Nowhere is this debt and difference more evident than in the distinction between the series' advertising material and its final narrative. One of the most frequently appearing images in the show's campaign was Kovacs silhouetted against a steep skyline adorned with neon advertisements. This very clearly situated the two texts in a dialogue, encouraging cross-comparison. It presents, just as *Blade Runner* did, a hard-boiled detective protagonist and sets out to follow his struggles in a classic combination of science-fiction and noir cinema that echoes throughout cyberpunk. After actively conjuring this connection, however, it is this hard-boiled aspect that *Altered Carbon* also ironically distances itself from.

Historically, hard-boiled fiction is constituted by certain elements that, as Sean McCann (2010) rightly notes, "are so widely known that they have achieved something close to mythic stature." He precedes this statement with a neat summary of general assumptions about the genre:

> tough-talking, streetwise men; beautiful, treacherous women; a mysterious city, dark; a disenchanted hero who strives, usually without resounding success, to bring a small measure of justice to his (or, more recently, her) world [McCann, 2010, p. 42].

Both *Blade Runner* and *Altered Carbon* certainly fit this description. Their cities are both mysterious and dark, lit only by an artful neon tinge. Priss, the beautiful and acrobatic cyborg target of *Blade Runner*'s detective Deckard, and Miriam Bancroft, the seductive yet suspect wife of Kovacs' employer, can both be described as femme fatales (the "beautiful, treacherous women" from McCann's description). Finally, both Deckard and Kovacs are disenchanted, tough-talking heroes who can only hope to administer a small amount of justice into their worlds.

This is reinforced in Cavallaro's discussion of the literary influences which anticipate cyberpunk, where she points to how "Chandler [a hugely influential hard-boiled fiction author] emphasizes the isolation and rootlessness of his hero" (Cavallaro, 2000, p. 9) (though this isolation, or rootlessness, is dramatically exaggerated in *Altered Carbon* with Kovacs appearing, primarily, as a man 250 years detached from both his environment and his own skin). The aspects of hard-boiled fiction described above are so close to mythic that the moment the genre begins to align with any of these tropes the audience will anticipate the inclusion of them in their entirety. This expected alignment with an established set of genre traditions becomes a useful tool for parodic works, however, enabling creators to play on audience expectations and disrupt a familiar structure in order to produce an effect.

The ironic distance that *Altered Carbon* establishes between itself and the legacy of *Blade Runner* is apparent from the very structure of its narrative. Kovacs is a resistance fighter made to wear the body of a detective. He is forced by circumstance to embody the traditional noir protagonist's role, regardless of his own wishes. This creates a dismissive, detached perspective toward the recognized structure that the show itself is "wearing"; it invites a direct comparison with *Blade Runner* in its visual style, and its future-noir hard-boiled detective, while simultaneously showing an utter disinterest in these features through its focal character; Kovacs, asleep for centuries and trained to be beamed to alien worlds, doesn't much care if the case is solved, or even if he lives or dies. This disjuncture is picked up by some of the reviewers of the show, but rarely in a positive tone. Muncy laments Kovacs' role as the protagonist due to what she calls:

> the simple problem that Kovacs has almost no stake in the life he's been given. He's detached and bitter, and justifiably so, but his lack of interest in the world leads the show to feeling untethered, distant, and focused on all the wrong things [2018].

In this regard, Kovacs' relation to the plot distances the viewer from the show which focuses on "the *wrong* things" for the detective structure it parodies. The highly praised additions which make *Altered Carbon* stand out, however, are enabled by the shifting of focus from a direct recreation of a detective story, strongly implying that we should see this as a feature, not a bug.

One such applauded addition is a set of scenes in which Detective Ortega, an officer with a Neo-Catholic family who don't believe in resleeving anyone who has died, brings her previously deceased grandmother to her home in a new body for a family celebration. These moments are given chances to shine and develop due to the distance *Altered Carbon* ultimately establishes from the fetishization of detectives and criminals so intrinsic to hard-boiled fiction. As a consequence of this, *Altered Carbon* is able to shift the exploration of the implications of transhuman technology from the violent detective's world, to the more recognizable family space, encouraging engagement with the concept of this technology's impact on their own lives.

As Hutcheon writes in her theory of parody, parody "may indeed be complicitous with the values it inscribes as well as subverts, but the subversion is still there" (Hutcheon, 1985, p. 106). Indeed, *Altered Carbon* does fall into some of the traps identified by its reviewers. The hard-boiled structure at times pulls the narrative away from its fresh additions to the genre. At the end of episode 1, for instance, Kovacs is confronted by the hitman Dimitri Kadmin, a fractured killer at the head of a gang of criminals hired to apprehend Kovacs. The scene, which quickly escalates into a well-choreographed fight sequence, leaves Kovacs triumphant but injured. Kovacs, however, initially accepts Kadmin's command patiently, but is taunted and beaten until he is ultimately forced into a violent engagement. If Kovacs is forced to play the role of the detective then he is also forced to respond appropriately as Kadmin does not accept his acquiescence. Sean McCann identifies the hard-boiled traits that dictate this response. He argues that the Western legacy, which hard-boiled fiction, in part, draws upon, exerts an influence wherein the detective must *battle* "the brute enemies of civilization—[in these worlds, the] swarthy denizens of the urban underworld" (2010, p. 45) Until this point, Kovacs has not proven his physical strength, aside from a brief flashback to a different life in a different body.

The fighting, however, serves only to distance Kovacs from the answers that he seeks and further embeds him into a structure for which he has no interest. This expectation of Kovacs' athletic and violent form of heroism stems, then, from both the demands of the storyworld and, metatextually, from the genres the show adapts, dictating the character choices and many of the topics of focus for *Altered Carbon* as a whole. Importantly, however, the framing of Kovacs' relationship to his role as a detective allows the show to express a frustration with, or simply ambivalence toward, this prescribed path. In this way, even as the show suffers from its expectations, it communicates discontent and in so doing ironically distances itself from the established structures that place these expectations upon them. This distance emphasizes the enactment of power on the human body enabled by the technology of *Altered Carbon*; how inescapable the performative demands of his body are on Kovacs and how despite his resistance inevitably he is dragged back to his imposed role. *Altered Carbon*'s prescribed culture is enforced by the bodies its people inhabit, especially for those such as Kovacs and Kadmin.

Violence, Sleeves and Family Drama

Altered Carbon's ironic distance from its noir history is again shown in episode 4, where, in one of the show's most discussed scenes, Kovacs' torture at the hands of Kadmin is contrasted by Ortega's family celebrations. Kovacs is placed in a virtual torture room where he is interrogated and mutilated on a seemingly endless loop that is broken up for the viewer with flashbacks to Kovacs' past and Detective Ortega's *Día de Los Muertos* celebrations. In this latter scene, Ortega's family, who are devoutly Neo-Catholic, a Christian sect in the show who believe resleeving deceased individuals puts the soul at risk of going to hell, are celebrating a holiday devoted to remembering friends and family members that have died. Ortega has resleeved her deceased Grandmother into the body of a criminal gang member so that the dead woman can attend the family celebration. This sparks an argument and discussion within the family about the moral and spiritual implications of resleeving.

This episode is important for a number of reasons. Firstly, it contrasts a scene from Morgan's original novel, Kovacs' torture, with a new scene unique to the show. Secondly, it intertwines the most extreme violence of the series with a lighter, often humorous exploration of the implications of resleeving. The inseparability of cyberpunk and violence is something Kevin McCarron (Featherstone & Burrows, 1995, p. 261) comments on, admitting that, despite its many critical and philosophical merits as a genre, the worlds presented in cyberpunk texts are often incredibly violent and misogynistic. The actions that cyberpunk protagonists take are frequently brutal in order to emphasize the uncaring culture they live within and are infected by. This often leads to nihilism as characters see themselves surrounded with meaningless, easy-to-replace people in overpopulated urban sprawls. It is also indicative of the popularity of violent action for many readers, viewers and players of cyberpunk fiction, with Morgan's own love of violence in his writing being well documented (Flood, 2018).

The torture scenes in both this episode and the novel have garnered a lot of critical discussion due to their shocking and potentially problematic natures. In the novel Kovacs is interrogated after being virtually resleeved into the body of a young woman; in the show he is tortured in the sleeve he occupies for the majority of the season. Laeta Kalogridis, the creator of *Altered Carbon*, reveals that she made this change to avoid the scene becoming "some torture porn thing" (quoted in Weber, 2018). Kalogridis goes on to state that she kept the scene in the series to continue the show's seemingly paradoxical discomfort with violence: "the worst violence is visited on [Kovacs]. Nobody else gets their legs burnt off while they're still alive with a blowtorch" she states (quoted in Eggertsen, 2018).

Violence begets violence for *Altered Carbon's* detective; Kovacs is forced into violent behavior and the repercussion of this is violence visited on himself. In these segments, Kovacs is mistaken for Detective Ryker, whose body acts as Kovacs' current sleeve, and a man described as every bit the violent, short-tempered, criminal-associate noir detective that *Altered Carbon*, and Kovacs, wish to be separated from. The show is uncomfortable with the violent legacy from which it springs. Violence is rarely rewarded neatly with success, but instead with the frustrated withholding of answers, as seen in Kadmin's death, and with an increase in violence reinscribed onto Kovacs' body.

Importantly, however, this scene is only partially the focus of the episode. Indeed the frequent scene changes between the torture and Ortega's party draw the two into comparison and create a disturbing backdrop of the potential terrors of resleeving. In Ortega's scenes, her Neo-Catholic family struggle with her Grandmother's return. The Grandmother, who is sleeved in the body of a threatening, tattooed, white supremacist, acts as a comedic juxtaposition of appearance and personality. Even so, this comedic element is problematized as the threatening appearance of the sleeve causes members of the family, even in this future world, to be fearful when Ortega's Grandmother plays with the young children. The inclusion of these scenes shifts the show's focus to a recognizable social dynamic and the impacts its futuristic technology can have on everyday social spaces. This cleverly restaged family drama is, however, broken by Kovacs' more literal experience of being physically torn apart. By juxtaposing these scenes, *Altered Carbon* is able to pay homage to its legacy, both its source text and the violent nature of previous cyberpunk works, while simultaneously expanding upon the social and cultural dynamics of personal life affected by high technology that otherwise may have been overlooked. Within this episode's structure the two interconnect and develop one another.

The potential for torture is experienced by those who tread the violent path, contrary to the reunion and celebration enjoyed by others at greater peace. Therefore, while *Altered Carbon* does fall into the expectation of providing brutal and gory spectacles for its viewers, its integration of this into new imagery distances it from a pure pastiche of the genre's expectations and allows a fresh, parodic focus to be applied to the philosophical and ethical questions inherent in its science fiction conceit: what would it be like if we could shed our skin?

Max Carnage

As described above, the similarities between *Altered Carbon* and *Blade Runner* have been frequently acknowledged. In order to further emphasize both the show's awareness of its heritage and the parodic intent behind its creation, however, we will close up this piece by turning our attention to its incorporation of less immediately apparent cyberpunk material, in particular the character of Max Headroom.

Headroom originally appeared in the British TV movie, *Max Headroom: 20 Minutes into the Future*, as a digitized television presenter, essentially an uploaded copy of a human mind with a wacky personality. *Altered Carbon* creates an ironic relation to this character, not by directly referencing the material but by positioning the actor who played Headroom, Matt Frewer, as the Panama Rose Fightdrome's ringmaster, Carnage. This subtle placement of an influential cyberpunk figure within the broader setting is indicative of the insightful parodic awareness *Altered Carbon* establishes with its intertextuality. To emphasize the parodic relationship in this connection, Matt Frewer's role in *Altered Carbon* will be compared to another recent cyberpunk text, *Ready Player One*, and how it uses the same character of Max Headroom. In the latter, references to and depictions of the character more neatly fit the criticisms levelled at *Altered Carbon*, demonstrating a relationship far more akin to pastiche than parody, and shows, in the juxtaposition, how *Altered Carbon* does something more interesting and insightful.

Ready Player One (2011) is a novel written by Ernest Cline, and adapted for film by Steven Spielberg (2018). Both texts are set in the near future, a cyberpunk dystopia where many citizens live in slums and so the majority of the world spends significant periods of time in a shared virtual reality called the Oasis. The story follows Wade, the main protagonist, and a group of other "Gunters" whose sole purpose is to find three secret keys to an Easter egg hidden in the Oasis that will grant them ownership of the company which controls it. Overall, the plot remains mostly consistent between the novel and film, with only superficial changes and omissions.

In the novel, Max Headroom is present in its entirety. Wade selects an Oasis copy of the character to essentially act as his personal assistant. The only reason given for choosing Headroom for this position is that he is supposedly cool because he is from the '80s, a decade venerated throughout the story as the billionaire creator of the Oasis nostalgically adored and replicated the pop culture of his childhood. Headroom, therefore, serves no new purpose in *Ready Player One* other than to signify awareness of '80s television. He does not progress the story, or open any new perspectives onto the storyworld or the reader's reality. All scenes including Headroom are therefore bland pastiches of this character rather than fresh contextualizations. This lack of significance is emphasized in the 2018 film where Headroom is entirely absent. The closest replacement is an AskJeeves-like Curator who is affiliated with any user of the Oasis rather than the desires of any single character.

Frederic Jameson feared a "nostalgia mode" (1991, p. 20) in postmodern pastiche, an inability to represent our own present and instead only retreading our inner memories of a past that is forever out of reach (p. 25). This inability signifies an eclipse of creative potential. None of the references made in *Ready Player One* are intended to reinterpret the sources upon which it draws, and the replaceability or elision of the intertexts in its adaptation only serves to highlight their empty worth as pastiche. *Ready Player One* also so selectively cherry-picks the elements of one decade's pop-culture that its positioning of itself as a repository of the influential texts of that period becomes a dangerously exclusive exercise, hyper-tailored toward the memories of white, male teenagers and their nostalgic fathers, a direction criticized by Jazmine Joyner (2018) on *Okayplayer*. Without drawing upon its references to do any real narrative or cultural work, they exist only to signify what icons are presumed to be important to the dominant readers or viewers.

Max Headroom is not important to *Ready Player One*; the connotations he carries are unexplored and unutilized, and so his use, along with the vast majority of references in both the novel and the film, becomes empty. His only purpose is to market a new product to an established demographic and perpetuate a singular perception of a past now beyond reach.

Altered Carbon's approach to intertextuality stands in pleasingly stark contrast to what we see in *Ready Player One*. Carnage is the boss and ringmaster of the Panama Rose Fightdrome, a combat arena utilizing specially bred sleeves which fight to the death. While not being exactly the same role, this draws upon Frewer's heritage in Max Headroom's boisterous showmanship; he is not given a talk-show, but he is still the host of this new, violent form of entertainment. Visual similarities are also apparent in Carnage's appearance with his excessively decorated suit, replete with colorful floral shirt and bowtie. His exaggerated appearance also compliments his status as one of only two fully synthetic sleeves encountered in the series, positioning him with a similar artificiality to Headroom's virtuality.

In choosing Frewer for this part in particular, *Altered Carbon* makes clear its subtle awareness of its cyberpunk ancestry, again encouraging a more ironic recognition; Carnage himself even remarks that "people love the classics" (*AC* 6, "Men with My Face"). Unlike *Ready Player One*, *Altered Carbon* re-envisions the role that Frewer/Headroom can play in a modern cyberpunk text. Carnage himself is a deceitful, menacing figure. He advertises terrifying spectacles, "never broadcasting, never recording anything" (*AC* 6, "Men with My Face"), while secretly undermining his word and recording every fight on VHS tapes. Frewer, therefore, is separated from his humorous ridicule; instead he more closely echoes the duplicitous storing of personal information so intricately important to contemporary society. His deceptive trait is a further, humorous nod to Headroom with its 1980s technology and links to video nasties and other old media panics. In this world, where the digitization of consciousness is commonplace, analogue technology becomes a subversive, dangerous element able to go undetected.

Frewer's role here is not glorified then, as in *Ready Player One*. There is a great contrast between Carnage and the humorous figure that was Max Headroom, with Carnage living up to his name. In episode 6, Kovacs and Ortega are thrown into Carnage's arena and pitted first against bestially designed sleeves with horns growing from their heads, and finally against Kovacs's original body, now a sleeve for Kadmin. This use of bodies positions the scene as a battleground of old versus new, of Kovacs working with Ortega to overcome his history, and this is framed and orchestrated by the actor who played Max Headroom. The scene becomes representative of *Altered Carbon*'s struggle to reshape the recognizable elements of cyberpunk into its contemporary context, striving to avoid stagnation and to contribute to its messages about our evolving technological environment. The presence of Frewer, departing from Headroom's smarmy self-importance which itself ridiculed the phony familiarity of game-show hosts, is a revelling in Carnage's deceitful greediness; the ridicule is gone and in its place is a vicious undermining of media providers. Carnage, the smiling presenter who promises anonymous viewership and betrays his customers, restructures the mockery of Headroom into a dangerously exploitative context.

In this comparison, then, *Altered Carbon* is distinguished by its manipulation and recontextualisation of its past. It takes elements of what came before, knowingly gestures toward them, and then reframes them for its own purposes. This demonstrates a parodic intention to signify difference whereas *Ready Player One* uses its intertextual references to shape itself as a pastiche of what came before, drawing comparisons to highlight its similarity to the source materials in order to be legitimized just from the association. *Altered Carbon* therefore demonstrates an impulse to knowingly satirize its cyberpunk ancestry in order to reignite and update the genre's longstanding fear of a technologically dependent transhumanist future.

Conclusion

Looking back over the examples provided above, it is clear that *Altered Carbon* is acting upon its cyberpunk heritage with a fresher perspective than its reviews might suggest. Unlike other modern cyberpunk films, such as *Ready Player One*, it refuses to simply recreate the gestures of the texts to which it refers. Instead, it plays upon the undetachable legacy of cult classics such as *Blade Runner* and the character of Max Headroom to reframe their concerns within its own context. It makes apparent its awareness of the inescapable canonicity of its predecessors and opens an intertextual space in which it can create ironic distance.

The danger surrounding this intent is that to imitate previous works, even with parodic intent, is to invite the criticism of being unoriginal. Hutcheon warns of this in her *Theory of Parody* where she acknowledges that postmodern parody "may indeed be complicitous with the values it inscribes as well as subverts, but the subversion is still there" (Hutcheon, 1985, p. 106). *Altered Carbon* is indeed complicit in its conformation with the genre; it uses the violence, the dystopian city, the lonely men, and the neon glare that has marked cyberpunk since its inception. The genre has remained popular for over 30 years and these elements constitute the major checkpoints new products have to hit if they wish to be readily identified as cyberpunk, and when the major visual signifiers of a genre are as powerful as those of *Blade Runner*, it becomes easy to write off any work which draws on them as an exercise in copying or empty pastiche.

Altered Carbon's mature attempts to revitalize '80s cyberpunk concerns with a fresh perspective shine through however. Its specific interpretation of cyberpunk clichés expresses distinction from its sources in its intent and message, and this aligns it far more closely with the concept of parody. The familiarity generated by its parody can help to orient an audience to new material, but it is important to identify the ironic differences the show establishes, particularly in comparison to other works close to its time of release. In so doing, *Altered Carbon* can be acknowledged as a creative progression of older cyberpunk perspectives, bringing forward the arguments of its past and resleeving them to address its own societal environment. This helps to ensure that cyberpunk fiction best reflects the concerns of an audience still finding its highly specific form relatable to their present and to the futures which they might see.

References

Altered Carbon, *Metacritic*. Retrieved from https://www.metacritic.com/.
Baker, B. (2019) *Science Fiction*. Basingstoke: Palgrave Macmillan, 2014.
Baker-Whitelaw, G. (2018, February 2) Netflix's 'Altered Carbon' proves cyberpunk has failed to progress. *The Daily Dot*. Retrieved from https://www.dailydot.com/.
Britt, R. (2018, February 5). "Altered Carbon" and "Blade Runner 2049" Don't exist because of futurism. *Inverse*. Retrieved from https://www.dailydot.com/.
Bullock, S. (2002). From the Vault: Richard Morgan Interview (2002). *Saxon Bullock*. Retrieved from http://www.saxonbullock.com/2014/04/never-mind-the-cyberpunks-an-interview-with-richard-morgan-2002/.
Cavallaro, D. (2000). *Cyberpunk and Cyberculture*. New Brunswick: Athlone Press.
Cline, E. (2011). *Ready Player One*. London: Random House.
Deeley, M. (Producer) & Scott, R. (Director). (1982). *Blade Runner* [Motion picture]. United States The Ladd Company.
Eggertsen, C. (2018, February 1). "Altered Carbon": Inside the Drama's 15-year road to Netflix. *Hollywood Reporter*. Retrieved from https://www.hollywoodreporter.com/.
Featherstone, M., & Burrows, R. (1995). *Cyberspace/cyberbodies/cyberpunk*. London: Sage.

Frewer, M. (Actor). (1985). *Max Headroom: 20 minutes into the future*. United States: Chrysalis.
Flood, A. (2018, February 13). Altered Carbon author Richard Morgan. *The Guardian*. Retrieved from https://www.theguardian.com/.
Hutcheon, L. (1985). *A Theory of Parody*. London: Methuen.
Jameson, F. (1991). *Postmodernism: Or, the Cultural Logic of Late Capitalism*. Durham: Duke University Press.
Johnston, K. (2011). *Science Fiction Film: A Critical Introduction*. London: Bloomsbury Academic.
Joyner, J. (2018). Why 'Ready Player One' and its erasure of black culture is harmful. *Okayplayer*. Retrieved from https://www.okayplayer.com/.
Kosove, A. (Producer), Johnson, B. (Producer), Yorkin, B. (Producer), Yorkin, .S. (Producer) & Villenueve, D. (Director). (2017). *Blade Runner 2049* [Motion picture]. United States: Warner Brothers.
Lavigne, C. (2013). *Cyberpunk Women, Feminism and Science Fiction: A Critical Study*. Jefferson, NC: McFarland.
Lenic, J.G. (Producer) & Kalogridis, L. (Creator). *Altered Carbon*. (2018–). [Series]. United States: Netflix.
McCann, S. (2010). The Hard-Boiled Novel. In *The Cambridge Companion to American Crime Fiction*. Nickerson, C.R. (Ed.). Cambridge: Cambridge University Press. doi:10.1017/CCOL9780521199377.005.
Merás, L. (2018). European Cyberpunk Cinema. *Arts* 7, no. 3: 45. DOI 10.3390/arts7030045.
Morgan, R.K. (2002). *Altered Carbon*. London: Gollancz.
Muncy, J. (2018, February 2). Altered Carbon may not be the cyberpunk show you're looking for." *Wired*. Retrieved from https://www.wired.com/.
Rickman, G. (2004). *The Science Fiction Film Reader*. New York: Limelight Editions.
Robinson, A. (2018, February 12). Altered Carbon's Blade Runner rehash misses the point of cyberpunk. *The Verge*. Retrieved from https://www.theverge.com/.
Ryan, M. (2018, January 30). TV Review: 'Altered Carbon' on Netflix. *Variety*. Retrieved from https://variety.com/.
Saunders, R. (Director). (2017). *Ghost in the Shell* [Motion picture]. United States: Paramount Pictures.
Spielberg, S. (Director). (2018). *Ready Player One* [Motion picture]. United States: Amblin Entertainment.
Starkey, A. (2018, February 2). Altered Carbon Review: A thrilling series just getting comfortable in its own sleeve. *Metro*. Retrieved from https://metro.co.uk/.
Virtue, G. (2018, February 5). Altered Carbon: has cyberpunk discovered life beyond Blade Runner? *The Guardian*. Retrieved from https://www.theguardian.com/.
Wachowskis (Directors) (1999). *The Matrix* [Motion picture]. United States: Warner Brothers.
Walker-Emig, P. (2018, October 16). Neon and corporate dystopias: why does cyberpunk refuse to move on. *The Guardian*. Retrieved from https://www.theguardian.com/.
Weber, R. (2018, February 15). Finished watching Altered Carbon? Here's the shocking part of the novel's torture scene its showrunner refused to film. *Gamesradar*. Retrieved from https://www.gamesradar.com/.

Another Kind of War

The Manufacturing of History in Altered Carbon

KENNETH MATTHEWS

One of the more quietly subversive elements of *Altered Carbon* is the manufacturing of the past by powerful characters in the present. Throughout the first season, the characters are affected by how the past is assembled around them. Takeshi Kovacs is acutely aware of how the manufacturing of the past occurs: "when the victors rewrite history, it's just another kind of war waged after the battlefield killing is done to murder the memory of the defeated" (*AC* 2, "Fallen Angel"). Kovacs realizes that the real way in which a society deals with the past is determined by the present, and the way that he interacts with his world reflects that knowledge. This idea is revisited repeatedly throughout the season in different ways and with varying degrees of insight from the characters.

This assemblage of a particular history in the series allows for a portrayal of a cyberpunk future that speaks effectively on contemporary concerns of misinformation in the post-truth political environment while maintaining a safe distance from any particular political agenda. The concepts of time and history are front and center for *Altered Carbon*. In a world where money buys near-immortality, traditional notions of history and past become a bit muddy; however, this change in tradition highlights the way real-world societies interact with and manipulate the past. While the word "manipulate" carries an insidious connotation, one should understand that it is a part of the default process that comes with the growth of a culture. By changing the way humans age and die, *Altered Carbon* provides the viewer with a different perspective on his/her own society and past. Viewing the series through a lens of New Historicism reveals a complex manufacturing of history that is dependent upon the complexity of power in the present of the narrative. To fully understand the way in which the show handles how time and history interact, one can look at the way that critics and theorists are reconciling their present with its manufactured history. The first part of understanding that reconciliation is understanding the problem that modern societies have with time.

The Problem of Time

Much of the modern thought on how a society interacts with media (newspapers, TV, the Internet, and social media) is so concerned with what is being transmitted through media that it fails to account for the medium itself. In "The Medium Is the Message" (1964), Marshall McLuhan offers insight into how a society interacts with a given medium by highlighting the fact that the content of a medium should not be the focus of analysis. The focus instead should be the medium itself: "This is merely to say that the personal and social consequences of any medium—that is, of any extension of ourselves—result from the new scale that is introduced into our affairs by each extension of ourselves, or by any new technology" (McLuhan, 1964, p. 19). That is to say that the things carried by the medium have far less societal impact than the carrier of those things. The importance of any individual consciousness carried in a stack cannot compare to the technology that allows human consciousness to be carried in what amounts to basically a flash drive. The results of that technology are wide-spread and encompass much of what *Altered Carbon* is actually about. The discussion of the feasibility of such technology is a matter of current debate, but for the sake of the narrative of the show, one must accept that humans have unlocked the ability to download consciousness. In doing so, however, humans have only modified an existing and powerful technology: literacy.

At first sight the link between literacy and any possible problem with time might not be obvious. Literacy allows for the recording of facts. It also moves a society away from a dependency on human memory and orality as the main means of data transmission. These advantages, however, come with unintended consequences. McLuhan's warning concerning technological advances is for every form of technology. Literacy is woven so tightly into modern society and thought, that it takes deliberate detachment to understand its influence and consequences.

In what can sometimes be a source of confusion, McLuhan decided to title his book *The Medium Is the Massage* (1967). In the book, he expands upon the ideas within his article "The Medium Is the Message," by taking advantage of a combination of pictures and text, with graphic designer Quentin Fiore providing pictures that either contextualize or problematize McLuhan's thoughts on technology. While the book aims to decenter the traditional modes of thought that accompany literacy, there are sections that explicitly state what McLuhan wants to convey. One of these sections discusses the relationship between literacy and modes of thought:

> Western history was shaped for some three thousand years by the introduction of the phonetic alphabet [sic], a medium that depends solely on the eye for comprehension. The alphabet is a construct of fragmented bits and parts which have no semantic meaning in themselves, and which must be strung together in a line, bead-like, and in prescribed order. Its use fostered and encouraged the habit of perceiving all environment in visual and spatial terms—particularly in terms of a space and of a time that are uniform, [continuous] and [connected] [McLuhan and Fiore 1967, p. 45].

According to McLuhan, the very use of writing has affected the way that literate societies view the world. If a society interacts on a daily basis with a medium that requires linearity to make sense and this society uses that medium as the way to transfer and retain vital information, then the processes in the brain that are required to operate in that manner take the front seat. The scope of this idea, again, is large enough that it changes entire societies' thought processes: a default of linearity in terms of time and history.

So far, the focus regarding understanding a history has been on cultural interactions between the present and the past, and how both constitute what a society thinks of as a history. This can be applied to the world of *Altered Carbon*. Despite being a show that relies on a large technological breakthrough for its core concept, the science is secondary to the world and people that have resulted from the technology. In fiction, this is acceptable; however, claiming that history is not fixed in the real world could benefit with some scientific backing. Fortunately, there are scientists that call into question the default of linearity. Take, for example, the concept presented by Stephen Hawking and Leonard Mlodinow in their book *The Grand Design*:

> Quantum physics tells us that no matter how thorough our observations of the present, the (unobserved) past, like the future, is indefinite and exists only as a spectrum of possibilities.
>
> The universe, according to quantum physics, has no single past or history. The fact that the past takes no definite form means that observations you make on the system in the present affect its past [2010, p. 82].

Hawking and Mlodinow claim that the unobserved past is indefinite, and the choices made in the present can affect the past. Obviously, they are referring to things outside the realm of everyday life, and reality demands of a person to function as if the past were solid. Their insight, however, cannot be ignored when one attempts to demonstrate that linearity is not the only way in which to negotiate the past and present. In terms of how these points interact in the world of *Altered Carbon*, understanding the fluidity of time will help to bring out the ways in which the past and present affect each other.

When considering what a stack actually does—regarding the scientific understanding of time—one can see that it really only reinforces the concepts of literacy and linearity. The missing time during which Laurens Bancroft "dies" is only possible because the technology relies on the linearity of literacy. Information is backed up from the stack which is little more than writing it down digitally. For Bancroft, information stops at the last point of backing up and continues from that point on with hours of information missing in-between. This however is his reality in which he must function. His linear brain stitches together an unbroken reality the same way that most modern people interact with and negotiate history as well. Linear thought dictates that despite large gaps in understanding and knowledge there is an order that occurs and a line of causality that continues in a forward motion, which is most often referred to as progress. While science seems to show that linearity is an imposed system that does not necessarily reflect the truth of the situation, it appears that traditional thoughts and attitudes on history rely on and benefit from the linear approach. There is, however, evidence to support the idea that this approach does not provide an accurate picture of reality and may, in fact, be a dangerous way to view history.

In the introduction to his book, *Archaeology of Knowledge*, Michel Foucault outlines the problematic way in which people traditionally interact with history:

> For many years now historians have preferred to turn their attention to long periods, as if, beneath the shifts and changes of political events, they were trying to reveal the stable, almost indestructible system of checks and balances, the irreversible processes, the constant readjustments, the underlying tendencies that gather force, and are then suddenly reversed after centuries of continuity, the movements of accumulation and slow saturation, the great silent, motionless bases that traditional history has covered with a thick layer of events [Foucault, 1989, p. 3].

Foucault focuses here on the artificial nature inherent within the traditional mode of interacting with a history, and the remainder of his book is built on the idea of disabusing the reader of that traditional mode of thinking. The linearly-focused mind wants to see a pattern of progress and an orderly march forward. Foucault, however, does not agree with this interaction:

> There are the epistemological acts and thresholds described by Bachelard: they suspend the continuous accumulation of knowledge, interrupt its slow development, and force it to enter a new time, cut it off from its empirical origin and its original motivations, cleanse it of its imaginary complicities; they direct historical analysis away from the search for silent beginnings, and the never-ending tracing-back to the original precursors, toward the search for a new type of rationality and its various effects [1989, pp. 4–5].

Foucault recognizes moments and acts that direct attention away from the traditional modes of thought concerning history. There are times that break this notion of progress and order and demand that the person interacting with history stop focusing on the attempts at finding the origins and embrace a "new type of rationality" instead. This breaking of "progress" calls attention to the fiction of ordered, purposeful linearity.

In the article "Theses on the Philosophy of History" (2017), Walter Benjamin writes about the dangers of fascism. During the time of the publication of his article, fascism was not just a word being bandied about in online comment sections. It was a reality that had burned a path of destruction across the globe, and the threat of capture by the Nazis would lead to Benjamin's suicide. Reconciling a world that espoused notions of progress and enlightenment while allowing the rise of fascism was of paramount importance to him. Though Benjamin is a Cultural Materialist, many of his ideas exemplify and demonstrate concepts that are key to the New Historicist's understanding of the way that the present interacts with and affects the past. For Benjamin, the historian should be able to look back over history and see the fabrications that led to the "present which is not a transition but in which time stands still and has come to a stop" (2017, p. 742). The historian cannot view "events like the beads of a rosary"; instead, one must "[grasp] the constellation which his own era has formed with a definite earlier one" and that will create a "conception of the present as the 'time of now'" (p. 743). For Benjamin, this was the point of action when time pauses. The historian can look back over the assembled mess of history and "seize hold of a memory as it flashes up at a moment of danger" (p. 738). This description provides a detailed example of the way in which a historian should interact with their present and past in order to navigate a history.

Throughout *Altered Carbon*'s first season the success or failure of individuals seems to hinge on how well they negotiate the present and past. The past and present are colliding in the story whether through memories and history or through actual characters reemerging from the past. The chance of characters and memories shifting temporally is increased by the technological plot device of the stack, but even with this breakthrough, the possibilities of the plot are limited to the current concepts on how to interact with the past in the present.

The distance afforded by fiction allows a society to examine its present through the fantastic future. This future, however, cannot function as a real glimpse into what may come because science fiction is only a cloudy mirror to the past. In *Simulacra and Simulation*, Jean Baudrillard outlines the problematic relationship between science fiction and the past:

> Perhaps science fiction from the cybernetic and hyperreal era can only exhaust itself, in its artificial resurrection of "historical" worlds, can only try to reconstruct in vitro,

down to the smallest details, the perimeters of a prior world, the events, the people, the ideologies of the past, emptied of meaning, of their original process, but hallucinatory with retrospective truth [Baudrillard, 2017, p. 123].

The quotation marks around the word historical emphasize the fictious nature of the modern interpretation of a history. One can know facts and figures about a society, but not experiencing the daily life or living through the events that influenced each decision within that society makes it impossible to know the truth of that time; therefore, real truth is replaced by the "retrospective truth." This is, of course, exemplified in *Altered Carbon* by almost everyone looking back on the time of the Uprising. Kovacs is consistently referred to as a terrorist. Part of this, is that he was on the losing side of history. The other part is that everyone he interacts with in the present has no way of overcoming the temporal distance between the present and Kovacs' time of origin.

In "New Historicisms" (2017) Louis Montrose summarizes and expands on the critical lens of New Historicism. Since so much of the lens focuses on the way that the present affects the past and an honest interpretation of that relationship, then a firm grounding in New Historicism, serves to benefit any discussion that aims to understand how the present affects our knowledge of the past. In his article, Montrose positions the poststructuralist orientation to history—regarding literary studies—as a "reciprocal concern with the historicity of texts and the textuality of histories" (Montrose, 2017, p. 823). This sounds like an aphorism, but there is a significant amount of meat to the statement, and Montrose continues to break it down:

> By the *historicity of texts*, I mean to suggest the historical specificity, the social and material embedding, of all modes of *writing*—including not only the texts that critics study but also the texts in which we study them; thus, I also mean to suggest that historical, social, and material embedding of all modes of *reading* [2017, p. 823].

Even the place of the critic, by necessity, must be considered part of the embedded historical specificity of the text, once again showing that textual understanding is bound up in the present, but Montrose goes on to explain the fabricative and textual nature of history:

> By the *textuality of histories*, I mean to suggest, in the first place, that we can have no access to a full and authentic past, to a material existence that is unmediated by the textual traces of the society in question; and, furthermore, that the survival of those traces rather than others cannot be assumed to be merely contingent but must rather be presumed to be at least partially consequent on subtle processes of selective preservation and effacement—processes like those that have produced the traditional humanities curriculum [2017, p. 823].

This of course echoes Kovacs' opinion of how history is manufactured. Both Montrose and Kovacs describe this as a process that is premeditated and deliberate. While there is certainly a great deal of premeditation involved, the fact is that so many of the negative consequences in the selection of surviving traces are, in fact, unconscious and therefore substantially more dangerous.

The Negative Effects of Transmitting a Culture

For Laurens Bancroft, Takeshi Kovacs is a cultural icon that encapsulates the past. For the Meth, Kovacs is not a real person in the sense that Bancroft and other Meths are real people. Kovacs is the "Last Envoy." Bancroft's preoccupation with items from the time of the "Uprising" is described throughout the season in terms that border on obsession. While Bancroft's murder investigation is important to him, it might be argued that he was just waiting for a reason to possess and use the most prestigious surviving item from the time of the "Uprising" which is, of course, Kovacs. Within this process of possession and use, Bancroft demonstrates the real-world issues inherent within the movement and transmission of culture. This especially applies to the way that cultural movements and transmissions interact with the present and the manufactured past. The movement of culture and the baggage that accompanies cultural relics are both key components to the way that a given culture creates and interacts with a past. As such, it is important that a culture be fully cognizant of the things being transmitted via cultural items.

To make understanding the dangers of such a transmission easier, one can look again to the work of Walter Benjamin. His insight into the place of a previous culture inside a separate culture's present understanding of the previous culture will highlight the dangerous precedent set by Bancroft and his real-world counterparts. Benjamin's insight begins by seeming to run parallel to Kovacs' view on creating history as the victor creates the history they want shown: "Whoever has emerged victorious participates to this day in the triumphal procession in which the present rulers step over those who are lying prostrate" (2017, p. 739). Benjamin, however, adds in a layer that is not normally addressed:

> According to traditional practice, the spoils are carried along in the procession. They are called cultural treasures, and a historical materialist views them with cautious detachment. For without exception the cultural treasures he surveys have an origin which he cannot contemplate without horror. They owe their existence not only to the efforts of the great minds and talents who have created them, but also to the anonymous toil of their contemporaries. There is no document of civilization which is not at the same time a document of barbarism [2017, p. 739].

According to Benjamin, the very act of selecting the cultural treasures adds the taint of barbarism. The items are not allowed to continue and to be of importance without being pushed forward (if only through approval) by the conquering power. This idea supports Montrose's concept of textual traces and their selection. The conquering power and those that benefit from it set the standard through things like legislation or signs of affluence (culture). Benjamin, however, is focusing on the unconscious process because it is harder to see, at least initially. It is embedded in a way that is reminiscent of McLuhan's concern with technology and the message that accompanies a new technological shift. The process that accompanies the movement of a cultural treasure hides its barbaric origin. The "Roman" alphabet that fills so many books cannot exist without its history of being subsumed or imposed through conquest. The victors not only decide what history to write, but they also choose what letters will write that history.

Kovacs' function as Bancroft's cultural icon turns the Envoy into a living, breathing cultural treasure, with all of the attached complications. He is a trophy for the Meth—a work of art from a bygone area. Bancroft is a conquering power in the story and his wealth allows him to purchase Kovacs. Much of the friction and excitement revolves around Kovacs trying to reconcile his place as an object. He carries with him the history and conflict that accompany any cultural treasure. As such, his very existence and every action he takes serve as extensions of Bancroft's transmission of the Meth's cultural treasure into the present.

If one understands how the manufacturing of history and the dangers of cultural transmissions work in the fiction of *Altered Carbon*—and in the real-world past—it should be possible for an individual to interact with the real-world present in a deliberate manner. This interaction is necessary if one intends to try to break the cycle of barbarism that accompanies conquest and the seizing of power.

Post-Truth and Fabricating History

As most good science fiction does, *Altered Carbon* allows important issues to be discussed without specific political motivation. The understanding of the manufacturing of history and the demonstrations of dangerous cultural transmissions displayed in the show support the idea that a society should be aware of how the present and the past interact. With that in mind, Walter Benjamin's concern with the transmission of fascism through culture should still be a concern today. The real-world implications of his writing show that severe, negative effects can accompany ignorance on this subject.

The 2016 election of Donald Trump capped off one the most divisive campaigns in U.S. history. These words from the Stanford History Education Group came fresh on the election's heels: "At present, we worry that democracy is threatened by the ease at which disinformation about civic issues is allowed to spread and flourish" (Stanford, 2016, p. 5). The bending of the truth and outright lies happened in many campaigns before, but the concerning new trend was the response to being caught on a lie: lying some more. Tell the constituents that the person accusing them of lying is a liar. Say it enough and you can create your own truth. This, of course, violates the ethical standards to which candidates should be held. In the book *Rhetorical Criticism: Perspectives in Action*, Forbes I. Hill describes how these situations should work regarding ethos:

> Persuasive discourse is constructed so that there are usually a large number of ethos claims. Ethos is basically an interpretation by the audience of qualities possessed by a speaker as the speaker delivers his message. Thus, by the way a speaker argues, an audience makes judgements about his intelligence, character, and goodwill. A speaker becomes unpersuasive if he has to claim directly, "I did not have sexual relations with that woman" [Bill Clinton] or "I'm honest in my dealings with people" [Mitt Romney]. If he needs to state it in this bald way, he has already lost credibility [2016, pp. 76–77].

Within the post-truth environment of the election, however, flagrant manipulations of the speaker were not met with any consequence. In fact, confronting the claim with enough force and misinformation seemed to actually benefit the speaker.

In his *New York Times* article "Googling Is Believing: Trumping the Informed Citizen," Michael P. Lynch wrote about the current political process and how misinformation affects it. The article begins by explaining Marco Rubio's attempts to discredit Donald Trump during a debate. Rubio had the audience google "Donald Trump and Polish workers" (2016). Lynch says that the number of searches for those terms and for "Trump University" went up, but the information provided by the searches did little to change the mind of Trump's supporters or even perturb Trump himself (2016).

Lynch writes that Rubios's tactic as well as the response from Trump and his supporters reveal "an interesting, and troubling, new change in attitude about a philosophical foundation of democracy: the ideal of an informed citizenry" (2016). One can easily see the connections between the dystopic future in *Altered Carbon* and the present political climate. As powerful Meths bend rules and society to their whims, they merely say that this is the way that things are done and have been done for ages. It is difficult for an individual to argue with someone who has outlived them by centuries and controls the political and legal landscape.

This fabrication of reality and history—both by modern politicians and by the Meths—resembles a warning issued by Friedrich Nietzsche in "The Will to Power":

> Exactly the same thing could have happened with categories of reason: they could have prevailed, after much groping and fumbling. Through their relative utility— There came a point when one collected them together, raised them to consciousness as a whole—and when one commanded them, i.e., when they had the effect of a command—From then on, they counted as a priori, as beyond experience, as irrefutable. And yet perhaps they represent nothing more than expediency of a certain race and species—their utility alone is their "truth"—[2017, p. 468].

When enough power and time is put behind an idea, it can come to be taken as truth, no matter how horrible the initial idea. One need only look at the Holocaust or slavery to see just how far this can be taken. For the characters in *Altered Carbon*, an example would be the way in which to many characters a death only mattered if the stack was destroyed. Any other damage to the "shell" was of no consequence. There were only a handful of characters that thought differently. For most of the society, the body a person was born into could be replaced and the "real person" still remain alive. As a result, a violent world evolved that skewed concepts of morality to a degree that left most of the characters broken in some way. Again, it is easy to distance oneself through fiction, but the real-world implications remain.

General Conclusion

The world of *Altered Carbon* shows how history is manufactured through the manipulation (both intentional and unintentional) of the past during the present. A default view of matters through linearity would have one believe that history is fixed and solid; however, an honest accounting of how the present affects the past is necessary to avoid problems that inherently accompany the progress of time. The least of said problems is a lazy acceptance of the negative attributes that accompany conquests. One should not think of armed conflict alone when thinking of conquests: again, the Roman alphabet has a history that involves armed conflict and quiet acts of colonization.

While this insight allows for a deeper understanding of the world of *Altered Carbon*, the implications for the real world should not be ignored. The science fiction presented by the show provides a safe look at the way that the past and present can interact. The show heightens these collisions by having characters and features that can actually stand in for these concepts. Takeshi Kovacs is a cultural treasure possessed and used by the conqueror. He brings with him the barbarism of the past and the confirmation of Laurens Bancroft's authority. While stacks allow a character to live well beyond the normal lifespan for a human, the only ones who can use this to be effectively immortal are the Meths. This longevity allows them to manipulate truth and society. This is not an issue in the real world, but it highlights the dangerous features of those who are in power. When a person can manipulate history and make enough people share his/her "version" of the past, then their "truth" becomes reality.

REFERENCES

Baudrillard, J. (2017). *Simulacra and Simulation*. Glaser, S.F. (Trans.). Ann Arbor: The University of Michigan Press.
Benjamin, W. (2017). Theses on the Philosophy of History. In *Literary Theory: An Anthology*. Rivkin, J., & Ryan, M. (Eds.) 3rd ed., Blackwell Publishing, pp. 466–470.
Foucault, M. (1989). *Archaeology of Knowledge*. Sheridan Smith, A.M. (Trans.). London: Routledge.
Hawking, S., & Mlodinow, L. (2010). *The Grand Design*. New York: Bantam.
Hill, F.I. (2016). The Traditional Perspective. In *Rhetorical Criticism: Perspectives in Action*. Kuypers, J.A. (Ed.). Lanham, MD: Rowman and Littlefield, pp. 69–90.
Lenic, J.G. (Producer) & Kalogridis, L. (Creator). *Altered Carbon*. (2018–). [Series]. United States: Netflix.
Lynch, M.P. (2016, March 9). Googling Is Believing: Trumping the Informed Citizen. *The New York Times*. Retrieved from http://opinionator.blogs.nytimes.com/.
McLuhan, M., & Fiore, Q. (1967). *The Medium Is the Message*. New York: Random House.
_____. (1964). The Medium Is the Message. In *Understanding Media: The Extensions of Man*. Critical ed., Gordon, W.T. (Ed.). Berkeley: Gingko Press.
Montrose, L. (2017). New Historicisms. In *Literary Theory: An Anthology*. Rivkin, J., & Ryan, M. (Eds.) 3rd ed., Hoboken: Blackwell Publishing, pp. 809–831.
Nietzsche, F. (2017). The Will to Power. In *Literary Theory: An Anthology*. Rivkin, J., & Ryan, M. (Eds.) 3rd ed., Hoboken: Blackwell Publishing, pp. 466–470.
Stanford History Education Group (2016, November 22). Evaluating Information: The Cornerstone of Civic Online Reasoning. http://www.west-info.eu/files/Executive-Summary-11.21.161.pdf.

The Present of the Dead

Spectral Ideology in Altered Carbon

Aldona Kobus

Introduction: "The future belongs to ghosts"

Jacques Derrida's 1993/1994 French and English publications of *Specters of Marx*, *Ghostly Matters* by Avery Gordon from 1997 and Wendy Brown's *Politics Out of History* from 2001 mark the beginning of the "spectral turn" in cultural theory (Blanco & Peeren, 2013b, p. 337). Since the 1990s haunting has become a pervasive conceptual metaphor (Blanco & Peeren, 2013a, p. 1), inspiring multiple interpretations of a broad variety of texts, although it is mostly applied to texts related to retrofuturism, cultural memory and the persistence of the past (Fisher, 2013, p. 44). The Derridean concept of hauntology is extremely useful in the analysis of cyberpunk, a genre which consists of: highly technologized daily life, cybernetic and biochemical modifications, a dystopian "end of history," neo-noir conventions and gothic atmosphere mixed together to represent a future that we do not wish for but that we know is coming.

In the Netflix series *Altered Carbon* (Lenic & Kalogridis, 2018–) the past that comes to haunt the future extends beyond the genre's conventions and becomes a central part of the series' body. The transmission of consciousness between sleeves through stacks has all the characteristics of haunting, as it does not allow the past to die and be mourned—and so be learned from. The impossibility of burying the past is what evokes specters. Various ghosts and ghost-like forms haunt the cityscape of Bay City. Takeshi Kovacs (Joel Kinnaman/Will Yun Lee/Byron Mann), the protagonist of the series, experiences his own form of haunting—presented by the voice and hallucinations of his long lost leader and lover Quellcrist Falconer (Renée Elise Goldsberry) as well as his sister, Raileen (Dichen Lachman).

This essay examines various forms of haunted existence presented in *Altered Carbon* and the purpose of the perpetual returns of the past. Deconstructivist approach is used here to analyze specters and states in every layer of the Netflix series: the "ghost" of Edgar Allan Poe (Chris Conner) and the ghostly presence of Lizzie Elliot (Hayley Law), the returns of the dead through resleeving, the haunting of Takeshi Kovacs and the return of the past in the ideology of Envoys. *Altered Carbon* is a curious example of a vision of the future told through the past. It corresponds well with Derrida's statement that ontology and ethics are only possible "between life and death" (Derrida, 1994, p. 14). *Altered Carbon* stays very true to Derrida's idea of hauntology by letting the past teach the heroes and the viewers difficult lessons, and representing the dangers of losing the connections to one's cultural and personal past.

Ghost's Demands: Contexts of Haunting

Hauntology (a portmanteau of "haunting" and "ontology") refers to a disjunction of time or history in which the presence of being is replaced by a differed (different, Othered) Thing (specter)—an embodied ghost that is neither dead nor alive, neither present nor absent. According to Derrida, the specter is "a certain phenomenal and carnal form of the spirit … neither soul nor body, and both one and the other" (1994, p. 5). Spirits and ghosts become specters by appearing, making themselves visible, taking the semblance of the body or returning to the body (spiritualizing the body). What exactly is the spirit, the uncanny Thing that haunts us? The past that becomes visible, reminding us about itself. Specters are making visible what is always present. Being haunted means to experience the everpresent elements of the past in the nowness (p. 20). By the means of haunting, the past becomes visible in order to hold us accountable, which means recognizing the past as "the all source from which something comes" and will come (pp. 18–19). The past is what is supposed to come, which is why time is defragmented, and chronological order is a historical fiction. One of the flagship slogans of *Altered Carbon*—"Let the dead speak!"—may be seen as a postulate of Derridean hauntology. The slogan appears in the series in a similar context, in relation to Proposition 653, a bill that would have murder victims resleeved in order to testify against their killers. This is, essentially, a literal approach to the Derridean metaphor. The past will bluntly hold us accountable.

The Derridean specter is always simultaneously a reminder/remnant of the past—*revenant* as well as *arrivant*, the forerunner of "what has not yet arrived" (Blanco & Peeren, 2013a, p. 13). The specter focuses on the future in its connection to the present and the past, the interactions between the present and the past, and the function of the past in the process of shaping the future. Wendy Brown sees haunting as something that "signals the unbidden imposition of parts of the past on the present, and the way in which the future is always already populated with certain possibilities derived from the past" (Brown, 2000, p. 36) and Blanco and Peeren add to that statement the notion of hunting as "the potential for different re-articulations of these possibilities" (2013a, p.13). Hauntology makes it possible for us to reinterpret the past and use it as the tool for change. Hauntology is as much about the past as it is about the future. Thus it is possible for Derrida to say, "the future belongs to ghosts" (Derrida, 2013, p. 38). Living with the spirits, being haunted means to reconsider how the past is present and absent at the same time, at any given moment "but also how the past can open up the possibilities for the future" (Blanco & Peeren, 2013a, p.14). It is that recognition of diversity (difference) in unrealized possibilities that makes the approach of hauntology deconstructivist. It also interestingly reverses the order of science fiction, which usually speculates about the possibilities of the future. However, this dimension of speculative fiction pertains equally to the present as a dimension of shaping the future. The time becomes a spiral, and its particular elements constantly overlap.

The popularity of references made between the Derridean concept of hauntology, and science fiction and cyberpunk, so genres based on temporal shifts and presenting potential visions of the future in the context of current problems and needs, does not surprise, either. In particular, cyberpunk provides a broad research field due to its pessimistic attitude. Corruption, gentrification and discrimination are a standard background of cyberpunk stories, in which only few can afford to access the technological miracles and the vision of the future promised by science fiction. *Altered Carbon* is not an exception. Only the class of immortals known as Meths (named in reference to the biblical Methuselah) can afford a luxurious lifestyle based on long-term (almost eternal) accumulation of capital. The others have to be satisfied with the bodies they were born into and the crumbs from the table of the scientific and technological revolutions. Cyberpunk presents systemic problems, but it rarely offers solutions; if it does, they are external, outside the corrupted justice system. Cyberpunk depicts the present as the future and the past; at the same time, it discusses the hereditary nature of the system that cannot be changed by any invention, and the deepening problems, most notably social and technological exclusion. This means that cyberpunk is, to a large extent, a retrospective genre, as it provides us with an experience of the future as something that is coming, which is effectively shown in *Altered Carbon*.

City of Ghosts: Bay City and the Origins of Cyberpunk

A prominent ghost-like presence within the series is Poe, the AI owner of the Raven Hotel. The AI is based on the famous writer Edgar Allan Poe. Not only are the AI's appearance and the style of the hotel faithful representations of the early American Gothic aesthetic, but it also speaks using crypto-quotes from the writer's poems and stories. He looks like Edgar Allan Poe and speaks his words, which makes him not so much a copy but rather the ghost of Poe himself—a ghost that is haunting the Netflix series as a reminder of cyberpunk's past.

Although Poe's appearance is holographic, he describes the hotel as his body (*AC* 3, "In a Lonely Place"). He is, at the same time, free and grounded. His consciousness can travel everywhere on the Net but his "body" is located in one place and therefore easy to destroy. His condition is in contradiction to the Meths' status, which can be described as a stable consciousness (or identity) in powerful and exchangeable bodies. While Poe's "body" is unchangeable, unlike the sleeves, he is similarly not limited by the location of said body. In this way, the AI already enriches the world presented in the series, as it becomes a counterpoint for the dominating discourse regarding humanity being threatened by stacks and sleeves. This coincides with the fascination with humanity shown by the AI. Poe is interested in humans, stating to the other AIs that he finds them fascinating. He also says that "studying humanity has become his greatest aspiration" (*AC* 3, "In a Lonely Place"). This makes him a pariah among other AIs, who consider humans lower life forms, mortal and limited, useful only as a source of profits, simultaneously merchandise and consumers (*AC* 3, "In a Lonely Place").

What distinguishes Poe not only from other AIs depicted in the series, but also from the very concept of artificial intelligence in science fiction, is his emotional approach. Isaac Asimov termed the discourse of AI in science fiction to be "Frankenstein's complex," as it focuses on the domination of machine over its creator. The opposite of this discourse are discussions over the fact that the AI will never equal humans due to its limitations, resulting from lack of emotionality. A computer has no emotions. Machines can be powerful, but they will not be human. This motif recurs in such fundamental works as *2001: A Space Odyssey* (Kubrick, 1968), *Alien* (Scott, 1979), *Blade Runner* (Ridley Scott, 1982), *Tron* (Lisberger, 1982), *The Terminator* (Cameron, 1984) and *The Matrix* (Wachowski sisters, 1999).

Poe's motivation is purely emotional. We learn about this before we even meet him, when Kristin Ortega (Martha Higareda) warns Kovacs against staying in the hotel run by an AI, saying that it is like "sleeping with a stalker"

(*AC* 1, "Out of the Past"). The AIs tend to be overprotective and very attached to their guests. However, this is not the case for other AIs presented in the series who are not Poe. He is defined by emotional connection and deep sensitivity. In spite of not being human, Poe is one of the most empathetic characters in the series, in stark contrast to the brutal and often cruel humans. He is the first to express emotions, which is presented in a scene when Vernon reunites with his wife, Ava (currently in a male sleeve). He even performs psychosurgery on Lizzie Elliot and helps her cope through her defrag. Poe can be described as a benevolent spirit of the series, providing the protagonists with every asset they might need. He is even capable of self-sacrifice and betrayal of his own kind for the sake of people he has come to love.

The choice of Edgar Allan Poe as a model for the AI serves not only to introduce stylistic elements of the Gothic into the series, but also to emphasize the emotional character of the AI. After all, the Gothic literary turn of the 18th century constitutes an expression of the unconsciousness of the Enlightenment, giving voice to the repressed emotions and fears, the irrational side of the human nature. This tradition was continued by the literary horror of the 19th century, including American Gothic authored by Poe. Thus, the AI in the series becomes a paradoxical creation, an emotional machine, capable of matching humans, and even surpassing them.

Artificial intelligence presents a case crucial for cyberpunk, that of privileging the mind over the body, the pursuance of freeing potentially limitless body from the prison of materiality. As such AI seems to be an equivalent of "the final frontier" of space in science fiction—the last untouched realm with the enormous impact on human imagination. Cyberpunk narratives regarding AI express not only the fear of losing humanity as a result of cybernetic modifications of the human body, but also anxieties and hopes connected with the possibility of machines "becoming human." At the point when our humanity is questioned, can a machine become more human than us? Poe's fascination with people illustrates this motif of genre speculations. In the end, Poe is presented as more human than a part of the privileged Meths class or street criminals, which makes it possible for him to state "you don't deserve to be human" (*AC* 10, "The Killers") toward an actual human being. At the same point, Lizzie says that "whatever it means to be human, Eddie… you are" (*AC* 10, "The Killers"). Undoubtedly, Poe is seen as human by some characters within the diegesis of the series. While *Altered Carbon* represents both threads of the discourse regarding artificial intelligence in science fiction, the positive one, within which AI becomes a response to human problems, becomes decidedly more emphasized, and expressed in an almost utopian way in the character of Poe.

In the series, Poe plays an important role in representing the genesis and the history of cyberpunk, which is highlighted by the visual transformations of this character. The changes that Poe's holographic representation undergoes in the series reflect the history of the genre, starting with Edgar Allan Poe's proto-crime stories (*The Murders in the Rue Morgue*, *The Mystery of Marie Rogêt* and *The Purloined Letter*), to the aesthetics of noir films (AC 3, "In a Lonely Place"), to the role of AI in contemporary cyberpunk. After learning about Kovacs' mission, Poe decides to get involved in it, drawing his knowledge from old crime stories and adjusting his appearance according to the style of film noir. This is a brief transformation, as Kovacs initially rejects his help, similarly to how in the first episode he refused Poe's offer to become his guide around the city. This offer was equally directed at the audience—the ghost from the past suggested that he could lead us through the futuristic landscape of the series, which can be deemed the essence of cyberpunk. Even in the diegesis of the series Poe is akin to an artifact of a past era. Nobody has stayed in his hotel for over fifty years, as institutions ran by AIs became old fashioned, or even dangerous for their clients.

Poe's aesthetics, his holographic advertisement and macabre decor of The Raven Hotel inscribe themselves into the landscape of the city. Bay City may be termed a single huge visual quote from the classics of the genre. Omnipresent holograms, dirty and crowded streets, street eateries full of hanging lanterns and constantly falling rain are references to such productions as *Ghost in the Shell* (Oshii, 1995) and *Blade Runner*—often to the point of distraction; moreover, every episode is titled after a famous noir film. Poe constitutes a reminder of the roots of cyberpunk, which references the intertextual dimensions of *Altered Carbon*. Bay City is a city of ghosts—not because it is extinct, deserted, but due to the genre weight it carries. What haunts the city is the history of cyberpunk, a certain impasse of narratives within this genre, or exhaustion of the formula. Even the opening credits of the series reference the famous first frames of the cult classic *Ghost in the Shell*: artificial skin falling down from what can be recognized as a synthetic body (here, a sleeve) is a very characteristic visual motif. The first shot of *Altered Carbon* is also a visual quotation from Mamoru Oshii's movie; a naked body floating in an undefined liquid, with an electric cable protruding from the base of the skull is a direct reference to the creation of major Motoko Kusanagi's body. Indeed, this is a charge that was levied at the series as such in critical reviews, as it was described as an imitative work. Such an approach disregard the metatextual dimension of the series, which positively transforms the clichés of the genre. Poe's emotional motivation constitutes an example of such a mechanism. The conviction that a machine may become human is a positive outlook on technological development, a generally atypical solution for the genre which usually focuses on problems and not solutions offered by the cyber-technological revolution.

Poe is a *revenant*, a reminder of the past. He not only represents but also embodies the origins and history of cyberpunk. He is the past itself showing us possibilities for positive reformulations of genres, tropes and conventions. The solution offered by Poe's subplot is not particularly original or subtle. A similar motif of overemotional AI was presented already in Steven Spielberg's *A.I. Artificial Intelligence* (2001). What makes Poe's plotline distinctive is its connection with the past of the genre, the ability to showcase something positive in the macabre, dark roots of cyberpunk. Poe is a specter created for the audience. He is haunting us. He is a constant reminder of the intertextual dimensions of the Netflix series, *Altered Carbon*'s self-consciousness.

Cassandra's Curse: Disjunction of Time, Disjunction of Genre

Another ghost-like character in the series is Lizzie Elliot, a girl trapped in her own mind. After her stack was damaged, she was kept by her father, Vernon, in a virtual-reality environment in order to stay alive. The defragmentation of her mind caused by traumatic experience prevented her from resleeving. Lizzie was stuck in a trauma loop, going through the moment of her sleeve's death over and over again. Eventually she is brought to The Raven Hotel for rehabilitation. As a result of Poe's therapy, the girl regains her equilibrium and is ready to return to her (synthetic) body. Poe's treatment is rather unorthodox—he teaches Lizzie to seek empowerment through martial arts, physical strength and the ability to fight back against oppressors. This arouses justified anxiety in her parents, who do not recognize their daughter in this new person.

Trapped in VR, Lizzie is haunted by her past but she is also haunting her father as an undead image of his mistakes that led to the murder of Lizzie's stack. For Vernon, Lizzie is a *revenant*, a reminder of the happy past that is lost, a time when the family was together. After losing his wife to jail and his child in a murderous assault, Vernon is unable to accept the change and work through it. He just wants to keep things as they used to be and, therefore, he traps Lizzie in agonizing stagnancy. Vernon creates the conditions of his own haunting. The question "who is being haunted by whom?" does not have a clear answer in this case. It might as well be said that Vernon is the malignant spirit that haunts Lizzie.

Lizzie's condition is characterized by enforced silence. She is silenced, unable to speak about what happened to her. She cannot name, and thus locate and work through her trauma. Lizzie's return to health means giving her back her voice. In the meantime, her body speaks, replaying the moment of the assault. However, the body has a virtual character, shaped by Lizzie's mind. The entire VR space is the body here: the dirty alley behind the brothel, in which the assault took place, or which Lizzie associates with the act of violence that happened to her. The VR construct shaped by Lizzie is a message in and of itself. Thus, Lizzie's condition is the condition of the hysteric: the VR environment is a hysterical symptom of a repressed (unspoken) trauma, according to Freud's definition of hysteria. For Freud, hysteria was produced by sexual trauma and repression (Devereux, 2014, p. 24). Hysteria is a vivid memory of a traumatic experience. Eventually Freud would connect hysteria with feminine subjectivity or, rather, the lack of it:

> Hysteria would emerge in Freud's writing ... as the effect of women's inability to achieve identity through the Oedipal moment of recognition: in effect, he suggested, women are always already psychically scarred by the recognition of their own "castration." The "lesson" is thus always already there in the psyche, at least from the Oedipal moment, an effect of the female genitalia conceived as loss and absence [Devereux, 2014, p. 24].

Freudian psychoanalysis is based on the understanding of female subjectivity and identity as the "negated obverse of men ... the castrated Other left behind in the men's completion of the Oedipal process" (Devereux, 2014, p. 25). Lizzie perfectly illustrates these assumptions. Her plotline begins with the condition of the speechless hysteric, whose virtual body expresses the symptoms that she is unable to articulate. The impossibility of articulating them only partially results from physical and mental indisposition (the sleeve's death and the trauma she went through). Partially it is also the result of placing Lizzie in the system of gender and racial oppression as a bi-racial female sex worker. Her entire being can be described as "collateral damage" of the cyberpunk genre, where sex workers are particularly often used to underline the brutality of futuristic worlds. She is almost predestined to victimhood by the power of genre's conventions. *Altered Carbon* itself does not escape this cliché with the character of Anemone, a ruthlessly murdered young prostitute (*AC* 3, "In a Lonely Place"). Lizzie is not a full-fledged subject in the world of heterosexist white hegemony, and as a result, she has no voice—because her story has no meaning. Lizzie's entire plotline serves to provide subjectivity to a character who, in androcentric cyberpunk (Cadora, 1995, pp. 357–359) would be constantly seen as an object.

During her recovery, Lizzie speaks mostly in riddles. She compares herself to Cassandra of Troy, implying she is "remembering things backwards" (*AC* 9, "Rage in Heaven"). For her, time is as defragmented as her mind; she confuses hellos and goodbyes as she is unable to keep the timeline straight. Therefore she becomes an *arrivant*, a herald of the past that is coming—she sees the past in the place of the future. However, her role as an *arrivant* is also to reveal what happened in the past, bring the past to life and, in that way, punish those who harmed her. Remembering the past serves to institute justice. This corresponds directly to Derrida's analysis, according to which law, instituting order, is the legacy of crime, due to the temporal shift between these acts—justice is always late, it happens after the crime, which means that law as such is the fruit of transgression (Derrida, 1994, p. 47). For Lizzie, this is a literal temporal shift, a confusion of the chronological order. For her, the past and the present merge into one course in which everything is the reason and the effect of everything else. Thus, the past and the present undergo constant mutual transformation, offering a potential for change. Undoubtedly, Lizzie is the character who changes the most during the series. The change is so radical that it almost terrifies her family; however, it is due to that change that they have a possibility of rebuilding lost happiness.

The time shift also belongs to the order of a crime story as a retrospective genre, whose aim is to discover what happened in the past in order to punish the perpetrators of a crime. Despite its cyberpunk shell, *Altered Carbon* remains a very correct, classic crime story, including elements such as an impossible murder (a locked room, weapon available only to two people outside the group of suspects) and a gathering of the people who have a motive in one room, where the detective makes his speech (*AC* 8, "Clash by Night"). Clichés of this kind serve to emphasize the genre roots of the series, and are included in the meta-textual dimension of the Netflix production.

The character of Lizzie embodies the tenets of hauntology in the most complete way. She is a specter, a ghost incorporated in a phantasmatic body (VR and synthetic), a *revenant* and an *arrivant* at the same time. As a specter, she makes visible what is present: the transgressions that Meths commit against the lower classes, and therefore, the degeneration of the entire hedonistic cast of the immortals. The crime committed against her is the result of the life Meths lead outside the law, their sexual, sadistic and economic crimes.

Lizzie's plotline ascribes itself into the meta-textual dimension of the Netflix series. Her character undermines the "dead sex worker" cliché. Victimhood is not the end of her story but rather the starting point. Her entire story arc concerns empowerment, which becomes a slogan used by Poe during her treatment to explain his unusual methods to Lizzie's parents. During the therapy, Lizzie regains a sense of power over her own body and mind. The fact that it all takes place in cyberspace, only in the landscape of the mind of a hurt woman, adds an interesting point to the conversation regarding the relationship between the body (sleeve) and the mind, happening within the series. Here, subjectivity means the ability to fight the brutality of the world, to protect oneself and one's close ones, which becomes Lizzie's main goal. Initially the girl resorts to violence and extra-systemic solutions, becomes a destructive force of vigilante justice. In the end, however, her role is to speak in the name of the law and to institute justice through official channels. Her true strength lies not in the ability to throw punches, but to speak, bear witness and publicly accuse.

Lizzie's empowerment does not concern giving her a physical advantage, but rather her voice being heard. She works through her trauma, makes it through the stage of mourning and finds her own language. The story she tells about herself and about what happened to her has a key meaning for the murder mystery in the series. It is not only a footnote to the long list of numerous crimes of the deprived social class that is in power. Subjectivity is found in the moment of killing a sexual degenerate as much as in speaking in the name of the law. Lizzie breaks Cassandra's curse and becomes a female voice heard in the public space, a female voice speaking in the name of the law, the expression of public indictment. Obviously, she first needs to pay a high price for such an opportunity. This is a scheme characterized by Mary Beard in her essay *Women & Power: A Manifesto* (Beard, 2017, p. 20)—a woman speaking, being listened to, is always connected with risk and a certain price. In this case, Lizzie's victimhood allows her to speak and, at the same time, is the very reason she needs to speak. However, it is not the first departure from this scheme. It was already Molly Millions in William Gibson's *Sprawl Trilogy* who was an example of a prostitute who not only managed to survive, but also became the protagonist of a series that defined cyberpunk as a genre. The characters of Lizzie and Molly have many points in common, both having made their way from being sex workers to invincible assassins. Here, *Altered Carbon* makes use of the past of cyberpunk, its roots, in order to redefine the binding schemes of the genre. Therefore, it utilizes in practice the tenets of Derridean hauntology, invoking the unused possibilities of the past—the roots of the genre—in order to change the current condition of cyberpunk, characterized by Cadora as an androcentric narrative. Similarly, many contemporary women writers, such as Lyda Morehouse, Pat Cadigan, Melissa Scott, Amy Thomson and Kathleen Ann Goonan, who write within the genre of cyberpunk, redefine its misogynistic roots. However, Lizzie's voice is significant not only within the genre, but also within the entire Western tradition of silencing women (Beard, 2017, pp. 18–20). Her plotline illustrates the mechanism of oppression described by Beard equally well as it does Derrida's metaphor of haunting. Lizzie is one of the dead who speak in the world of *Altered Carbon*, testifying on the subject of their own death. Thus, similarly to Poe, she constitutes an attempt at re-evaluating the attitude toward the techno-cybernetic revolution in cyberpunk, showcasing a positive relationship with a technology that changes lives. Simultaneously, she introduces a feminist undertone to the series, telling the story of woman becoming a subject, although she still repeats patriarchal schemes in that regard.

Living with Ghosts: The Haunting of Takeshi Kovacs

Takeshi Kovacs is the most haunted character in the series. At first his conversations with his long-dead lover and sister could be described as visual and auditory hallucinations of "sleeve sickness," a side effect of waking in the new sleeve. Over the course of the series, this explanation loses its rationale, as Kovacs engages in conversations with Quell long after the effects of resleeving have passed. Her ghost appears when the protagonist is in need of emotional support and reminds him about lessons Quell taught him 250 years ago. She is the source of emotional comfort for Kovacs as well as the cause of suffering—an undead embodiment of mourning that is still in progress. The haunting of Takeshi Kovacs depicts the work of mourning in action, an attempt at coming to terms with a loss and doing justice to the past. According to Derrida, mourning is not only an emotional process, but an ontological one, a utilization of the remains of the past (Derrida, 1994, p. 29).

The first ghost seen by Kovacs is the specter of his own sister, Reileen, who is entirely conscious of her spectral nature. In her introduction, she informs him that she is not real (*AC* 1, "Out of the Past"). The appearance of the ghost is preceded by retrospective shots of happy moments from their childhood on Harlan's World, an Earth colony on another planet. The specter carries with herself a memory of not only the past, but, above all, of the lost innocence of a child. She also emphasizes Kovacs's loneliness and isolation in the new world in which he was awoken—in the dystopia of capital collected in the hands of immortal beings outside the law, whose arrival was foreseen by Quell.

Eventually Kovacs even faces a clone of his own original sleeve in an underground combat arena, an experience that emphasizes just how far both he and time are out of joint. While being haunted, Kovacs has a vision of throwing away Quell's journal, which he had received from Bancroft. However, he keeps the notebook, which is a significant gesture, meaning that Kovacs agrees to live with the ghosts. Reileen is a perfect *revenant*, an embodied past more than a ghost of an actual person, evidencing how little Kovacs actually knew about his sister when she was alive. Still, she is a *revenant* asking about the future. The question "What you gonna do, Takeshi-kun?" (*AC* 1, "Out of the Past") could be asked by the audience as well when it comes to character motivations. But Rei is asking in the name of the past: "What will you do with me? Reject or keep me?," which is a crucial question in the Derridean hauntology.

Moreover, the conversation with the sister's ghost reverses the order of haunting, signaling that Kovacs is a spectral figure as well:

> REI: What are you doing here, big brother?
> KOVACS: I should be asking you that.
> REI: That's easy. I'm not real. What's your excuse?

Rei asks questions in the name of the past, although we are used to the opposite order. However, according to hauntology, ghosts (the past) initiate the conversation, as it happens in the case of Rei and Kovacs. The ghost appears to ask "what you gonna do [with me]." Moreover, asking about his excuse, Rei emphasizes Kovacs's status as a relic of the past, and thus, a specter. Her appearance has more rationale than resurrecting the last Envoy in the world of *Altered Carbon*, 250 years after the fall of Uprising. In this way, it is highlighted that Kovacs is also a *revenant*, a remainder of a past order.

The ghost of Quell first appears before Kovacs when he considers suicide as a convenient solution for his heartbreak caused by Quell's death. Kovacs is still mourning her, but she is the one to teach him how to transform the work of mourning into something constructive. She does that by reminding him of his identity as an Envoy:

> QUELL: Two hundred and fifty years in long enough. Move on.
> KOVACS: No. You hear me? Never. Not ever.
> QUELL: Than do what you were born to do. What I trained you to do. Make things change…. Finish the mission.

The specter of Quell is as suicidal as Kovacs in this scene. Her demand that Kovacs should "move on" means her spectral form would disappear. After the work of mourning is done and the lesson from the past is learned, there is no need for the specter anymore. Quell pleads to be buried in the past, where she belongs. Her specter is a *revenant*, reminding Kovacs of his lost identity as an Envoy but also about what she would call the "natural order of things"—the necessity of death. The scene has emotional as well as ideological undertones, connected with Quell's teachings regarding the necessity of mortality as the human condition. Quell perfectly understands hauntology, a process, into which she was drawn after her death. Her ghost desires peace. This can happen only if Kovacs makes use of his past as a reservoir of tools for changing the future.

The role of Quell's specter as emotional support for the protagonist is particularly visible in Episode 4, where Quell's appearance in the virtual construct of a torture chamber is intertwined with retrospections from the training of Envoys. The past here is not only recalled, but, above all, made present. It constitutes a starting point for a difficult situation in the present—or, rather, the present is a repetition of the past. What Kovacs experiences has already happened. Retrospective Episodes 4 and 7 showcase how the temporal order becomes upended in the diegesis of the series. Kovacs does not recall the past as much as he continuously experiences it. The pain of torture experienced in the past and the present overlap, and the air he breathes is full of ash from the battlefield where Quell died. The past is not dead, but only now discovered on the level of content. We pay equal attention to discovering what happened (Kovacs's story, the mystery behind Bancroft's murder) and seeing what is yet to come (how Kovacs will solve the murder case). On the level of the message, this means that the past and the present have switched places.

Kovacs's haunting is also interesting in reference to the gender context of showing ghosts on contemporary television, which has been aptly diagnosed by Nelly Strehlau writing about "Women's Ghosts" and "Men's Demons":

> the rendering of men's and women's encounters with haunting can be usefully if simplistically illustrated by a comparison between original *Ghostbusters* (1984), whose male heroes fight dangerous but largely impersonal apparitions, and *Ghost* (1990), whose female protagonist needs to be saved from peril by the ghost of her murdered lover. When approaching the issue of haunting through contemporary American television, a similar opposition may be detected between storiesconcerning male and female characters and their encounters with thespectral, uncanny, otherworldly. Both in the series that treat those stories literally and in the ones that present them figuratively, male protagonists tend to fight demons and monsters more commonly than they come across ghostly apparitions. Some stories which centre around male protagonists, such as those of *Supernatural*, *Grimm*, *The Walking Dead* or *Constantine*, depict a variety of monsters as elements of the world, while more realistic stories, such as *Breaking Bad*, *Justified*, *House MD* or *The Sopranos*, depict addiction or toxic masculinity as demons faced by its heroes [Strehlau, 2017, p. 42].

Kovacs's haunting does not inscribe itself into this identified context of male struggles with ghosts. Quell is not a demon the protagonist needs to face, she does not personify his inner struggle, but, rather, only his suffering, unsolved emotional problems, and, above all, the process of mourning that has not been worked through. This makes Quell's specter closer to the role played by ghosts in the context of haunting of female characters:

> the hauntings range from ones associated with children or sexual partners … to parental figures, particularly mothers … as well as historical *revenants*…. The ghosts of children (whether past or prospective) and revenants of lovers most frequently serve to contain the female characters in more rigid gender and social roles, interpellating them to fulfill their duty to the ghost … [In contrast] historical and maternal specters by demanding a reckoning, ensure the possibility of reconciling with the one's past … leading the female characters into a more hopeful future [Strehlau, 2017, pp. 51–52].

Quell's and Reileen's specters personify everything that Kovacs had lost, above all, a child's innocence, love and family, as well as his purpose in life, thus referring to the core of his identity not only as the Envoy, but also as a person. Kovacs's essential motivation is making certain that nobody will experience what he had suffered together with his sister. His identity is defined through his relationships with women—with his mother and sister and with Quell. Mother and sister merge into one, Rei wears their mother's necklace, a carrier of emotional associations with love and safety. In a certain way, Quell also plays the role of a mother, providing Kovacs with his new identity as an Envoy. The mother's ghost appears in the series indirectly, through these two women characters. This is significant inasmuch as Strehlau emphasizes the importance of a mother's ghost in providing subjectivity to a woman character (2017, p. 52); a similar role is played in the series by this spectral figure, never shown but always present, like the past itself, according to Derridean hauntology. Kovacs states that what their mother taught them gives him guidelines even more primal for his identity than Quell's teachings (*AC* 7, "Nora Inu").

Kovacs's haunting inscribes itself into the female model of hauntology identified by Strehlau, but the specters of his sister and lover do not limit the protagonist to a defined social role prescribed for a man. In that case, the haunting would serve to inscribe Kovacs into the function of a noir film detective, cynical and tired with life. Rather, the emotional work enforced on him by Quell's haunting drives him away from this role, reminding him about the importance of feelings and relationships. She forces him to build a community rather than retreat from it, which is the Envoy's *modus operandi*: "Find ways to inspire loyalty in a few capable locals, even if many of them will ultimately be expendable" (*AC* 7, "Nora Inu"). The problematic part is that Kovacs will not accept the "expendable" part even if it scares him to become attached again. This is visible in Episode 6, "Man with My Face," where Kovacs argues with Quell's ghost as Ortega's life is in peril:

> QUELL: It's in the details. Don't tell me you haven't noticed a pattern here.
> KOVACS: She's not gonna die.
> QUELL: That would be a change for you.
> KOVACS: I won't let it happen. Not this time, not ever again.
> QUELL: This is what you do, love. Stride across the centuries, and death follows, churning in your wake.
> KOVACS: That's poetic.
> QUELL: I'm a figment of your tortured psyche, I say what you're thinking.
> KOVACS: A man who never loves gives no hostage to fortune, to paraphrase a great scientist.
> QUELL: A men who never loves isn't truly a man. To paraphrase you.

The specter of Quell plays the role of devil's advocate here, forcing Kovacs to display an emotional response. She wants him to admit to himself how much he cares about Ortega. It works, causing Kovacs to temporally banish Quell's ghost. For Kovacs to fulfill the duty to Quell's ghost means to be alive again, to feel again, to love again. Not only to be an Envoy but also to be (a) human. She is "leading [Kovacs] into a more hopeful future" (p. 52) with a possible new love interest. The specter of Quell is also an *arrivant*, showing the possibilities open to the protagonist once the work of mourning is complete. However, Quell's role as an *arrivant* exceeds far beyond emotional support for Kovacs, or the subjective dimension of haunting.[1] Her ghost visits not only the protagonist, but also the very series whose narration she co-creates. In this sense, the haunting by Quell is ideological, it heralds the return of the Uprising and the Envoys, signals that their mission had not been finished. For Kovacs, this means destroying the order built on the stacks and sleeves technology, on social inequality based on immortal accumulation of capital. Indeed, Quell's specter marks Kovacs as an *arrivant*, postulating that finishing that task is the reason he was woken up 250 years after the failure of the Uprising. This perfectly summarizes the function of a ghost as an *arrivant*, thus described by Gordon:

> The ghost is ... pregnant with unfulfilled possibility, with the something to be done that the wavering present is demanding. This something to be done is not a return to the past but a reckoning with its repression in the present, a reckoning with that which we have lost, but never had [Gordon, 1991, p. 83].

In the case of *Altered Carbon* "that which we have lost but never had" is the world from Quell's vision, which Kovacs believes in. Sometimes reckoning with the past means not coming to terms with the loss as much as a refusal to acknowledge the failure and an attempt at resuscitating the past, embodying it anew and making it into the future. In this sense, the ideology of hauntology has a reactive dimension, although not necessarily a conservative one. This is particularly so given that the past never returns unchanged—the seed of change is hidden within the past itself. Its reconstruction is always a reconstruction with change, with the possibility of another, an update of the seeds of difference in the reconstructed events (Derrida, 1994, p. 49). This is also perfectly illustrated by *Altered Carbon*—Kovacs finishes the mission given to him by Quell with the support of ghosts and the past, using the Rawling Virus, which had destroyed the Uprising, in order to put an end to the impunity of the Meths.

"Let the dead speak!": The Ideology of Haunting

Quell is the first voice to speak in the series, shapeless and off-frame, co-creating the narration of *Altered Carbon*. What first speaks to the audience is thus a ghost, and it is a ghost teaching a lesson—"First thing you'll learn is that nothing is what is seems" (*AC* 1, "Out of the Past"). At this point, Quell's appearance has no narrative justification; rather, it points to the role of the past in building the structure and the content of the series, especially since what is happening on the screen illustrates her words. What can be initially taken as an erotic scene is, in fact, something else. In *Altered Carbon* the past literally teaches us lessons from the very first minutes, postulating that we get rid of expectations—also those connected with genre conventions, the basic expectations the audience has for any text of culture.

The issue of voice and silencing is extremely important in *Altered Carbon*. In the diegesis of the series, hegemony consists in silencing—people and specters, pacifying the subversive potential of the past through twisting it, which also means being silent about it. The hegemonic ideology of the *Altered Carbon*'s society is based on accepting, or even glorifying the stacks and sleeves technology. This can be evidenced not only by the class of wealthy Meths, relying on this technology to uphold their status and wealth, but also by numerous elements of the diegesis, including the legal order which separates crimes leading to real death (destruction of the stack) and "organic damage," that is, damaging the bodily shell (also in an irreparable way), which does not destroy the stack. The gladiator fights, performed for the entertainment of Meths (resolving with upgrading or downgrading the sleeve respectively in the case of winning or losing), also constitute a part of the hegemonic order. The immortality of people chosen due to their economic advantage has become a commonly accepted fact, as has the exclusivity of the Meths' status.

The character of a lawyer, Omumou Prescott (Tamara Taylor), serves to exemplify this exclusivity. Her main goal is to become one of the Meths, but regardless of how close she seems to be to attaining it, for her clients she does not differ in any way from other relatively mortal people from the lower classes. In their eyes, her role is always limited to being an intermediary between the class of the chosen ones and regular mortals. Her voice is also silenced when she is accused of killing one of the Meths; a cleverly made up lie turns out to be more important than her years of work and supposed friendship with wealthy clients. She is not one of them, so her words have no significance.

In the world of *Altered Carbon* being silent means dying. Religious coding of stacks preventing "resurrecting" the dead due to their religious convictions and the failure of Proposition 653, the aforementioned law according to which murder victims could be resleeved and testify against their killers, are the basic examples of connecting silence and death. Real death is connected with silencing and only those who have the means to avoid it permanently have a voice that counts. The failure of the Uprising also resulted in the silencing of Quell's message, and she was trapped in catchy slogans. A museum exhibition summarizes her as a "Zealot, radical, terrorist" (*AC* 2, "Fallen Angel"). In the eyes of history, the Envoys became brutal murderers of women and children, and the fall of the Uprising—an example of the Protectorate's heroism. History has been rewritten in a way that deprives it of its subversive dimension and unambiguously deems the winner to be right. Kovacs terms the twisting of history as "another kind of war waged to murder the memory of the defeated" (*AC* 2, "Fallen Angel"). Silence (being quiet and forgotten) is once again connected with death. It is thus even more important that Quell is the first voice to speak in the series. *Altered Carbon* constructs a world in which silence is death only to give voice to the dead.

"Let the dead speak" is also the counter-hegemonic slogan of those who demand to implement Proposition 653. It can be also considered the basic tenet of Derridean hauntology. The past is not dead as long as it speaks. The dead should speak—metaphorically, according to Derrida, and literally in the world of *Altered Carbon*. As Derrida notes:

> At a time when a new world disorder is attempting to install its neo-capitalism and neo-liberalism, no disavowal has managed to rid itself of all of Marx's ghosts. Hegemony still organizes the repression and thus the confirmation of a haunting. Haunting belongs to the structure of every hegemony [Derrida, 1994, p. 46].

Silencing is what creates the discourse of haunting. By refusing to acknowledge the subversive dimension of the Uprising, the Meths bring on their own destruction. The past they had destroyed comes back to torture them and uses the tools they had used themselves to destroy the Envoys—this time to hold the class of the immortal accountable for their lawless deeds. It is the irony of history—a tool of hegemony being used to undermine it. In reality, it is the neoliberal, capitalist hegemony of the Meths that creates its own specters. This is why Bancroft and the other Meths became engaged in resleeving Kovacs and bringing him back to the world of the living. Yet again *Altered Carbon* illustrates the mechanism of haunting, deftly weaving Derrida's theses regarding the spectral nature of the past into the plot.

However, the ideological core of the series remains Quell's ghost and her counter-hegemonic message of struggle against immortality as a condition contradictory to humanity. Her political position is spelled out, in a speech directed at the Envoys:

> It's not the Protectorate we're fighting. It's immortality itself. The creation of stacks was a miracle and the beginning of the destruction of our species. A hundred years from now, a thousand, I can see what we will become. And it's not human. A new class of people so wealthy and powerful, they answer to no one and cannot die. Death was the ultimate safeguard against the darkest angels of out nature. Now the monsters among us will own everything, consume everything, control everything…. If we do not stop the curse of eternal life in our realm our children would inherit despair. The ebb and flow of life is what makes as all equal in the end. The Uprising must end immortality [*AC* 7, "Nora Inu"].

Here, Quell touches upon three significant points that also appear in Derrida's *Specters of Marx*, namely, the immorality of capitalism, the mechanism of accumulating capital that puts the class of the owners outside of the law and the issue of the structure of inheritance. Immortality is connected with the lack of responsibility for anything. It puts the new class of "people" outside of the law, which results from the very structure of the law, characterized by Derrida as based on a temporal shift and succession of generations. The law may appear later, after a crime (Derrida 1994, p. 24); it is the domain of the coming generation which is "in a necessarily second generation, originarily late and therefore destined to *inherit*" (Derrida, 1994, p. 24). And "One never inherits without coming to terms with some specter" (p. 24). In other words, the law is the domain of the specters. This refers to a mechanism that Derrida termed "the visor effect": a state in which the spectral Other looks at us and we feel the gaze of those who have already died or have not yet been born. Future generations are also spectral in nature, as they pertain to our present. Quell understands this paradox perfectly. *Visor effect* is an asymmetry: we are watched by something we cannot see, something whose eyes we cannot meet, engage in a mutual relationship. It is this gaze of the past and the future generations, mixing the chronological order, providing it with retrospective nature, that creates the law. Immortality achieved through the technology of stacks and sleeves eliminates generational succession, which is interestingly thematized in *Altered Carbon*. The children of the Meths are sentenced to eternal childhood; they cannot grow up and take the place of their parents, because the latter do not change and do not die. The resulting frustration leads to pathological situations in which children steal the sleeves from their parents in order to live their adult lives. The only way to experience adulthood is to impersonate the parent, which means that they cannot be an adult version of themselves. They are playing dress-up with bodies, which is ultimately a child's game. Without the succession of generations, time stops. There is no past and future, only the eternal "now." There is no specter that demands our responsibility, the gaze of the Other, or the visor effect. There is no law. Therefore, the Meths are structurally located outside the law, and thus immoral. *Altered Carbon* uses this immoral structure of immortality, connecting it with the accumulation of capital, in order to showcase the immorality of capitalism as a system in which the well-being of some is achieved at a price of exploitation of everyone else. For Quell, immortality and inexhaustible wealth, the excess of goods impossible to consume through hundreds of years of one's life (the status of a billionaire in the reality of late capitalism) are one and the same.

Quell refers directly to the issue of generational succession: "Our children would inherit despair" (*AC* 7, "Nora Inu"). Inheritance is a key notion in *Specters of Marx*. Derrida presents it in the following way: "There is no inheritance without a call to responsibility. An inheritance is always the reaffirmation of a debt, but a critical, selective, and filtering reaffirmation, which is why we distinguished several spirits" (Derrida, 1994, p. 114). For Derrida, being who we are is, above all, inheriting, regardless of our awareness of this state of things. We are submerged in the past, and thus, we inherit. *Heredito ergo sum.* Inheriting means responsibility, a value which Quell also refers to when talking about the responsibility toward future generations, which will inherit our despair. Derrida also notes that "Reaction, reactionary, or reactive are but interpretations of the structure of inheritance" (p. 68). Quell's pursuit of destroying the stacks and sleeves technology inscribes itself into the reactive dimension of the structure of inheritance. The Uprising aims to restore the previous order of things, restore the past in order to provide humankind with a future. Reactivating the past is a reversal of the chronological order, but also a necessity, something essential to retain the law. Quell postulates a life with ghosts, in a dialogue with spectral presence. The specter remains that which gives us the most food for thought. This spectral way of production consists in making us work on ourselves. The specter poses a challenge for us, and Quell characterizes the human condition as a tendency to answer to the specter's challenge, to accept responsibility. Kovacs continues her work—he forces the Meths to confront the past, its spectral character, and to accept responsibility for their deeds. The Uprising did not fail, but, rather, it came back as a specter—stronger and more difficult to resist in the form of haunting.

Conclusions: The Work of Specters

This essay examines Netflix's series *Altered Carbon* in the context of the Derridean concept of hauntology, the notion of an ever-present past that makes itself visible through ghost-like figures. Thus comprehended, ghosts are quintessencial "unsolved cases," above all, as lost possibilities of the past, seeds of *différence*, otherness and difference. The ghost represents the "radical and necessary heterogeneity of an inheritance, the difference without opposition that has to mark it, a 'disparate' and a quasi-juxtaposition without dialectic (the very plural of what we will later call Marx's spirits). An inheritance is never gathered together, it is never one with itself" (Derrida, 1994, p. 18). The elements of haunting are dispersed throughout the text of the Netflix production, present in its structure and content, in the way the plot is presented and in its fragments.

Altered Carbon may be treated as a thoughtful and blunt illustration of Derridean hauntology. In the series, haunting takes place on many levels, starting with the attempt at reconstructing cyberpunk on the basis of the source inspirations of the genre. As Karen Cadora has noted, cyberpunk has met a dangerous impasse, resulting from the clash between the content and the message: "Cyberpunk's deconstruction of the human body first appeared to signal a revolution in political art. However, closer examinations of the movement have revealed that its politics are anything but revolutionary" (Cadora, 1995, p. 357). This is a result of the androcentric approach of the genre which does not keep up with current social changes in gender politics and in real life. The paradox of androcentric cyberpunk comes down to its lack of ability to transpose into the future current issues, which it ignores or does not understand. *Altered Carbon* uses ghost-like characters to deconstruct the structure of cyberpunk, firstly in order to return to the roots of the genre—a noir crime story and gothic novel—and thus to look for different ways of developing the genre. The character of Poe not only refers to proto-crime stories, which are at the source of cyberpunk, but also points toward a more emotional and empathetic origin hidden in the roots of the genre. The gothic affect speaks in the series like a specter of a forgotten pathway from the past, driving the actions of the characters much more than the rational interpretation of their deeds. The motivation of the antagonist of the series has a strictly affective dimension, which brings her closer to a character from a gothic novel. Kovacs's actions are also based on emotions and affects, the notorious "Envoy intuition" as an (irrational) method of diagnosing the environment. Visual quotations from leading cyberpunk titles emphasize the intertextual nature of the series. The character of Lizzie Elliot is another attempt at departing from the androcentric narration of contemporary cyberpunk, performed in the spirit of feminist revision, although this gesture still leaves much to be desired. *Altered Carbon* is an example of a story about the future told through the past, be it through retrospective scenes, the crime mystery or the lessons that the past teaches the characters.

On the level of content, the message of hauntology is conveyed bluntly. The protagonist does not only experience haunting but he also haunts. Ghosts appear as voices from the past, heralds of the future, setting in motion the potential for change contained in the repressed past, as *revenants* as well as *arrivants*. Such roles are played by the specter of Reileen, the character of Takeshi Kovacs, the ghost of Quellcrist Falconer and the ghost-like presence of Lizzie Elliot. Spectral nature is also the characteristic feature of the Elder civilization, the cosmic race on whose achievements the stacks and sleeves technology is based; it is present in the series through a number of artifacts that are a reminder of the twisted paths of inheritance. The futuristic technology of stacks and sleeves is rooted in the past, not only as a legacy of the Elder civilization, but also as a carrier of consciousness as memory. Human consciousness in the world of *Altered Carbon* inscribes itself into William James's theory of consciousness. Cortical stacks serve as a receptacle for the human consciousness or Digital Human Freight. Said consciousness is composed from memories of the user. For James, the pure ego is what provides the thread of continuity between our past, present, and future selves. Thus, consciousness is memory, meaning that it is always the consciousness of the past. This is another element of the omnipresence of the past in the series.

Specters teach subsequent theses of Derrida regarding the upending of the chronological order, the structure of the law, inheritance and responsibility. They constitute an example of embodied past whose presence becomes visible in order to hold us accountable to that which was and that which will come. The slogans appearing in the series may be seen as the leading tenets of hauntology, especially the key postulate "Let the dead speak." In *Altered Carbon*, the dead speak in a loud voice, be it in the narration or through individual acts of haunting. What they say is surprising, mysterious and key to understanding the message of the series, which is making us aware of the necessity of living with ghosts. Thus, the Netflix production may be treated as an embodiment of Derrida's theses and an entertaining, interesting way of familiarizing a broader audience with the tenets of hauntology.

NOTE

1. Blanco and Peeren emphasize the importance of subjectivity of haunting: "Ghost are not interchangeable (in terms of the effect and the affect produced) in what guise their appear and to whom. This subjectivity inflects both structural positions in the scenario of the haunting: being haunted by one's father is not the same as being haunted by one's mother, one's child or a stranger" (Blanco, Peeren, 2013b, p. 309).

REFERENCES

Blanco, M.P., & E. Peeren. (2013a). Introduction: Conceptualizing Spectralities. In *The Spectralities Reader: Ghosts and Haunting in Contemporary Cultural Theory*. Blanco, M.P., & Peeren, E. (Eds.) London: Bloomsbury, pp. 1–28.
____, & ____. (2013b). Spectral Subjectivities: Gender, Sexuality, Race / Introduction. In *The Spectralities Reader: Ghosts and Haunting in Contemporary Cultural Theory*. M.P. Blanco, M.P., & Peeren, E. (Eds.) London: Bloomsbury, pp. 309–316.
Brown, W. (2013). Specters and Angels at the End of History. In *Vocations of Political Theory*. Frank, J.A., & Tamborino, J. (Eds.). Minneapolis: University of Minnesota Press, 2000. pp. 25–58.
Cadora K. (1995). Feminist Cyberpunk. *Science Fiction Studies*, Volume 22, No. 3.pp. 357–372.
Derrida, J. (1994). *Specters of Marx: The State of Debt, the Work of Mourning and the New International*. Kamuf, P. (Trans.) New York: Routledge.
____, & B. Stiegler. (2013). Spectrographies. In *The Spectralities Reader: Ghosts and Haunting in Contemporary Cultural Theory*. Blanco, M.P., & Peeren, E. (Eds.). London: Bloomsbury, pp. 37–51.
Devereoux, C. (2014) Hysteria, Feminism, and Gender Revisited: The Case of the Second Wave. *English Studies in Canada*, Volume 40, No. 1. pp. 19–45.
Fisher, M. (2013) *The Metaphysics of Crackle: Afrofuturism and Hauntology*. Retrieved from https://dj.dancecult.net/index.php/dancecult/article/viewFile/378/391

Gordon A. (1991). *Ghostly Matters: Haunting and the Sociological Imagination*. Minneapolis: University of Minnesota Press.
Lenic, J.G. (Producer) & Kalogridis, L. (Creator). (2018). *Altered Carbon* [Series]. United States: Netflix.
Strehlau N. (2017). Postfeminist Specters: What Is Haunting Television Heroines?. *Theoria and Historia Scientarium*, Volume 19, No. 1. pp. 39–53.

Nevermore!
Poesque Thanatophobia as Counter-Narrative

FERNANDO GABRIEL PAGNONI BERNS
and EMILIANO AGUILAR

Populated with neon lit streets, a hard-as-nails detective, deep chiaroscuros and glamorous *femme fatales*, *Altered Carbon* is a throwback to the aesthetics of the noir film. What is more, the show's neon lit streets, technologically-saturated landscapes and bleak climate evoke the spirit of the cyberpunk genre. Still, there is another narrative informing the series: the Gothic. Elastic in concrete definitions as the Gothic is, we can define it as a revolt against the Enlightenment's view of the world and relations, which localized the reason and the realistic as the main ethos of both, the world and art, in favor of recovering an earlier model like that proposed by Romanticism, where the subjective, forces of nature and the world of dreams/nightmares prevailed through climates of horror and dread. The force of the Gothic is especially present through the figure of Edgar Allan Poe (Chris Conner) an elegant artificial intelligence character who runs the hotel that serves as Takeshi Kovacs' (Joel Kinnaman) base of operations.

Poe's presence comes with two of his most famous poems: "The Raven" and "Annabel Lee." Both poems revolve around something missing in this dystopian future: death. This way, Poe's presence can be read as a counter-narrative that parallels, challenges and tenses the neoliberal discourse informing the show, where life is something that can be extended to the infinite, simultaneously fitting within the market logic as a commodity. Life becomes banal under the market logic of this dystopic landscape, as cycles of illness and death are postponed for those who can pay for this deceleration. Poe's shadow, on the other hand, reveals a deep thanatophobia—excessive fear of human finitude—and an erotically charged attachment to death. Like Poe, death still lurks at the margins, a Gothic meditation on the inevitability of the end of human life.

The real-life Poe believed that humans felt an overwhelming, deep fear of death and many of his stories revolve around the terror of dying, and the horror of decay. The haunting presence of "The Raven" evokes the inevitability of the phrase "nevermore," a bold statement in a society that has forgotten the meaning of death. It reminds us that fear of dying implies also fear of living. In this essay, we will analyze the different spectral echoes of Poe resonating in the show. We believe that all the pieces, once united together, create a complex tapestry that unites the Romantic death and the thanatophobia informing Poe's works. In parallel, our current world is also shaped by such dichotomy: pharmaceutical and medical developments prolong life to new, unexpected lengths.

Still, this prolongation is accessible to those who can pay for it, while large numbers of people still struggle with poverty and insubstantial living conditions. On the other hand, international terrorism exposes our vulnerabilities and the nearness of (our) death (Kennedy, 2018, p. 812). We are all at constant risk of being killed, no matter our health and age. Thus Poe's presence within the series irremediably returns us to a certainty: *we exist to die.* As death is presented throughout the show as exciting exoticism and/or eroticism, Poe's Gothic nature works as a counter-hegemonic narrative that disrupts the neoliberal logic of infinite life.

Poesque Influence: On Thanatophobia

The term "Poesque" refers to the influences that the great Gothic American writer Edgar Allan Poe cast upon the literary and artistic works created by those who followed him chronologically. The recurrence to "decadence and morbidity" (Vale de Gato, 2012, p. 92) informs the works of a wide array of varied artists, as presented by: Sean Moreland's edited collection *The Lovecraftian Poe* (2017), the edited collection put together by Lois Davis Vines *Poe Abroad* (on Poe's influence in remote countries such as Italy, Croatia or Poland) or Marco Caracciolo's essay on video games inspired by Poe's poetics.

Futuristic and deeply rooted in cyber-punk aesthetics as *Altered Carbon* is, however, Poe's influence permeates the narrative. The TV series displays a set of thematic and stylistic features that could be easily bound to the Poesque, from Poe's explicit presence as a major character in the series, with direct references to his works—the hotel that Poe manages bears the name of one of the writer's most famous works, "The Raven"—to the presence of death as nothingness. Patrick McGreevy goes as far as saying that "Edgar Allan Poe was perhaps more obsessed with death than any other nineteenth-century writer" (2013, p. 57). A culture of death has been evident in the Gothic (Davison, 2017, p. 14) which has had important implications in Poe's work. Arguably, Poe has paid a great heed to death and the supernatural, as well as the imaginary of decay and cemeteries in his tales and poems.

A causal relationship can be established between the author and the process of dying, as Poe himself had "to face up to traumatic deaths" (Marín-Ruiz, 2010, p. 37). Poe became an orphan at the age of three. His surrogate mother, Jane Stith Stanard, died in 1824 and his foster mother, Frances Allan, in 1829. His marriage with her young cousin Virginia Clemm in 1836—arguably, the only happy period in his life—ended in 1847 after his wife's slow death of tuberculosis. Her death took five excruciatingly painful years, thus predisposing Poe to "a number of symbols that identified women with death" (Hernandez Del Castillo, 1981, p. 59).

Arguably, this nearness to death alone cannot explain Poe's obsession with the finitude of life. What interests us here is the fact that Poe's relationship with death has been interpreted through the lenses of morbidity, decay and dread even when this relationship is, in fact, fraught with contradictions.

On the one hand, death seems to be an object of some kind of erotic desire, a severe case of necrophilia (Aggrawal, 2011, p. 44; Hernandez Del Castillo, p. 109; Roderick, 2016, p. 25). The return of beautiful women from the grave or the evocation of pale deceased girls insinuates a Romantic version of death. Poe's epitome of poetic beauty was "the death of a beautiful woman" (McGaan, 2014, p. 152). This is Poe's "most poetical subject in the world" because of two aspects. Firstly, this particular figure "organizes Poe's imaginative world as an ideological condition." Secondly, this figure "is a gravity field for the cultural condition of the nineteenth century, the epoch of High Romanticism and its immediate aftermath" (McGaan, 2014, p. 152). "The Raven," so embedded in *Altered Carbon*, revolves profusely around the subject of a sad, sensitive, but lovely engagement with death. Poe's works seems to caress death, whereas deathbeds are the most romantic objects. The poet perceived death as beautiful mourning, a link between loss and beauty, between passing away and pristine bodies. David Stamos argues that the evocation and experience of beauty in Poe's works "is heightened by discord" (2017, p. 107); death is an absolute that elevates rather than destroys.

In "The Philosophy of Composition" Poe explains that death is the inevitable movement to a higher plane of being. Thus, death is the most intense instance of perfect beauty, the latter coming from the "pleasurable elevation of the soul." Further, melancholy is "the most legitimate of all the poetical tones" (2014, p. 522). In his poem "Lenore," the titular dead heroine is called the "the most lovely dead that ever died so young!" (2000, p. 335).

Mourning concerns repentance, so Poe not only brings back death, but also conjures up ethical considerations about how we should live and treat others.

On the other hand, popular tales such as "The Premature Burial," "The Masque of the Red Death" or "The Fall of the House of Usher" reveal a deep dread of death, sickness and decay. Being buried alive is, together with "the death of a beautiful woman," one of the topics to which the author will come back most. In fact, the fear of being buried alive, expressed in "The Fall of the House of Usher" has been "one of the chief selling points of Poe's fiction from his earliest tales such as 'Loss of Breath' (1832) through twentieth-century interpretations of his work in a wide range of media" (Hartmann, 2008, p. 35). "The Premature Burial," in turn, reveals death as metamorphosis that leads to redemption; the proximity of the grave should not give horror to enlightened people (Goldhurst, 1996, p. 156) but only those superstitious or with guilty minds. The extreme fear of death that shapes Bay City (and, presumably, the whole globe) reveals a society ingrained with an economy and ethos which have wrought much destruction.

With his work revealing an eroticism of death but, also, a deep fear of dying, it can be argued that Poe's works are an oscillating meditation on the nature of death. Death itself played a central role in shaping the author's work through an intense duality: a melancholic impulse that imagines death (of a woman) as sublime elevation, opposed by an equally strong dread of human finitude. Between these two opposite poles—death as human elevation and dying as agony—rises the fear of being alive but dead, being buried alive. It is from this dread of being buried alive—agonizing death, illness, decay—that the terror of death actually arises. Real death is not that fearful, but its existence, living through the angst of knowing our finitude, certainly is.

In this sense Poe's "tales are not finally so much about the death of their characters as about those characters' inability to die" (Elmer, 1995, p. 109). The real horror comes more from the irrational fear of death, of being buried alive, of corporeal decadence, than death itself. Philosopher Karl Jasper argues that knowing our human finitude does not produce fear but rather angst: *knowing* our finitude, "the horror of not being" (Jaspers, 1970, p. 198), understood as what lies beneath, is not ours to see.

Thus, Poe's necrophiliac dramas speak less about "a fear of the irrevocable termination of life than the correlative anxiety before the interminable nature of death" (Elmer, p. 109). This "angst" appears in tales such as "Berenice" (1835), "Morella" (1835), "Ligeia" (1838), "Usher" (1839), "Some Words with a Mummy"(1845), and "The Cask of Amontillado" (1846). Something still living and pulsating even if buried is referenced in "The Tell-Tale Heart" (1843). All these tales are suggestive of man's thanatophobia, ending up buried alive being the most extreme of horrors.

The fear of dying makes the majority of the characters of *Altered Carbon* (especially the Meths) embrace a life of perpetual good health through the practice of resleeving. To prolong their immortal state, many of them are capable of breaking any ethic boundaries, including killing or gaining economic power while crushing others in the process, a neoliberal fantasy made true.

In our future we might see new sophisticated methods of prolonging the human life-span. This "science-fiction" technoscience, however, comes with a neoliberal cost, as medical expenses increase, leaving many citizens marginalized. One of the major impediments to achieving global medical and pharmaceutical welfare is the limited access to affordable medicines in underdeveloped or peripherical areas of the world. "The neoliberal global economic policies create additional hurdles for both access to medicines and building up of industrial capacity for pharmaceutical production in the global south" (da Silva, 2009, p. 104). It is not by chance, thus, that the main representatives of those who oppose the neoliberal politics of eternal life in the series are Latin American. Kristin Ortega (Martha Higareda) and her mother are both proponents of life as an experience with a limited timespan. Ortega finds the idea of prolonging life frivolous, except if it allows to put a killer in jail; her family, however, is staunchly against resleeving. Those who follow Neo-Catholicism—like Ortega's mother—are not allowed to be "brought back," since it is considered a sin. In concordance, those who protest against resleeving wear make-up that evokes the sugar skulls of *Día de Los Muertos*. Their understanding of death is that of celebration and mourning rather than a commodity.

Against this scenario of neoliberal lifespan, death still exists, even though it is postponed and thus, turned invisible. Poe itself mentions that nobody comes to his hotel anymore: it seems that people mostly want to avoid any reference to death. Navigating between the Romantic sublime of perfect beauty and/or thanatophobia, both "Poes" are saturated by death. Poe's presence slips morbidity and death within a narrative that actively tries to suppress it. Along with gloomy and recondite places, as well as deep chiaroscuros, the imagery strongly linked to death—the festivity of the *Día de Los Muertos*, incubators for clones which works as sarcophagi, stains of blood still dripping on the wall—contributes to recreating a death-related atmosphere.

As argued by Michael Burduck, "Poe shows how fear often creates demonic effects" (1992, p. 227). Indeed, the grueling, dystopian character of Bay City stems from the deep, irrational fear of dying. Carrying this fear on their shoulders, the characters are practically dead, obsessed with eternal life, rather than really living. After all, the show begins with a rich man, Laurens Bancroft (James Purefoy) hiring Kovacs to help him solve his own murder.

Bancroft is actually alive, but dead. Besides trying to find the traitor living within his intimate circle, what creeps out Bancroft the most is his own mortality. All the clues point to suicide, but Bancroft is adamant in his resolution: he would never have attempted to take his own life, his fear of death is almost overpowering.

Like Bay City, our contemporary world navigates through the edge of contradiction. Medical and scientific developments have improved our life quality as never before and greatly increased our life span. In other words, people live longer and in better health than ever. The remarkable increase in life expectancy is illustrated, through a fantastic lens, by *Altered Carbon* and its politics of resleeving. On the other hand, our contemporary life is inextricably linked with the angst of "becoming nothing" as our days are fraught with terrorist attacks, random shootings and natural disasters that make our existence particularly "fragile." Death can arrive in an unexpected crash of an airplane into a skyscraper, a letter containing mortal powders or through an earthquake. As Teresa Brennan argues, "the new anxieties over terrorist attacks are only the latest in a series of fears generated by globalization" (2003, p. 1). Indeed, "increasing chronic ill health, longing working hours, greater debt … [and] cutbacks in welfare and education and health benefits" (Brennan, 2003. p. 1) filled our world with the fear of death.

In other words, death has been largely removed from everyday life, as perfect health has become a commodity interchangeable through the economic market. Still, death is casting a larger shadow, haunting us with the realization that we all live in a world where everyone seems vulnerable, no matter how healthy we feel. The terrorist assault on the Trade World Center in 2001 was a heart attack suffered by one of the most powerful, healthy organisms at a global scale.

Gerald Kennedy finds multiple connections between Poe's works and terrorism. Analyzing "The Fall of the House of Usher," Kennedy explains that "Poe constructs the terrorist plot in 'Usher' by ratcheting up the doubling to expose the ultimate object of terrorism—the fear of death awakened by 'mortality salience'" (2018, p. 817). Kennedy brings forth Baudrillard and his bold statement: terrorists "have succeeded in turning their own deaths into an absolute weapon against a system that operates on the basis of an exclusion of death" (Baudrillard, 2002, p. 16). Thus, the presence of Poe in Bay City works as the return of the repressed: not matter how much people work to entomb their fears/angst of death; it will always find a way to return, even from the fringes of narratives of everlasting life. Our steadfast rejection of human finitude is Gothic in nature; behind a shinning surface of medical and scientific Enlightenment, darkness patiently awaits.

Gothic at the Margins, Poe at the Center

Even if Poe is a major character in the series, his presence sometimes feels like the "comic relief" of classical horror cinema. Ironic, elegant and decadent, Poe is a square peg in the cyberpunk landscape of *Altered Carbon*. However, he reeks of death, even if he is not at all threatening to his guests. The choice of his hotel's name is very telling: "The Raven" refers to the most brilliant piece of mourning and sorrow about the death of a beautiful woman, a "ceaseless memory" of those loved and lost (Kopley & Hayes, 2004, p. 195).

Altered Carbon opens with an image of death and beauty: the first episode begins with a rapid editing of Kovacs' naked body floating aimless in water. Thanks to the editing, audiences can rest their gaze upon pieces of a muscular body: a nipple, a beautiful face. The real state of its owner, however, is cloaked in mystery, since we do not know if he is alive or dead. The episode's title, "Out of the Past," is linked to melancholia, to the Gothic attachment to times of yore. Indeed, the Poesque Gothic is deeply embedded in the main narrative: Kovacs is unable to escape the deeds of his past; neither is he able to forget previous commitments—with his sister Reileen (Dichen Lachman) or with his love interest Quellcrist Falconer (Renée Elise Goldsberry). The past weighing on the present is a Gothic motif.

"In Gothic, history weighs like a nightmare on the present" (Scruggs & VanDemarr, 1998, p. 135), destroying classical historiography conceptualized as a chronological order of historical progression. This linear progression is further debilitated by the series' plot device, which recurrently jumps from the past to the present; the changes of bodies—and actors—increase the sense of fragmentation of time. When Kovacs wakes up in the present, at first he fights the doctors, because he is still mentally battling his last pre-death fight, thus blending together the present and the past. Momentarily, his past is still alive when, in fact, he has been dead for years. Further, the woman presiding over the inmates of Alcatraz (where Kovacs is revived as a prisoner) warns against the first effects of being resleeved; hallucinations and dizziness. Through the narrative, Kovacs will talk with a spectral version of his sister (before knowing the truth of her survival) and his previous love interest— another blending of daydreaming, hallucination and imagination. All of them are Gothic motifs.

Since Poe was a writer interested in the Gothic, he was also interested in the past surviving in the present. In his poem "A Dream" (1827), Poe makes a lament for those who live trapped in the past: "Ah! what is not a dream by day/ To him whose eyes are cast/ On things around him with a ray/ Turned back upon the past?" (2014, p. 429). Incidentally, Takeshi Kovacs' loneliness in the vastness of the overpopulated streets is reminiscent of "The Man of the Crowd" (1840), whose narrator, recently recovered from a disease, becomes obsessed with an old man whom he starts to follow, provoking a "delirious immersion in the crowd" (Nicol, 2013, p. 75). Like Poe's narrator, Kovacs is a kind of outcast lost in the streets, using drugs and losing his consciousness. Like the narrator in the poem, Kovacs' behavior reflects the urban environment of his time, highlighting issues related to the miseries of the new century, such as human trafficking, famine and homelessness.

This first episode presents another Gothic trope, as the show focuses on "the dark unconscious as the underside of the bright modern polis" (Horner & Zlosnik, 2001, p. 79). The "original" Kovacs approaches a window showcasing a beautiful day of sun at the beach. This reality, however, is fake: after touching it, the window is revealed to be a digital screen. The reality is a bleak urbanity of grayness, pollution, and neon advertisements. The sublime elevation proposed by Poe takes place through entrepreneurship, as rich people live at the skies, in the Aerium, a city free from smog, with last remnants of nature.

The artificial Poe mentions that in the skies it is possible to observe the mud lying below, another evocation of the dualism so favored by the Gothic. This dualism contrasts beauty and horror, life and death, as well as dream and reality as excluding spheres which, nevertheless, blend with one another. The people at the Aerium mostly wear white, a color which codes them as angels, superior beings who observe with disdain the below, the mud of common people. The Aerium, however, is not free from the haunting presence of death: Laurens Bancroft's big studio displays a big stain of blood, a reminder of death that the millionaire is not able to push himself to clean up. The stain, covered by a blanket, localizes death within a space that is steadfast in its rejection of finitude.

The stain is not the only signpost of death haunting the narrative: the episode "Force of Evil" (*AC* 4) offers a glimpse into All Hallows Eve. Being of Mexican descent, Ortega and her family celebrate *Dia de Los Muertos*, the Day of the Dead, a holiday that focuses on gatherings of family and friends to pray for, and remember friends and family members who have died. The gathering, decorated with ornate sugar *calaveras* (skulls) is mostly used as an important channeling of mourning and so, enhances the presence of death within the narrative.

The police department is, arguably, the other place where death is geographically localized. The place contains the people in charge of investigating murder cases. Even if filled with sophisticated technology, the building is obviously a cathedral—the facade clearly visible in episode 3, "In a Lonely Place"—including high arcades, colored stain glasses and rose windows. Bay City has pushed death to the margins, conflating all the reminders of human finitude in strategically localized spaces. Like in dreams, the images overlap together, the shining modern screens are at odds with—yet somehow they complement—the gothic architecture, creating a reservoir for death amidst the city.

Another Gothic/Poesque trope, the double, is an important element of the narrative. In the episode "Rage in Heaven," Kovacs manages to create a clone of himself to infiltrate Head in the Clouds and, at the same time, monitor the attack from the hotel. The idea the duplicate, like the double, illustrates a psychological dualism that is the result of "internal struggles" (Jones, 2019, p. 236); Kovacs is prey to internal contradictions as he loves his sister but has to put an end to her machinations and, at the same time, plays a game of love and hate with Lieutenant Ortega.

The apex of Gothic is, however, The Raven hotel, a place where the tired traveler can be cloaked "in darkness" as Poe himself (itself?) claims in his advertisements. The Raven hotel is strikingly anchored to Edgar Allan Poe's times. The entrance hall is decorated with huge candelabras, ancient chairs and real candles, while Poe wears clothes taken from the nineteenth century. It is mentioned that the concept of AI hotel itself is a relic of the past, a place where nobody stays anymore. Like the Police department, the hotel has been pushed to the margins.

Still, it is not only the past that is evoked; Poe's welcome includes calling his hotel the most macabre place in all of Bay City. The Raven Hotel is the place of mourning and death, a counter-narrative against the hegemonic ethos, because of its ultimate faith in death and interest in humans (whom Poe finds fascinating). The hotel and Poe conform a "closed system," which was one of the writer's favorite topics (Peeples, 2002, p. 186). These spaces are prone to disruption, however, and the humanity brought by Kovacs is the foreign element, which is of special interest to Poe. People outside the hotel can escape the finitude of life; The Raven Hotel, however, stinks of death. Even the walls are decorated with crows flocking the skies.

The hotel is a building where literal death can be enacted. In the first episode ("Out of the Past"), a hit mob comes to kill Kovacs. He is bludgeoned almost to the point of death, his blurry vision—only discerning the crows populating the walls and ceiling, all of them a reminder that people—all people—can still die. After paying as a guest, however, Kovacs is defended by the hotel, who (which?) brutally kills all the hired guns. Thus, the hotel not only evokes death; it produces it as well. Poe himself grabs an old fashioned shotgun and starts blasting at the goons.

Besides death, the hotel also evokes hope. When Poe lights up the candles in the first episode, a close shot reveals the brand of the box of matches: "Fire of Fire," another subtle reference to Poe and his poem "Tamerlane": "You call it hope-that fire of fire!" (96). The reference to hope is not capricious, as Kovacs is seconds away from finding a good partner and a friend in his battle against his many foes. As base of operations, The Raven Hotel is, indeed, the last hope that Kovacs has at finding redemption.

Nevermore! Mourning the Female in a World Without Death

As mentioned earlier, the feminine is a potent trope in Poe's fiction. The (dead) female incarnates the ideal of the sublime and poetry, beauty and fear. This feminine ideal, however, is attached to death, as many female protagonists hold "capacities for life beyond the grave" (Weekes, 2004, p. 148); Reileen, Kovacs' sister, fits well within this trope. Melancholic remembrance is a form of poetical beauty, albeit a desperate one, so "the woman must die in order to enlarge the experience of the narrator" (Weekes, 2004, p. 148). Kenneth Silverman believes that in his tales Poe "nourished himself on a young woman's death, in the sense that art was for him a form of mourning, a revisitation of his past and of what he had lost, as if trying to make them right. Since nothing could, he returned to the subject of 'the one and only supremely beloved' again and again" (1993, p. 21).

The dead woman as an experience of mourning is also constitutive of the Gothic: unlike stories where the female characters are merely caricatures, "those women who take part in the Gothic tales display a beauty which is both corporeal and spiritual. Though rickety and slender they may seem, their bodies are regarded as beautiful since they fulfill the Romantic model of fragile and paleskinned woman" (Marín-Ruiz, 2010, p. 38). The motif is deeply embedded in Poe's fiction and, by extension, in *Altered Carbon* as well, another trace of the poet's presence "infecting" Bay City with death.

In the episode "Out of the Past" (*AC* 1), a thug calls The Raven Hotel "possessive like a crazy girlfriend." This attachment to "possessive girlfriends" evokes Poe's necrophiliac impulse and his poems dedicated to deceased women who still cast their shadows upon him. The (dead) female presence is referred to again in the second episode, depicting the floating corpse of a beautiful, young pale-skinned woman which a fisherman finds in the waters. The title of the episode, "Fallen Angel," takes us again to the Poesque motif of the death of a beautiful woman, whose passing is synonymous of beauty and spiritual elevation. The hair and the white delicate dress, softly undulating around her, elevates her to a signpost of the Romantic aesthetics and the Gothic obsessions haunting Poe. Horrid or beautiful, Poesque death slips within the neoliberal fabric of *Altered Carbon*.

This particular pale-skinned body belongs to Mary Lou Henchy (Lisa Chandler), a prostitute who worked at the Head in the Clouds brothel. She was hired by Bancroft to fulfill his sexual fantasies, which include choking women to the point of death, returning viewers to the imagery of eroticism, beauty, elevation and human finitude. When Mary Lou's mother goes to the police department to ask questions about the disappearance of her daughter's body from the morgue, she is unconsciously referencing Poe's work: the woman claims she has been unable to say goodbye to her daughter; furthermore, she is unable to accept that she will never see Mary Lou again. The feeling of melancholy that eschews closure takes viewers to the last word that one of the hitmen hunting down Kovacs says before being brutally killed by Poe; "nevermore!," a statement that not only explicitly connects the narrative to the poem "The Raven" but, also, to death and mourning in a world that has obliterated the former.

The pain that comes with "nevermore!" also haunts Vernon Elliot (Ato Essandoh), who has lost his daughter, Lizzie (Hayley Law), and blames Bancroft for her disappearance. Lizzie is not just another "Poe's girl," a lament about a lost female's young life, as the connection with the poet runs deeper. "Many of Poe's female characters—Annabel Lee, Eulalie, Helen, Lenore, Ligeia, Morella—favors the letter 'L,' an aspect of Poe's use of sound that poets from Konstantin Balmont to Thomas Hardy have appreciated" (Kopley & Hayes, 2004, p. 200). Lizzie is another of Poe's Ls. The AI Poe immediately takes a paternalistic attitude toward the traumatized girl, a form of engagement with a sharp proximity to romance.

In a conversation with *The Hollywood Reporter* (2018) the actor playing Poe, Chris Conner, explains that "Annabel Lee" was "a tremendous help" in getting him to understand Poe's relationships with the women of the show, particularly Lizzie. The actor confesses that there is an ambiguity framing the relationship: "I think there's a paternalistic aspect to his relationship with Lizzie, but there's a creepy side to it as well," as Poe seems to want to "erotize" her. Mary Lou, the "fallen angel," also contains an "L" in her name. Furthermore, Lizzie lives within another of Poe's tropes: the locked room, that the writer popularized in his time. Like in "The Murders in the Rue Morgue," there must be a rear exit, some alternative point of fugue since the "main exit" has been shut down.

"The Raven" and "Annabel Lee" are the two explicit connections between Poe's work and *Altered Carbon*. Not by chance, since both poems revolve around death and the melancholic attachment with someone dead. The mention of both poems marks human finitude, thus inscribing death in *Altered Carbon*. The death of others makes us realize our own mortality, our own finitude. Without the nearness of death, there is only hedonism and selfishness. The society depicted in *Altered Carbon* is the culmination of a neoliberal dream: the commodification of eternal life that takes, to the extreme, our neoliberal climate of health as something that can be bought. Against this backdrop, we need a remembrance of death, something anchoring us firmly in this world and in our own existence as ethical beings.

Ultimately, the Aerium evokes Prince Prospero's Abbey from "The Masque of the Red Death": a place filled with people who feast while being delusional about death. The "Red Death" is so frightening to them because it reminds them of the inevitability of human finitude. In the last episode, "The Killers," Poe slips death into the Aerium. Dying in the act, Poe sends a murderous, black-clad (the color meaning death) Lizzie to kill almost everyone in the abbey that Prospero/Laurens Bancroft tries to keep oblivious to death. Prospero/Bancroft are Gothic villains, those who upset "the normal order of life" (Fisher, 2004, 88), and who would bring death as a punishment. "He and his followers vainly combat an antagonist who, to them, would be terrifying, but who, to more realistic minds, would be a grim, but essential, part of life" (Fisher, 2004, p. 88). In the end, death is inescapable.

In considering selected moments and elements invested with death, this essay argued that such spectacles work counter to the claims of neoliberal politics. Following Poe's acts of mourning, death is framed in ways that uncover the economic nature of cultural narratives about the prolongation of life. While the horror/death scenes work to shock viewers, they also oblige them to face the reality of death in a world filled with health that can be bought and sold. This neoliberal fantasy of everlasting life and youth is complicated and interrupted by the politics of a global world that bleeds us to death. Healthcare is better than ever, but the consequences of keeping the rhythm of an increasing life-span are, (un)surprisingly, mental burnouts and heart attacks. Edgar Allan Poe, his very presence meaning death, but also, deep interest in the human soul, is supposed to make us remember that human finitude is not just a biological process but, also, a counter-narrative that weighs in our way of (ethical) living.

REFERENCES

Aggrawal, A. (2011). *Necrophilia: Forensic and Medico-legal Aspects*. Boca Raton: CRC Press.
Baudrillard, J. (2002). *The Spirit of Terrorism and Requiem for the Twin Towers*. London: Verso.
Brennan, T. (2003). *Globalization and Its Terrors: Daily Life in the West*. New York: Routledge.
Burduck, M. (1992). *Grim Phantasms: Fear in Poe's Short Fiction*. New York: Garland.
Caracciolo, M. (2019). Edgar Allan Poe Simulations: On Dream Logic: Game Narratives and Poesque Atmospheres. In *Intermedia Games—Games Inter Media: Video Games and Intermediality*. Fuchs, M., & Thoss, J. (Eds.). New York: Bloomsbury, pp. 167–188.
da Silva, Anna. (2009). Calling the Shots: Global Network of Trade in Vaccines. In *Hegemonic Transitions, the State and Crisis in Neoliberal Capitalism*. Atasoy, Y. (Ed.). New York: Routledge, pp. 104–125.
Davis Vines, L. (Ed.). (1999). *Poe Abroad: Influence, Reputation, Affinities*. Iowa City: University of Iowa Press.
Davison, C.M. (2017). Introduction—The Corpse in the Closet: The Gothic, Death and

Modernity. *The Gothic and Death.* Davison, C.M. (Ed.). Manchester: Manchester University Press, pp. 1–19.
Elmer, J. (1995). Terminate or Liquidate? Poe, Sensationalism, and the Sentimental Tradition. In *The American Face of Edgar Allan Poe.* Rosenheim, S., & Rachman, S. (Eds.). Baltimore: The Johns Hopkins University Press, pp. 91–120.
Fisher, B. (2004). Poe and the Gothic Tradition. In *The Cambridge Companion to Edgar Allan Poe.* Hayes, K. (Ed.). Cambridge: Cambridge University Press, pp. 72–91.
Goldhurst, W. (1996). Tales of the Human Condition. *A Companion to Poe Studies.* Carlson, E.W. (Ed.). Westport, Connecticut: Greenwood, pp. 149–167.
Jaspers, K. (1970). *Philosophy*, Vol. 2, Ashton, E.B. (Ed.). Chicago: The University of Chicago Press.
Hartmann, J. (2008). *The Marketing of Edgar Allan Poe.* New York: Routledge.
Hernandez Del Castillo, A. (1981). *Keats, Poe, and the Shaping of Cortazar's Mythopoesis.* Amsterdam: John Benjamins Publishing.
Hollywood Reporter. (2018, February 15). How *Altered Carbon* Brought Its Breakout Character to Life. Retrieved from https://www.hollywoodreporter.com/
Horner, A., & Zlosnik, S. (2001). Strolling in the Dark: Gothic Flânerie in Djuna Barnes's *Nightwood.* In *Gothic Modernism.* Smith, A., & Wallace, J. (Eds.). New York: Palgrave, pp. 78–94.
Jones, P. (2019). Counterparts: Poe's Doubles from 'William Wilson' to 'The Cask of Amontillado.' In *The Oxford Handbook of Edgar Allan Poe.* Kennedy, J. & Peeples, S. (Eds.). New York: Oxford University Press, pp. 236–251.
Marín-Ruiz. R. (2010). Two Romanticisms but the Same Feeling: The Presence of Poe in Gustavo Adolfo Bécquer's *Leyendas.* In *A Descent into Edgar Allan Poe and His Works: The Bicentennial.* González Moreno, B., & Aragón, M. (Eds.). Bern: Peter Lang, pp. 35–44.
McGaan, J. (2014). *The Poet Edgar Allan Poe: Alien Angel.* Cambridge, Massachusetts: Harvard University Press.
McGreevy, P. (2013). Reading the Texts of Niagara Falls: The Metaphor of Death. In *Writing Worlds: Discourse, Text and Metaphor in the Representation of Landscape.* Barnes, T., & Duncan, J. (Eds.). New York: Routledge, pp. 50–72.
Nicol, B. (2013). The Urban Environment. In *Edgar Allan Poe in Context.* Hayes, K. (Ed.). Cambridge: Cambridge University Press, pp. 75–95.
Kennedy, G. (2018). Poe's Terror Analytics. In *The Oxford Handbook of Edgar Allan Poe.* Kennedy, G., & Peeples, S. (Eds.) Oxford: Oxford University Press, pp. 809–828.
Kopley, R., & Hayes, K. (2004). Two Verse Masterworks: "The Raven" and "Ulalume" In *The Cambridge Companion to Edgar Allan Poe.* Hayes, K. (Ed.) Cambridge: Cambridge University Press, pp. 191–204.
Lenic, J.G. (Producer) & Kalogridis, L. (Creator). *Altered Carbon.* (2018–). [Series]. United States: Netflix.
Moreland, S. (Ed.). (2017). *The Lovecraftian Poe: Essays on Influence, Reception, Interpretation, and Transformation.* Bethlehem: Lehigh University Press.
Peeples, S. (2002). Poe's Constructiveness and 'The Fall of the House of Usher.' In *The Cambridge Companion to Edgar Allan Poe.* Hayes, K. (Ed.). Cambridge: Cambridge University Press, pp. 178–190.
Poe, E.A. (2014). A Dream. In *Edgar Allan Poe: The Dover Reader.* Kopito, J. (Ed.). New York: Dover, pp. 429–431.
_____. (2014). Annabel Lee. In *Edgar Allan Poe: The Dover Reader.* Kopito, J. (Ed.). New York: Dover, pp. 466–467.
_____. (2000). Lenore. In *Complete Poems.* Mabbott, T.O. (Ed.) Urbana: University of Illinois Press, pp. 330–338.
_____. (1876). Tamerlane. In *The Poetical Works of Edgar Allan Poe.* New York: W.J. Widdleton Publisher, pp. 136–145
_____. (2014). The Philosophy of Composition. In *Edgar Allan Poe: The Dover Reader.* Kopito, J. (Ed.). New York: Dover, pp. 519–530.
_____. (2014). The Raven. In *Edgar Allan Poe: The Dover Reader.* Kopito, J. (Ed.). New York: Dover, pp. 456–460.

Roderick, P. (2006). *The Fall of the House of Poe: And Other Essays*. New York: iUniverse, Inc.
Scruggs, C., & VanDemarr, L. (1998). *Jean Toomer and the Terrors of American History*. Philadelphia: University of Pennsylvania Press.
Silverman, K. (1999). Introduction. In *New Essays on Poe's Major Tales*. Silverman, K. (Ed.). Cambridge University Press.
Stamos, D. (2017). *Edgar Allan Poe, Eureka, and Scientific Imagination*. Albany, NY: SUNY Press.
Vale de Gato, M. (2012). Around Reason Feeling: Poe's Impact on Fernando Pessoa's Modernist Proposal. In *Poe's Pervasive Influence*. Cantalupo, B. (Ed.). Bethlehem: Lehigh University Press, pp. 91–108.
Weekes, K. (2004). Poe's Feminine Ideal. In *The Cambridge Companion to Edgar Allan Poe*. Hayes, K. (Ed.). Cambridge: Cambridge University Press, pp. 148–162.

About the Contributors

Emiliano **Aguilar** graduated with an MA from the Universidad de Buenos Aires (UBA)—Facultad de Filosofía y Letras (Argentina). He has published chapters in *New Heart and New Spirit*, *Orphan Black and Philosophy*, *The Man in the High Castle and Philosophy* and *Giant Creatures in Our World*, among others.

Burcu **Baykan** is an assistant professor of visual communication design with a specialization in contemporary art theory and practice at Bilkent University, Turkey. She has been a graduate fellow at Trinity College Dublin where she earned her Ph.D. in 2017. Her dissertation is a Deleuze-Guattarian investigation of contemporary body-based visual arts, including performance art, video art, installation, sculpture, bio-art, and the interdisciplinary collaborations within these fields.

Dariusz **Brzostek** is an associate professor of cultural studies at Nicolaus Copernicus University in Toruń, Poland. His main research interests are sound studies, science and technology studies, science fiction, and horror studies. His research is concerned with early Polish electronic music, counterculture in Poland, Communist-era science fiction, and the history of jazz. He has published two books in Polish: *Literature and Non-Reason* (2009) and *Listening to the Noise* (2014).

Adam **Edwards** is a second year Ph.D. student in the English Department of the University of Birmingham. His research is in the cyberpunk genre, in particular its modern incarnations, which incorporates analysis of its intersection with transhumanist ideology and development, and issues of human entanglement with technology as depicted in its depictions of embodiment. This project charts the development of the genre into modern incarnations.

Aline **Ferreira** is an associate professor at the University of Aveiro in Portugal where she teaches English literature and cultural studies. Her interests comprise the intersections between literature and science, bioethics, feminist utopias and women's studies. She is working on a book provisionally titled: *The Sexual Politics of the Artificial Womb: Fictional and Visual Representations*.

Alexander N. **Howe** is a professor of English at the University of the District of Columbia, where he offers courses on American literature, popular culture, and film. He is the author of *It Didn't Mean Anything* (McFarland 2008) and numerous articles about detective and science fiction. His work focuses on hybrid bodies and modes of detection in dystopian fiction and film.

Michał **Klata** is an MA student in English studies at the University of Warsaw, with a separate master's degree in sociology (also from the University of Warsaw). He is completing his thesis on the representation of James Bond's relations with women in the film series, with his main focus on the shifts in the politics of gender.

Aldona **Kobus** is a professor in the department of cultural studies at Nicolaus Copernicus University in Toruń, Poland. She specializes in fan studies, popular culture studies and research concerning women's authorship. She received her Ph.D. based on the dissertation *Models of Authorship in Western Culture*, dedicated to the notion of authorship in the context of cultural and market forces. She is also the author of *Fandom: Fanowskie modele odbioru* (2018).

Esra **Köksal** is a master's student in the Program of Media and Visual Studies, at Bilkent University, Turkey. Her research interests include theoretical and ecological implications of new media, expanding to science fiction, climate fiction and eco-criticism. Her master's thesis, "The Afterlife of Electronic Waste," takes a Deleuzian-Guattarian perspective on artworks created with electronic waste.

Kenneth **Matthews** teaches English composition courses at Northern Oklahoma College in Tonkawa, Oklahoma. His primary research interest is the relationships between rhetoric, the classroom, and modern civic responsibility.

Łukasz **Muniowski** holds a Ph.D. in American Literature from the University of Warsaw, Poland. He has written numerous academic articles on various topics, including gentrification, geek culture, American literature, video games and television series. His primary academic interest is sports, and his doctoral thesis examines careers of leading NBA players.

Fernando Gabriel **Pagnoni Berns** (Ph.D. student) is a professor at the Universidad de Buenos Aires (UBA)—Facultad de Filosofía y Letras (Argentina). He teaches courses on international horror films. He is the director of the research group on horror cinema "Grite" and has published chapters in the books *Divine Horror*, *To See the Saw Movies*, *Critical Insights: Alfred Hitchcock* and *Gender and Environment in Science Fiction*.

Damla **Pehlivan** is an independent researcher from Izmir, Turkey. She graduated from Ege University's American Culture and Literature Department in 2018. Her research interests include contemporary theory, especially Freudian and Lacanian psychoanalysis and theoreticians such as Žižek, McLuhan and Baudrillard.

Lars **Schmeink**, Ph.D., works in digital learning at the HafenCity University, Hamburg, and has been a visiting professor at the Hochschule für Musik und Theater Hamburg and the University of Cincinnati. He is a researcher of the fantastic and the author of *Biopunk Dystopias* (Liverpool, 2016) and coeditor of *Cyberpunk and Visual Culture* (Routledge, 2018) and *The Routledge Companion to Cyberpunk Culture* (Routledge, 2020).

About the Contributors

Kwasu David **Tembo** obtained a Ph.D. from the University of Edinburgh's Language, Literatures, and Cultures Department. His research interests include media studies, comics studies, literary theory and criticism and philosophy, particularly the so-called "prophets of extremity"—Nietzsche, Heidegger, Foucault, and Derrida. He has published on Christopher Nolan's *The Prestige*, in *The Cinema of Christopher Nolan* (Columbia University Press, 2015), and on Superman, in *Postscriptum* (2017).

Index

AC 1 "Out of the Past" 53, 54, 62, 64, 70, 71, 74, 91, 93, 95, 106, 109, 110, 112, 113, 159, 165, 169, 186
AC 2 "Fallen Angel" 43, 62, 65, 70, 87, 93, 96, 115, 144, 170, 171
AC 3 "In a Lonely Place" 21, 35, 44, 70, 73, 75, 110, 111, 115, 158, 160, 162
AC 4 "Force of Evil" 63, 75, 77, 106, 112, 123, 184
AC 5 "The Wrong Man" 46, 69, 70, 76, 78, 83, 85, 95, 109, 112, 115
AC 6 "Man with My Face" 22, 77, 140
AC 7 "Nora Inu" 76, 98, 99, 113, 168, 171, 172
AC 8 "Clash by Night" 36, 77, 79, 124, 163
AC 9 "Rage in Heaven" 35, 70, 72, 115, 162
AC 10 "The Killers" 35, 36, 37, 72, 74, 79, 114, 159
Aggrawal, Ani 179, 188
Anttiroiko, Ari-Veikko 82, 86, 88
Armstrong, Karen 106, 116
Asimov, Isaac 158

Balsamo, Anne 56, 66
Bancroft Laurence 2, 9, 21, 28, 29, 32–36, 39, 43–46, 54, 63, 69, 71, 73, 74, 75, 78, 79, 82–88, 91, 92, 94, 111, 115, 147, 150–153, 165, 167, 171, 181, 182, 184, 187, 188
Bancroft, Miriam 34, 35, 41–46, 69, 70, 74, 87, 91, 92, 134
Barthes, Roland 29, 31, 38
Bataille, Georges 4, 27, 28, 29, 33, 34, 38
Baudrillard, Jean 116, 148, 149, 154, 182, 188
Bay City 8, 20, 27, 29, 31, 36, 53, 54, 62, 86, 91, 155, 158, 160, 180, 181, 182, 184, 185, 186
Beard, Mary 164, 175
Benjamin, Walter 29, 31, 32, 38, 148, 150, 151, 154

biopolitics 4, 6, 29–31, 38, 69, 90; biopower 4, 29, 30, 31, 71
Blade Runner 8, 15, 18, 25, 39, 48, 91, 96, 104, 129, 130–135, 138, 141–143, 158, 160
Blade Runner 2049 3, 91, 96, 104, 129, 142, 143
Blanco, Maria del Pilar 155–157, 175
Bloom, Harold 116
Bordwell, David 42, 45, 48
Bostrom, Nick 98, 103
Braidotti, Rosi 99, 103
Brennan, Teresa 182, 188
Brown, Wendy 155, 157, 175
Buben, Adam 97, 103
Burduck, Michael 181, 188

Caccamo, James 70, 80
Cadora, Karen 2, 11, 69, 80, 162, 164, 174, 175
Caracciolo, Marco 178, 188
Carnage 70–72, 79, 129, 138–141
Cavallaro, Dani 130, 134, 135, 142
Cedeström, Carl 84, 86, 88
Chion, Michel 123, 125
Cholbi, Michael 96, 103
consciousness 1, 3–7, 9, 16, 27–33, 36, 51–55, 58, 61, 63–68, 73, 74, 84, 87, 91, 94, 95, 97, 101, 110, 124, 141, 145, 153, 155, 158–161, 174, 175, 184
Corbin, Charles B. 82, 88
Corbin, William R. 82, 88
cortical stacks 1–5, 7, 9, 11, 15–17, 20, 21, 24, 27–33, 37, 38, 40–44, 47, 53–55, 60–65, 68, 69, 71, 78–82, 84, 86–95, 98, 105, 108, 113, 145, 147, 148, 153, 155, 158, 161, 169–174
Crary, Jonathan 83, 89
Crittenden, Roger 39, 48
cyberpunk 1–5, 8–11, 16, 25, 33, 39, 44, 48, 51, 52, 63, 66, 68, 69, 78, 79, 80, 127, 129,

130–135, 137–144, 155, 157–164, 173–175, 177, 183
cyberspace 52, 58, 63, 69, 74, 117, 142, 163
cyborg 5, 52, 55–57, 59, 60, 61, 65, 66, 73, 105, 112, 116, 120, 134

Damásio, António 95, 103
da Silva, Anna 181, 188
Davis, Colin 8, 121, 122, 125
Davis, Erik 107, 116
Davis, John K. 98, 103
Davis, Vines L. 178, 188
Davison, Margaret 179, 188, 189
De Natale, Robert 39, 48
Derrida, Jaques 8, 122, 125, 155, 156, 157, 162, 163–165, 169, 171–173, 175
Descartes, René 5, 58, 81, 89, 95, 103
Devereux, Cecily 162, 175
Dia de Los Muertos 20, 64, 77, 124, 137, 181, 184
Digital Human Freight (DHF) 53, 54, 60, 63, 91, 105, 108, 175
Dow, Suzanne 17, 25

Ehreinreich, Barbara 82, 85, 89
Eisenstein, Sergei 4, 39, 40, 41, 48
Elliot, Lizzie 9, 10, 35, 63, 71, 72, 77, 96, 124, 125, 156, 159, 161–164, 174, 187, 188
Elliot, Vernon 36, 37, 72, 77, 124, 159, 161, 187
Elmer, Jonathan 180, 189
embodiment 3–6, 8, 15–18, 20, 21, 23, 51–53, 55, 57–59, 61–63, 65–69, 71–74, 77, 78, 133, 165, 175
Empathin 42, 46, 70, 87; Merge Nine (Merge9) 70, 87
Enlightenment 57, 148, 159, 177, 182
envoys 22, 24, 28, 32, 40, 42, 54, 63, 70, 75, 84, 98, 112, 115, 150, 151, 156–171
Epicurus 97, 98
Eros and Thanatos 4, 10, 41, 46, 47, 48

Falconer, Quellchrist (Quell) 22, 41, 42, 47, 63, 98, 99, 102, 113, 115, 155, 165–174, 183; Quellism 7, 105, 106, 112–116
Farkas, Carol-Ann 86, 89
Ferkiss, Victor 107, 116
Fink, Bruce 25, 124, 125
Fiore, Quentin 145, 146, 154
Fisher, Benjamin Franklin 188, 189
Fisher, Mark 155, 175
Flieger, Jerry Aline 23, 25
Foster, Thomas 78
Foucault, Michel 4, 6, 28, 29, 30, 33, 38, 147, 148, 154
Frelik, Paweł 4, 11, 52, 66

Freud, Sigmund 7, 23, 25, 41, 48, 97, 103, 123, 125, 162
Fukuyama, Francis 83, 88, 89
Fuller, Steve 107, 111, 116

Ghost in the Shell (1995) 8, 48, 160
Ghost in the Shell (2017) 3, 129, 143
Gledhill, Christine 19, 25
Gnosticism 7, 107–117
Goldhurst, William 180, 189
Gordon, Avery 155, 169, 176
Gothic 10, 80, 122, 155, 158, 159, 174, 177–179, 182–186, 188, 189
Grant, Edward 116
Gruman, Gerald Joseph 97, 103

Haraway, Donna 5, 52, 55–57, 59–61, 65, 66, 116
hard boiled fiction 3, 9, 15, 18–21, 24, 134–136, 143
Hartmann, Jonathan 180, 189
Hasan, Ihab 110, 116
hauntology 8, 9, 10, 155–157, 163–166, 168–171, 173–175
Hawking, Stephen 146, 154
Hayes, Kevin J. 183, 187, 189
Hayles, Nancy N. 5, 52, 53, 55–68, 76, 78, 80, 99, 103
Head in the Clouds 35–38, 44, 71, 72, 94, 96, 185, 186
Heidegger, Martin 97, 103
Heise-von der Lippe, Anya 73, 75, 76, 80
Hernandez Del Castillo, Ana 179, 189
Hill, Forbes I. 152, 154
Hitchcock, Alfred 123
Hollinger, Veronica 51, 66
Horner, Avril 184, 189
Horsley, Lee 19, 25
Hutcheon, Linda 8, 132, 133, 136, 142, 143
Huxley, Aldous 91, 102, 103
Iridium Package 36, 37, 72

Istvan, Zoltan 95, 96, 102, 103

Jack It Off 71, 75
James, William 174, 175
Jameson, Fredric 8, 88, 132, 140, 143
Jantzen, Grace 97, 103
Jasper, Karl 180,189
Johnston, Keith M. 130, 143
Jonas, Hans 107, 108, 113, 114, 115, 116
Jones, Paul Christian 185, 189

Kalogridis, Laeta 15, 25, 27, 35, 38, 48, 51, 66, 68, 80, 89, 90, 103, 116, 125, 137, 143, 154, 155, 176, 189

Index   197

Kaplan, Ann   19, 25
Kawahara, Reileen   24, 34, 70, 72, 75–77, 92, 94, 96, 165, 167, 174, 183, 186
Kennedy, Gerald   178, 182, 189
Kopley, Richard   183, 187, 189
Kovacs, Takeshi   2, 3, 9, 10, 11, 21, 22, 24, 28, 32, 35, 36, 40, 41–47, 54, 60, 61, 63–66, 69–71, 73–79, 82, 84, 85, 87, 91, 92, 95, 98, 99, 114, 115, 119, 124, 125, 130, 134–138, 141, 144, 149–151, 155, 156, 158, 160, 165–169, 171, 177, 181, 183–187
Kroeber, Karl   106, 116

Lacan, Jacques   3, 15, 17, 22–26, 38, 124–126
Lasch, Christopher   114,116
Lavigne, Carlen   143
Lefebvre, Henri   83, 89
Lessl, Thomas M.   111, 117
Li, Jack   98, 103
limit-experience   4, 27–29, 31, 33, 35–37
Lincoln, Abraham   99, 103
Lucretius   97
Lundin, Roger M.   110, 117
Lynch, Michael P.   152, 154

Marín-Ruiz, Ricardo   179, 186, 189
Max Headroom   8, 79, 80, 129, 133, 139–141, 143
McAvan, Emily   117
McCann, Sean   134, 136, 143
McCarron, Kevin   137
McGaan, Jerome   179, 189
McGreevy, Patrick   178, 189
McLuhan, Marshall   145, 146, 151, 154
Messerly, John G.   94, 97, 98, 100, 103
Meths   1, 2, 4, 6, 7, 28–31, 33–35, 37, 38, 45, 54, 62, 69, 71, 73, 75, 76, 79, 81- 87, 91, 93, 99, 100, 105–107, 109–114, 116, 150, 152–154, 157–159, 163, 169–173, 181
Miller, Jaques-Alain   23, 25
Mlodinow, Leonard   146, 154
Montrose, Louis   149, 151, 154
Moravec, Hans   25, 58, 68, 73, 80
More, Max   16, 25
Moreland, Sean   178, 189
Morgan, Richard   1, 8, 11, 27, 51, 66, 68, 72, 78, 80, 84, 89, 91, 103, 118, 119, 120, 126, 129, 134, 137, 142, 143
Mosco, Vincent   117
Mulvey, Laura   4, 39, 42, 44, 45, 48
Muncy, Julie   1, 11, 69, 80, 130, 135, 143
Muri, Allison   58, 66, 73, 74, 80

Neo-Catholics (Neo-C)   8, 20, 24, 72, 93, 94, 124, 135, 137, 138, 181
Nicol, Bran   184, 189

Nietzsche, Friedrich   153, 154
noir   2, 10, 15, 18, 19, 20, 24, 25, 39, 52, 134, 135, 137, 138, 160, 168, 174, 177; neo-noir   3, 15, 18, 20, 155
Noonan, Jeff   99, 103

Optical Neural Interface (ONI)   60
Ortega, Kristin   3, 15, 20, 21, 22, 24, 43, 44, 46, 47, 62, 64, 70–79, 84, 93, 96, 109, 124, 125, 135, 137, 138, 141, 158, 168, 181, 184, 185

Pagels, Elaine   109, 112, 117
Peeples, Scott   185, 189
Peeren, Esther   155, 156, 157, 175
Place, Janey   19, 25
Plato   96
Poe (AI)   9, 10, 42, 44, 63, 156, 158–161, 163, 174, 177, 178, 181, 184, 185, 187, 188
Poe, Edgar Allan   2, 10, 42, 131, 156, 158, 177–189, 190; novels   2, 160, 180, 182, 186, 187, 198; poems   177, 178, 179, 180, 183, 185, 187, 189
posthumanism   2, 5, 6, 15, 16, 17, 22–25, 52, 53, 55–59, 66, 78–80, 93; transhumanism   2, 68, 80, 93, 103, 133
post-truth   9, 144, 151, 152
Prescott, Oumou   35, 170
Proposition 653   94, 156, 170, 171
PsychaSec   82, 87, 92, 96

The Raven Hotel   36, 41, 44, 75, 158, 160, 161, 185, 186
Ready Player One   129, 139–143
Roderick, Philip L.   179, 190
Roudinesco, Elisabeth   33, 38
Rowlands, Mark   97
Ryker, Elias   3, 15, 21, 22, 24, 32, 44, 46, 47, 54, 60, 64, 70, 76, 77, 79, 119, 138

Salecl, Renata   22–24, 26
Sandberg, Anders   95, 104
Scruggs, Charles   183, 190
Sheppard, H.J.   117
Shilingford, Jenepher P.   86, 88, 89
Shilingford, Mackin Anne   86, 88, 89
Silverman, Kenneth   186, 190
sleeve   1–10, 16, 17, 20, 21, 24, 27–38, 40–42, 44–46, 49, 53, 54, 60–65, 68–74, 76–96, 98, 100–102, 105, 108, 121, 123, 124, 129, 137, 138, 140, 141, 143, 155, 156, 158–163, 165, 169, 170, 172–174, 183
Smith, Adam   88, 89
Solomon, Robert C.   86, 88, 89
Songspire Trees   74, 108
Spicer, Andre   84, 86, 88

Spielberg, Steven 129, 139, 143, 161
Stamos, David 179, 190
Strehlau, Nelly 167, 168, 176
Stross, Charles 120, 126

thanatophobia 10, 177, 178, 180, 181
Thompson, Kristin 42, 45, 48

Vale de Gato, Margarida 178, 190
VanDemarr, Lee 183, 190
Vint, Sherryl 11, 66–69, 74, 78–80, 99, 104, 117
virtual reality (VR) 35, 38, 52, 58, 63, 71, 72, 75, 139, 161, 162, 163
Voegelin, Eric 111, 117

Wachowski Lana 91, 104, 133, 143, 158
Wachowski, Lily 91, 104, 133, 143, 158

Walker-Emig, Paul 130, 143
Weber, Max 106, 137, 143
Weekes, Karen 186, 190
Wei Clinic 63
Welk, Gregory J. 82, 88
Welk, Karen A. 82, 88
Williams, Bernard 97, 104
Wood, Donald C. 82, 89
Wright, Colin 17, 25

Yuen, W.K. 39, 44, 48

Zandbergen, Dorien 106, 117
Žižek, Slavoy 25, 88, 119, 121, 123, 125, 126
Zlosnik, Sue 184, 189
Zupančič, Alenka 23, 26

www.ingramcontent.com/pod-product-compliance
Lightning Source LLC
Chambersburg PA
CBHW032045300426
44117CB00009B/1194